S0-BNK-024

The IDG Books Creating Cool™ Series Advantage

We at IDG Books Worldwide created *Macworld Creating Cool HTML 3.2 Web Pages* to meet your growing need for quick access to the most complete and accurate computer information available. Our books work the way you do: they focus on accomplishing specific tasks — not on learning random functions. Our books are not long-winded manuals or dry reference tomes. In each book, expert authors tell you exactly what you can do with new technology and software and how to evaluate its usefulness for your needs. Easy to follow information, comprehensive coverage, and convenient access in language and design — it's all here.

The authors of IDG books are uniquely qualified to give you expert advice as well as to provide insightful tips and techniques not found anywhere else. Our authors maintain close contact with end users through feedback from articles, training sessions, e-mail exchanges, user group participation, and consulting work. Because our authors know the realities of daily computer use and are directly linked to the reader, our books have a strategic advantage.

Our experienced authors know how to approach a topic in the most efficient manner, and we know that you, the reader, will benefit from a "one-on-one" relationship with the author. Our research shows that readers make computer book purchases because they want expert advice. Because readers want to benefit from the author's experience, the author's voice is always present in an IDG book.

In addition, the author is free to include or recommend useful software in an IDG book. The software that accompanies each book is not intended to be a casual filler but is linked to the content, theme, or procedures of the book. We know that you will benefit from the included software.

You will find what you need in this book whether you read it from cover to cover, section by section, or simply one topic at a time. As a computer user, you deserve a comprehensive resource of answers. We at IDG Books Worldwide are proud to deliver that resource with *Macworld Creating Cool HTML 3.2 Web Pages*.

Brenda McLaughlin
Senior Vice President and Group Publisher

Internet: YouTellUs@idgbooks.com

Macworld® Creating Cool™ HTML 3.2 Web Pages

Macworld® Creating Cool™ HTML 3.2 Web Pages

by Dave Taylor

IDG Books Worldwide, Inc.
An International Data Group Company

Foster City, CA ♦ Chicago, IL ♦ Indianapolis, IN ♦ Southlake, TX

Macworld® Creating Cool™ HTML 3.2 Web Pages

Published by
IDG Books Worldwide, Inc.
An International Data Group Company
919 E. Hillsdale Blvd
Suite 400
Foster City, CA 94404
www.idgbooks.com (IDG Books World Wide Web Site)

Library of Congress Catalog Card No.: 96-79587
ISBN: 0-7645-4013-0

Printed in the United States of America
10 9 8 7 6 5 4 3 2 1
IB/RX/RS/ZW/FC
Distributed in the United States by IDG Books Worldwide, Inc.
Distributed by Macmillan Canada for Canada; by Contemporanea de Ediciones for Venezuela; by Distribuidora Cuspide for Argentina; by CITEC for Brazil; by Ediciones ZETA S.C.R. Ltda. for Peru; by Editorial Limusa SA for Mexico; by Transworld Publishers Limited in the United Kingdom and Europe; by Academic Bookshop for Egypt; by Levant Distributors S.A.R.L. for Lebanon; by Al Jassim for Saudi Arabia; by Simron Pty. Ltd. for South Africa; by Pustak Mahal for India; by The Computer Bookshop for India; by Toppan Company Ltd. for Japan; by Addison Wesley Publishing Company for Korea; by Longman Singapore Publishers Ltd. for Singapore, Malaysia, Thailand, and Indonesia; by Unalis Corporation for Taiwan; by WS Computer Publishing Company, Inc. for the Philippines; by WoodsLane Pty. Ltd. for Australia; by WoodsLane Enterprises Ltd. for New Zealand. Authorized Sales Agent: Anthony Rudkin Associates for the Middle East and North Africa.
For general information on IDG Books Worldwide's books in the U.S., please call our Consumer Customer Service department at 800-762-2974. For reseller information, including discounts and premium sales, please call our Reseller Customer Service department at 800-434-3422.
For information on where to purchase IDG Books Worldwide's books outside the U.S., please contact our International Sales department at 415-655-3172 or fax 415-655-3295.
For information on foreign language translations, please contact our Foreign & Subsidiary Rights department at 415-655-3021 or fax 415-655-3281.
For sales inquiries and special prices for bulk quantities, please contact our Sales department at 415-655-3200 or write to the address above.
For information on using IDG Books Worldwide's books in the classroom or for ordering examination copies, please contact our Educational Sales department at 800-434-2086 or fax 817-251-8174.
For authorization to photocopy items for corporate, personal, or educational use, please contact Copyright Clearance Center, 222 Rosewood Drive, Danvers, MA 01923, or fax 508-750-4470.

is a trademark under exclusive license to IDG Books Worldwide, Inc., from International Data Group, Inc.

About the Author

Dave Taylor has been involved with the Internet since 1980, when he first logged in as an undergraduate student at the University of California, San Diego. Since then he's been a research scientist at Hewlett-Packard Laboratories in Palo Alto, California; a software and hardware reviews editor for *SunWorld* magazine; and an interface design consultant. He is president of Intuitive Systems in Northern California (www.intuitive.com).

So far, Dave has designed more than 1,000 Web pages. He has published more than 750 articles on the Internet, UNIX, Macintosh, and other computing topics. His books include *Global Software* and *Teach Yourself Unix in a Week*. He coauthored *The Internet Business Guide* and is a columnist for *InfoWorld*, *LOGIN*, and a regular contributor to *Computer Currents* and *MacWEEK*. He is well known as the author of the Elm Mail System and, more recently, the Embot mail autoresponder program.

He holds a Masters degree in Educational Computing from Purdue University, and an undergraduate degree in Computer Science from the University of California, San Diego.

On the Web, Dave has created the award-winning Internet Mall™, the Purdue University Online Writing Laboratory, the WebStar public Web site prize, and dozens of commercial Web sites.

ABOUT IDG BOOKS WORLDWIDE

Welcome to the world of IDG Books Worldwide.

IDG Books Worldwide, Inc., is a subsidiary of International Data Group, the world's largest publisher of computer-related information and the leading global provider of information services on information technology. IDG was founded more than 25 years ago and now employs more than 8,500 people worldwide. IDG publishes more than 275 computer publications in over 75 countries (see listing below). More than 60 million people read one or more IDG publications each month.

Launched in 1990, IDG Books Worldwide is today the #1 publisher of best-selling computer books in the United States. We are proud to have received eight awards from the Computer Press Association in recognition of editorial excellence and three from *Computer Currents*' First Annual Readers' Choice Awards. Our best-selling *...For Dummies*® series has more than 30 million copies in print with translations in 30 languages. IDG Books Worldwide, through a joint venture with IDG's Hi-Tech Beijing, became the first U.S. publisher to publish a computer book in the People's Republic of China. In record time, IDG Books Worldwide has become the first choice for millions of readers around the world who want to learn how to better manage their businesses.

Our mission is simple: Every one of our books is designed to bring extra value and skill-building instructions to the reader. Our books are written by experts who understand and care about our readers. The knowledge base of our editorial staff comes from years of experience in publishing, education, and journalism — experience we use to produce books for the '90s. In short, we care about books, so we attract the best people. We devote special attention to details such as audience, interior design, use of icons, and illustrations. And because we use an efficient process of authoring, editing, and desktop publishing our books electronically, we can spend more time ensuring superior content and spend less time on the technicalities of making books.

You can count on our commitment to deliver high-quality books at competitive prices on topics you want to read about. At IDG Books Worldwide, we continue in the IDG tradition of delivering quality for more than 25 years. You'll find no better book on a subject than one from IDG Books Worldwide.

John Kilcullen
President and CEO
IDG Books Worldwide, Inc.

Eighth Annual Computer Press Awards ≥1992

Ninth Annual Computer Press Awards ≥1993

Tenth Annual Computer Press Awards ≥1994

Eleventh Annual Computer Press Awards ≥1995

Dedication

To Ashley, the twinkle in my eye.

Credits

**Senior Vice President and
Group Publisher**
Brenda McLaughlin

Director of Publishing
Walt Bruce

Acquisitions Manager
John Osborn

Acquisitions Editor
Nancy E. Dunn

Marketing Manager
Melisa M. Duffy

Executive Managing Editor
Terry Somerson

Editorial Assistant
Sharon Eames

Production Director
Andrew Walker

Supervisor of Page Layout
Craig A. Harrison

Development Editor
Susannah Davidson

Copy Editor
Tracy Brown

Technical Editor
Stuti Garg

Project Coordinator
Ben Schroeter

Layout & Graphics
Mario Amador
Andreas Schueller

Quality Control Specialist
Mick Arellano

Proofreader
Christine Sabooni

Indexer
Ty Koontz

Production Administration
Tony Augsburger
Todd Klemme
Jason Marcuson
Christopher Pimentel
Leslie Popplewell
Theresa Sanchez-Baker
Melissa Stauffer

Book Design
Theresa Sanchez-Baker

Foreword

Just the other day, I was roaming through the halls of the Louvre, looking at great works of art such as the *Mona Lisa.* An hour before, I had toured the exhibits of the University of California at Berkeley's Museum of Paleontology, and learned about Dilophosaurs from a well-versed professor. And just a short while before that, I previewed Disney's upcoming summer flicks before actual movie audiences would. The remarkable thing about all these feats was that I accomplished them without ever leaving my home (or workstation, for that matter). The killer application of the network-of-networks is the World Wide Web, and you're nobody unless you have a cool home page on the Web.

Sporting the first truly user-friendly multimedia features for the Internet, the Web represented about one percent of all Internet traffic in 1993. In 1994, it grew to 12 percent of all traffic and is now at a sky-rocketing 20 percent. A year ago there were 1,265 estimated Web sites; today there are nearly 20,000!

As further evidence of its rapid growth, most of the commercial online services opened their doors to the Web, with Prodigy leading the pack in January 1995. Since then, nearly half a million Prodigy users have grabbed the Web browser software needed to enjoy this graphically intense corner of the Internet. Now that Microsoft has shipped Windows 95, many more users are just a click away from becoming Web surfers.

A year ago I had but a few Web sites in my Internet Services List and had barely trod into the realm myself. Today, my list is growing almost exclusively as Web sites. As a further testimonial, I am now employed as a Web Developer for SpectraCom, Incorporated in Milwaukee.

The future has arrived, and Dave Taylor has created a book to help newbie Web developers (such as myself!) design cool Web pages in what once was a desert but is now an oasis of information and enjoyment. Dave is well known for providing the Internet with valuable information sources and tools, such as the Elm Mail System and the Internet Mall, and his trustworthy experience will once again be valuable in aiding university eggheads, corporate suits, and homegrown fanatics to exploit the capabilities of the Web and HTML.

— Scott Yanoff

Scott Yanoff is famous on the Net for creating and maintaining the valuable Internet Services List, *aka* Yanoff's List, *which you can visit at:*
`http://www.uwm.edu/Mirror/inet.services.html`.

Acknowledgments

No writing project can be done while the author is locked in a room, though if the room had a good Net connection, we might be able to negotiate something! Seriously, innumerable Internet folk have proven invaluable as I've written the different editions of this book, some for their direct help, and others for simply having produced some wickedly cool Web pages that helped inspire me when things were moving a bit slowly. Chief among those is the ever-omniscient James Armstrong, who helped me verify the internal details of the more obscure HTML tags. My editors at IDG Books continually offered valuable suggestions that helped me fine-tune the prose herein. And the gangsta' team of Rick Tracewell, Tai Jin, and Marv Raab also helped with their insight on page design and Web graphics layout, as well as suggestions for cool Web sites not to miss.

Adobe Systems, Macromedia, Pixar, and **Broderbund** were most generous with their assistance; many of the graphics presented in this book were created by **Photoshop, Illustrator, FreeHand, TypeStyler, Typestry,** and other top-notch commercial applications, originally on the Macintosh. Screenshots were done with **Capture** and the book was originally written mostly on an **Apple PowerBook Duo 210**, with everything verified with the fabulous **PowerComputing PowerWave 132** on my desk. The Windows 95 additions were developed on a **Maryland Systems TANGENT** flying with **Windows 95** at 166Mhz. Shareware gets a nod too; **Graphic Converter** proved helpful for ensuring that the images were in the correct form, and **Transparency** made them transparent. **Internet Explorer, Mosaic,** and **Netscape** were all quite capable Web browsers, although I prefer Explorer because it's cool! Also, thanks to **NetTech Systems** of San Mateo for my ISDN connectivity.

Finally, warm hugs to **Linda, Jasmine,** and **Karma** for ensuring that I took sufficient breaks to avoid carpal tunnel syndrome or any of the other hazards of overly intense typing. The time off-line would be a lot less fun without ya!

Contents at a Glance

Table of Contents

Introduction

Who should buy this book? What's covered? What's not? How do I read this book? Why should I read this book? Who am I?

Welcome!

"Wow! Another Internet book. What makes this one different?"

That's a fair question. I wrote this introduction to answer that question. I want you to be confident that *Macworld Creating Cool HTML 3.2 Web Pages* will meet your needs as well as provide fun and interesting reading.

What This Book Is About

In a nutshell, *Macworld Creating Cool HTML 3.2 Web Pages* is an introduction to HTML. HTML stands for *HyperText Markup Language*, and it is the markup language that enables you to create and publish your own multimedia documents on the World Wide Web. Millions of users on the Internet and online services such as America Online, CompuServe, and Prodigy are learning how to use the visually exciting World Wide Web from within Internet Explorer, Navigator, Mosaic, and a quickly growing list of other programs.

You can create attractive documents that are right on the cutting edge of interactive publishing. That's why I went through the pain of learning HTML. For me, learning was hit-or-miss, because the only references I could find were confusing online documents written by programmers and computer types. For you, it will be easier. By reading this book and experimenting with the software and samples included on the CD-ROM, you can learn not only the nuts and bolts of HTML but also how to design and create useful, attractive Web documents and spread the word about them on the Net.

To make things even more fun in this book, I pop into various cool and interesting Web sites and show you the HTML code used to create those pages. In the end, cool Web documents aren't necessarily those that have extensive or pretty graphics. With a little verve and some witty prose, you'll see how you can present purely textual information via the Web in a way that's interesting, visually engaging, helpful, and fun — in other words, *cool*.

These things are what this book is all about.

What This Book Isn't About

This book doesn't introduce you to or tell you how you can get on the Internet. (It does, however, include a brief and painless introduction to the World Wide Web.) If you seek detailed information about the Net or want to find out how to "get on", you can find many interesting and useful books from IDG Books Worldwide and elsewhere on those topics. And because of space restraints, this book *explores* some very advanced HTML topics — such as how to create forms or build HTML pages on-the-fly — but doesn't explore them in depth.

Instead, *Macworld Creating Cool HTML 3.2 Web Pages* is a fun introduction to the art and science of creating interesting Web documents that you'll be proud of and that other users will want to visit and explore.

Oh! And I can't help you figure out who you are. I'm still working on figuring out who I am.

Text Conventions Used in This Book

Stuff you type appears in bold, like this: **something you actually type.**

Filenames, names of machines on the Net, and directories appear in a special typeface, like the following one, which lets visitors sign a White House guest book:

```
http://www.whitehouse.gov/White_House/html/Guest_Book.html
```

HTML-formatted text appears in the same special typeface, like this:

```
<HTML>
<TITLE>How to Write Cool Web Pages</TITLE>
<IMG SRC="intro.gif" ALT="How To Write Cool Web Pages">
```

I use three icons in this book:

 Tip icons point out expert advice on tricks and techniques.

 Warning icons alert you to information that may help you avoid trouble.

 Note icons point out details that may deserve special attention in the long term.

Who This Book Is For

Even if you don't have a connection to the Internet, you can use this book and software to learn HTML and the techniques of creating cool Web pages. All you need is a simple text editor, such as SimpleText, which comes with your Mac, and a Web browser like Netscape Navigator or Microsoft Internet Explorer, both of which are conveniently packaged on the CD-ROM in the back of the book.

If you're already online and have a Web browser hooked up, you can easily explore local files (files on your computer) and then log on to explore the many fascinating examples of Web page design on the Internet itself.

A Sneak Peek at Some Actual HTML

Are you curious about what this HTML stuff looks like? The following figure shows what a portion of the outline for this book might look like as a simple HTML document, as seen in Netscape:

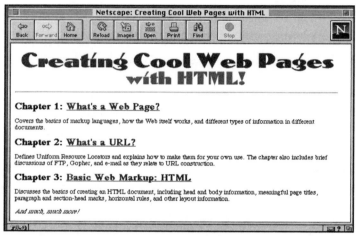

Figure 0-1: A Web page viewed in Netscape.

The following is the raw HTML document that lurks behind Figure 0-1:

```
<HTML>
<HEAD>
<TITLE>Creating Cool Web Pages with HTML</TITLE>
</HEAD><BODY BGCOLOR=#FFFFFF>
<IMG SRC="intro.gif" ALT="Creating Cool Web Pages with HTML">
<HR>
<H2>Chapter 1: <A HREF="chap1.html">What's a Web Page?</A>
</H2>
Covers the basics of markup languages, how the Web itself
works, and different types of information in different
documents.<H2>Chapter 2: <A HREF="chap2.html">What's a
URL?</A></H2>Defines Uniform Resource Locators and
explains how to make them for your own use. The chapter
also includes brief discussions of FTP, Gopher,
and e-mail as they relate to URL construction.
<H2>Chapter 3: <A HREF="chap3.html">Basic Web Markup:
HTML</A></H2>
```

```
Discusses the basics of creating an HTML document,
including head and body information, meaningful page
titles, paragraph and section-head marks, horizontal
rules, and other layout information.
<P>
<I>And much, much more!</I>
</BODY>
</HTML>
```

By the time you're halfway through this book, you'll be able to whip up the kind of material in Figure 0-1 yourself, guaranteed. And by the time you *finish* this book, you'll know other ways to organize information to make creating Web versions of print material easy. You'll also learn why the particular HTML layout seen in Figure 0-1 isn't necessarily the best way to present information in a hyperlinked environment such as the Web.

```
Want to contact the author? Send e-mail to
taylor@intuitive.com or visit my home page on the Web at
http://www.intuitive.com/taylor.
```

The home page for this book is at:
`http://www.idgbooks.com`.

If you're ready, let's go!

What Is a Web Page? What's a Browser?

It's important for you to have a basic understanding of what a "web" of information is all about right off the bat. Before we look at the basics of creating cool Web pages, therefore, let's take a close look at what the Web is, how it works, and what HTML itself is all about. I promise to be brief!

What Is the Web Anyway?

To understand the World Wide Web, it's a good idea to first consider how information is organized in print media. Print media, I think, is a fair model for the Web and how it's organized, though others may feel that adventure games, movies, TV, or other information-publishing media are better suited for comparison to the Web.

Linear media

Think about the physical and organizational characteristics of this book for a second. What characteristics are most notable? The book has discrete units of information: pages. The pages are conceptually organized into chapters. The chapters are bound together to comprise the book itself. In some sense, what you have in your hands is a collection of pages organized in a format conducive to your reading them from first page to last. However, there's no reason why you can't riffle through the pages and create your own strategy for navigating this information.

Are you still with me? I call the book example *linear information organization*. Like movies, most books are organized with the expectation that you'll start at the beginning and end at the end.

Hypermedia

Imagine that instead of physically turning the page, you can simply touch a spot at the bottom of each page — a forward arrow — to flip to the next page. Touching a different spot — a back arrow — moves you to the preceding page. Further, imagine that when you look at the table of contents, you can touch the description of a chapter to immediately flip directly to the page where the chapter begins. Touch a third spot — a small picture of a dictionary — and move to another book entirely.

Such a model is called *hypermedia* or *hypertext,* terms coined by mid-twentieth century computer visionaries, most notably Ted Nelson in his book *Computer Lib*. Some things become apparent in this more dynamic approach to organization. One immediate benefit is that the topical index suddenly becomes *really* helpful; by being able to touch an item of interest, whether explanatory narrative or descriptive reference material, you can use the same book as a reference work in addition to the linearly organized tutorial that it's intended to offer. It's like the best of two worlds — the linear flow of an audio or video tape, and the instant access of a music CD.

Another benefit of hypertext involves footnotes. Footnote text doesn't have to clutter up the bottom of the page; with hypertext, you merely touch the asterisk or footnote number in the text, and a tiny page pops up to display the footnote.

One more bonus: you can touch an illustration to zoom into a larger version of that illustration or maybe even convert the illustration to an animated sequence.

What makes the Web really fun and interesting is the fact that the pages of information you connect to can reside on a variety of systems throughout the world. The pages themselves can be quite complex (and, ideally, cool and attractive) documents. Imagine: instead of writing "You can see the White House Web page to learn more," and leaving everyone stranded and unsure of how to proceed; Web documents enable direct *links,* so readers can click on the highlighted words in the sentence and immediately zoom to the White House.

Cool spots on the Web

Figure 1-1 shows a typical text-only Web document that you'll explore later in the book. Notice particularly the underlined words, each of which actually is a link to another Web document elsewhere in the Internet.

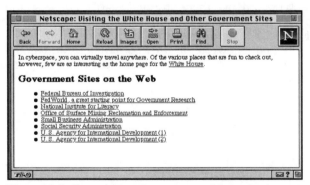

Figure 1-1: Some interesting spots to visit on the Internet.

If you're on the Internet, and you click on the phrase <u>The National Institute for Literacy</u>, you travel (electronically) to the center in Washington, DC, as shown in Figure 1-2.

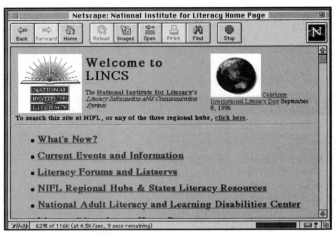

Figure 1-2: The National Institute for Literacy.

What do I mean by click on? I'm sure you already know: clicking is "touching" a spot on the screen; placing the mouse pointer over a word or picture and then pressing the mouse button. Clicking works whether you're running on a Macintosh, a Windows machine, or a UNIX workstation running X Windows.

What makes links so compelling is that there aren't thousands or tens of thousands of Web documents, there are *millions of them* — so many, in fact, that no one has ever visited all of them. So many documents are available that finding information is perhaps the single greatest challenge on the Internet. (Whew — I almost wrote *on the information highway.* I'll try to avoid that cliché, even though the metaphor actually can be helpful in considering traffic patterns, connection speeds, and various other arcana.)

Non-HTML Web information

Although it's certainly true that much of the information on the World Wide Web consists of rich multimedia documents written in HTML (hypertext markup language) specifically for the enjoyment of Web readers, the majority of documents actually come from other types of information-publishing services on the Internet. These documents are presented in the most attractive formats possible within the Web browsers themselves.

FTP

The simplest of the information services on the Internet is FTP (File Transfer Protocol). FTP has been around for a long time, long before the Web was envisioned. Traditionally, working with FTP is a pain, and the interface has always been only a tiny step away from programming the computer directly. For example, from a UNIX host, you would have to type the following sequence of steps to connect to the Digital Equipment Corporation FTP archive called gatekeeper.dec.com (user input is in boldface):

```
% ftp gatekeeper.dec.com
Connected to gatekeeper.dec.com.
220 gatekeeper.dec.com FTP server (Version 5.97 Fri May 6
14:44:16 PDT 1996) ready.
Name (gatekeeper.dec.com:taylor): anonymous
331 Guest login ok, send ident as password.
Password:taylor@intuitive.com
230 Guest login ok, access restrictions apply.
ftp> dir hypertext
200 PORT command successful.
150 Opening ASCII mode data connection for /bin/ls.
total 11
dr-xr-xr-x 2 root    system     512 Dec 28 12:57 docs
-r-r-r- 1 root     system    2435 Feb 8 00:26
gatekeeper.home.html
-r-r-r- 1 root     system     455 Dec 29 22:17
gatekeeper.temphome.html
lrwxr-xr-x 1 root    system      20 Feb 8 00:20 home.html -
> gatekeeper.ho
me.html
dr-xr-xr-x 2 root    system     512 Feb 8 23:13 includes
dr-xr-xr-x 2 root    system     512 Feb 8 00:35 info
dr-xr-xr-x 2 root    system     512 Feb 8 00:35 orgs
dr-xr-xr-x 2 root    system     512 Dec 29 22:05 pics
dr-xr-xr-x 2 root    system     512 Dec 28 12:57 util
226 Transfer complete.
remote: hypertext
619 bytes received in 0.28 seconds (2.2 Kbytes/s)
ftp>
```

Calling such a procedure complex would be an understatement. FTP is fast and easy to use, after you learn all the magic, but when working with computers, you should be able to focus on *what* you want to accomplish, not on *how* you need to accomplish it.

Compare the preceding example with the following procedure for using Netscape to access the same archive directly (see Figure 1-3). Instead of typing all that information, you simply *open* location: `ftp://gatekeeper.dec.com/hypertext`.
In this example, `ftp` indicates what kind of service is available, the `://` is some fancy (if mysterious) notation, and `gatekeeper.dec.com/hyper text` is the name of the computer and the directory to view. Press Enter.

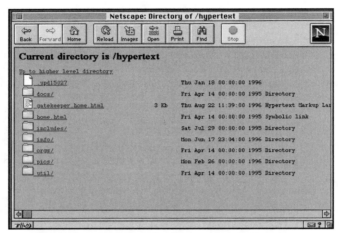

Figure 1-3: Netscape visits DEC's Gatekeeper FTP archive.

The location format (`ftp://gatekeeper.dec.com/hypertext`) is called a URL, which stands for Uniform Resource Locator.

Ready to visit a directory or folder listed? Click on it, and you'll move to that spot. Ready to grab a file? Just click on the file, and Netscape automatically figures out the file type, asks what you want to call the file on your PC, and transfers it across. No fuss, no hassle.

Easy FTP isn't a unique feature of Netscape, but a capability of *all* Web browser packages. Figure 1-4 shows the same place (Digital's FTP site) in Internet Explorer.

Here's where the difference between the *paper* and the *words* becomes important: the type of service that you can connect with is what I'll call the *information transfer level*, and the actual information presented is the *content*. Some Web documents available on the Internet aren't actually saved and available directly within the Web itself, but are accessible directly via FTP. Figure 1-5 shows an example: the first portion of a Web page that is accessible only with an FTP program or, of course, with your Web browser reading FTP information.

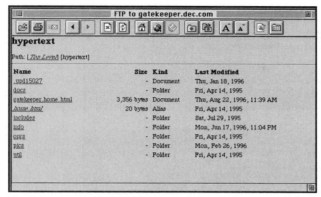

Figure 1-4: Internet Explorer visits DEC's Gatekeeper FTP archive.

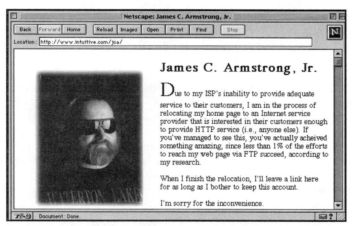

Figure 1-5: An HTML document via FTP.

Gopher and telnet

Web browsers also can traverse *Gopher* information space and help you *telnet* to other computers, that is, they let you explore the menu-based Gopher system and connect to remote computers as if you were on a direct-connection terminal. To see how helpful those capabilities can be, consider how things were done in the days before the Web took a stab at unifying the various interfaces. Figure 1-6 shows a screen from the Mac program TurboGopher. The application is easy to use, but it can't help you with FTP, Web documents, or anything else.

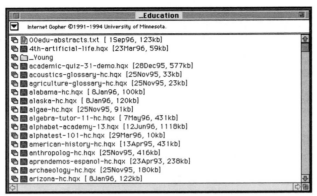

Figure 1-6: TurboGopher is a limited alternative to Web browsers.

Telnet is fairly easy to use. From your UNIX host, you simply type the word **telnet** followed by the name of the computer you want to connect to. But there's the rub: how do you remember all the computer names? The capability to be an easy, unified starting point for the different Internet services is a real selling point for a Web browser.

Figure 1-7 shows a Web page in which the links actually are pointers to different types of Internet services. Using this Web page, you don't have to remember the name of the remote computer or how to get to the place.

As you learn how to design and create Web documents, you also will learn how to choose among the various services on the Net and how to use them.

Click here to continue. (Just kidding.)

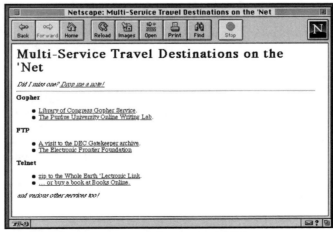

Figure 1-7: Multiple services from a single Web page.

Introduction to Netscape Navigator

Two events were the highlight of 1995 from an Internet perspective: the massive hype surrounding the introduction of Microsoft Windows 95, and the initial public offering of stock in a small startup company called Netscape Communications. Netscape exploded onto the scene and quickly became one of the highest valued small companies in the U.S. What really excited everyone about Netscape was Navigator, the cutting-edge Web browser that the company was freely distributing to the Internet community, a Web browser that had been born as NCSA Mosaic and rapidly took on a life of its own.

Fast forward two years, and Netscape continues to lead the pack — retaining its reputation as the leader of the Web business with its powerful server software and the ever-improving Netscape Navigator application. In fact, the browser is evolving fast, very fast, so fast that at any given time the company has a formal release version of Navigator, a beta release of the next version for users, and a second beta release for developers. There's a major release about every six months, which means that it's a constant effort to keep up.

Navigator includes lots of fun stuff, including a chat system, a Net-based telephone package, and more, but what isn't included is a way to plug into the network or a dialup connection to the Net.

The nuts and bolts of a dialup network connection are a bit beyond the scope of this book, but suffice to say that if you can connect to the Internet from your Mac, odds are very good that you'll be running something called PPP, or Point-to-Point Protocol on top of either MacTCP or Open Transport. If you consider a telephone and how you get that to work, PPP is the equivalent of the language your phone speaks so that it can talk with the wire coming out of the wall. Of course, you can't use a phone without a phone service, and a phone from Europe, for example, might not understand the signals sent on a phone wire in Japan, so indeed, it's a combination of all three — phone, signal standards, and phone service — that combine to give you a dial tone and calling service.

In exactly the same fashion, the requirements for you to have Internet connectivity are the dial tone (a dial-up line from an access provider like America Online, Netcom, or Best Communications), a shared signal standard (in this case PPP), and a telephone (a Web browser like Navigator or Internet Explorer).

Launching Netscape Navigator

If you're reading this book, odds are you've already spent some time exploring the Web and are ready to publish your own material online. If you haven't, you'll be glad to find out that it is quite easy to become an expert "surfer" online — once you have a network connection, of course — and that even with the differences between Navigator and Internet Explorer, the basic functionality is quite similar.

At any given time, you are looking at a document on your screen that has static information (text, graphics), active information (animations, audio, video), and links to other pages. To jump to another page, you move your mouse over the 'hot link' (either text or a graphic) and click. As you travel about, the browser remembers where you've been, so the Back button becomes a quick way to zoom to a previous page you visited, so you're not forced to always be moving forward. It's the equivalent of being able to shift your car into reverse on the highway, but without the screech of other cars and danger involved!

Navigator works identically if you're surfing a set of Web documents that are on your local disk as it does for remote pages around the world, just lots faster off your disk or CD-ROM drive. Because of this capability, Navigator and Internet Explorer are invaluable aids as you develop your own Web pages on your computer.

Find Navigator on the enclosed CD-ROM or on your computer if you've already installed it, and launch it by double-clicking on the icon or filename. Odds are it will immediately try to connect via the network to the Netscape home page (www.netscape.com). Instead, we want to open one of the HTML files on the included CD-ROM, so you can explore each of the examples in this book as you read along. To do that, choose Open File in Browser from the File menu in Navigator. You should see a dialog box similar to Figure 1-8.

If the browser insists on using a network connection that you might not have (which is perfectly okay; you'll still be able to work with all the Web pages in this book and build your own) then you might well need to 'cancel' out of the connection dialog before you can open a local file in Navigator.

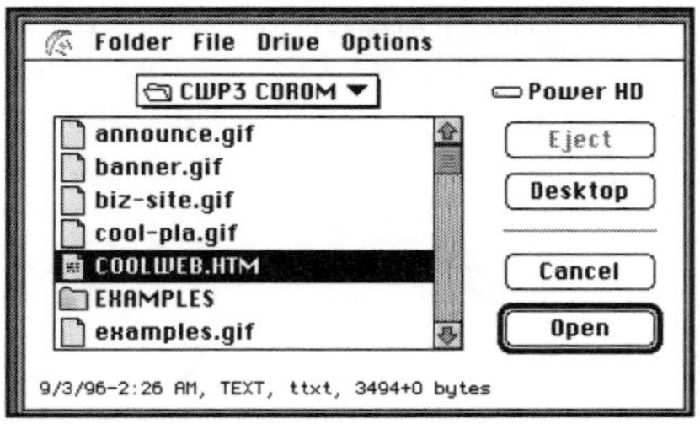

Figure 1-8: Find the file 'coolweb.htm' and click on Open.

Once you've successfully moved to the CD-ROM drive and found the file coolweb.htm, you should see some fun graphics that are a more colorful version of Figure 1-9. The toolbar display on your screen might vary slightly from what I have here in the book, in particular you might have more stuff on your toolbars, but that's easy for you to change from the Options menu (Show Toolbar, Show Location, and Show Directory buttons settings change the appearance of the program window).

Throughout this book I'll be using the main release of Netscape Navigator 3.0 for the vast majority of my examples. By the time you read this book there will undoubtedly have been a few more beta releases along the way, but most importantly I think that there will have been a more stable release of Navigator 3.0. If that isn't what we include on the CD-ROM, which we'll be building as late as possible, then you can always get the most up-to-date copy of Navigator from Netscape's Web site at:
`http://www.netscape.com/`
Be warned: the release I downloaded was over 5 MB, so it takes quite awhile to transfer!

Figure 1-9: Creating Cool Web Pages with HTML home page in Navigator.

If you have the toolbar selected with Navigator, then you'll see a set of buttons along the top of your window, either with or without one-word text descriptions underneath (it's a preference setting you can change from the Options/General Preferences area). If you look at Figure 1-10 you can see my quick guide to all these buttons on the Navigator browser.

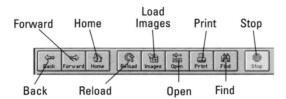

Figure 1-10: Navigator basic toolbar buttons.

- **Back**   Click on this and you'll jump to the page prior to the one you're viewing currently. You can go back quite a ways if you've been exploring for awhile.

- **Forward**   If you've gone back too far, forward will move you ahead on your list of visited pages.

- **Home**   A quick shortcut to get to the default page. You'll see how to change that to your favorite Web site or HTML file later in this chapter.

- **Edit**   If you're running the Gold version of Navigator, there's a nifty page editing capability included that you can access by clicking the pencil icon. I tend to stick with the regular browser because it's smaller and faster, so this particular button isn't shown in the screen shots.

- **Reload**   Many pages on the Web update frequently to reflect visitor activity, system activity, or perhaps just changes in weather maps or stock values. Clicking on the circular arrow Reload button enables you to request a new copy of the current Web page.

- **Images**   On a slow network connection you might find it considerably faster to surf the Web if you opt not to automatically download and display the graphics associated with a Web page. Many times this can cause great confusion, because most page designers don't take into account non-graphical users, but if you're exploring, it can speed things up quite a bit. Once you find a page that looks interesting, a click on the Images button will request all the graphics and build a complete page for you.

- **Open**   Here's how you type in a specific URL from a book or magazine article. While Microsoft Internet Explorer enables you to open files from the Open button dialog box, Navigator doesn't; the only way to open local files is to use the cryptic file: URL (which you'll learn in Chapter 2) or to use the Open File in Browser option from the File menu.

➡ **Print** Ready to keep a hard copy of the page you're viewing? Click the printer icon and it'll come out beautifully.

➡ **Find** Depending on how you have your Navigator browser configured, clicking on Find should quickly take you to a specific Web search engine like Alta Vista, Yahoo!, or Infoseek. You can change the search page to one of your favorites from the preferences area.

➡ **Stop** When you're waiting and waiting for a page to finish downloading, it's nice to know that you can tell Navigator "Okay, I've seen enough" by clicking the Stop button.

Changing the default page

One thing you might find very helpful as you read through this book is to change the default page in Netscape Navigator so that you start right up with the coolweb.html file rather than having to find it on your system each time. It's pretty straightforward and involves five steps:

1. Open Navigator and move to the coolweb.htm file as explained above.

2. Select Show location from the Options menu so that you have a URL displayed in a small box atop the window. My system shows `file:///MyDisk/CWP3%20CDROM/coolweb.htm` Yours may vary slightly.

3. Click and highlight the entire URL in the location box, then press Command-C to copy the information to the clipboard.

4. Now we're just about done. Choose general preferences from the Options menu and under the Appearance tab you should see a bunch of options that look like Figure 1-11. In the middle of the dialog box is an option of Browser starts with. Choose home page location, highlight any URL that might be in the white input box immediately underneath, and press Command-V to paste the address of your desired starting page into that field.

5. Click OK and you're done!

Now that you know how to change your default home page, you can modify it at will, perhaps to point to your own page on the Web once you create it, or to start you out at any of the variety of great pages online.

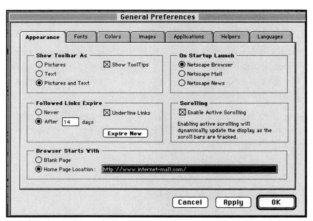

Figure 1-11: Changing default home page in Netscape Navigator.

Introduction to Internet Explorer

You'd have to live under a rock not to catch the hoopla surrounding the unveiling of Windows 95. Windows 95 is much more than an operating system; it's a whole new environment for PC users, an environment that is focused on making the computer easier to use and the interface more seamless and consistent. It's not a Mac, but it's getting closer. But then again, if you ask me, there was quite a distance to travel based on the, uh, "rustic" Windows 3.x interface.

Just as Netscape constantly revises their browser, Microsoft has been on an aggressive upgrade path with major releases distributed as fast as the company can complete them. What's surprising is that Microsoft seems to be pulling ahead. The first version of Microsoft Internet Explorer for the Mac was okay, but it lacked many of the best features of Navigator. Currently, the 3.0 release of both browsers had remarkably similar features and the differentiation revolved around the add-on pieces like group conferencing (Microsoft has a better design, Netscape has a better implementation), Net-based telephony (Microsoft has a better system), and interactive chat (they're about even). There are almost no HTML tags that are only available in one browser, unlike the first generation of these applications, which is good; very sophisticated Web page designs work for both. It is frustrating that currently only the 2.1 release of Internet Explorer was available for the Macintosh, though the 3.0 release had been out for awhile on the Windows platform. By the time you read this, however, you'll be able to use 3.0 for your Mac.

Launching Internet Explorer

Once you're ready to start browsing the Web, or even just the files I've included with this book, you need to find and launch either Explorer or Navigator. You can most easily do so by double-clicking on its icon on your desktop, launching the application.

The first time you start up Explorer it's going to try and connect to the Microsoft home page on the World Wide Web, which could be a problem if you don't already have your Internet connection up and running. If that happens, don't worry; just choose cancel when it either pops up a dialog box asking for a phone number or otherwise indicates that it's waiting for a Net connection. You'll end up looking at a blank page, but all the controls will be there. Now, from the File menu, choose Open_File... (or use the Command-O keyboard shortcut). That launches a standard Mac file selection dialog, as shown in Figure 1-12.

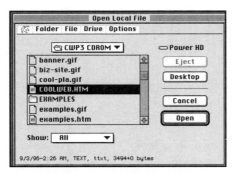

Figure 1-12: Find the file coolweb.htm and click on Open.

Now we're getting somewhere! Internet Explorer should promptly open up the file and the associated graphics, displaying it all in one neat window. You might have different toolbars shown on your screen, by the way, but it's easy to change back and forth from the View menu. Figure 1-13 shows how the *Creating Cool Web Pages with HTML* Web page should look on your screen.

If you have the toolbar selected, you'll see a set of small buttons that can help you move your way around the Web. From the left, they let you move backwards and forwards in the set of pages you've viewed, stop the transfer of a slow page, refresh the current page (that is, get a new copy of the page and rewrite the screen. This will prove a huge help to you as you develop your own Web pages) and instantly zip back to your home or default page. The globe icon with the magnifying glass enables you to pop straight to your favorite Web search engine, the folder icon with the star in the center enables you to open your list of favorite sites, and the printer icon enables you to print the current Web page on the screen. A cool

Figure 1-13: Creating Cool Web Pages, the HTML version.

feature that's unique to Internet Explorer is represented by the final button: the capital "A" with the small up and down arrows will enlarge all the type on the current Web page, up to the maximum size, then shrink it, stepping up and down in size, once per click. That is, if you're look at a Web page and the text is just too tiny to read comfortably, click on this button to make all the text larger. Figure 1-14 gives you an easy summary of these different buttons.

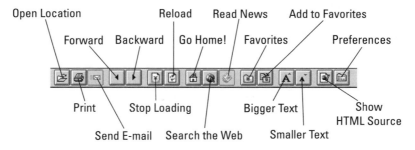

Figure 1-14: Handy shortcuts from the toolbar.

Changing the default page

Now that you have the program running, one useful trick before we begin our exploration of HTML and the mysteries and adventure of building cool Web pages: let's change your default page to the CoolWeb page you currently should have on your screen. When you're done learning how to write cool Web pages, you can then change it to your own page, or perhaps to a useful site on the Internet itself.

To change your default page, you'll want to choose Options from the Edit menu. In the Options box that opens, you'll notice one labeled Home/Search Page. Choose it, and now you should see something remarkably like Figure 1-15.

Options	
Browser Display	The Home Page and Search Page buttons on the tool bar (or items on the Go menu) can be customized to open any pages you want.
Web Content	
Home/Search Page	Your [Home Page ▼] is currently:
Font	http://www.msn.com/
Security	┌ Change Address ─
Mail	To change your Home Page to be the page you are currently viewing, click Use Current. [Use Current]
News	To have no Home Page, click Use None. [Use None]
Helpers	To change your Home Page back to its original location, click Use Default. [Use Default]
Proxy	
Advanced	

☐ Use Internet Config settings [IC Settings...]   [Cancel]   [OK]
(This will disable some preferences above.)

Figure 1-15: Changing your default start page.

Because you're currently viewing the page that you want to make your default, simply click on the topmost of the two buttons, Use Current.

That's all there is to it. Now the next time you start up the Internet Explorer, you'll find the cheery *Creating Cool Web Pages with HTML* page conveniently accessible.

Take a few minutes now to scroll around and click on the 'examples' button to see how I've laid out the dozens of example files so that they parallel what's shown in this book. Remember that you can always use the back arrow on the toolbar to go back to the previous page you were viewing.

Moving On

In this chapter, you quickly toured some of the sites available on the Net and saw how you can use Web pointers to access more than just HTML documents. You learned that you can use Web browsers to transfer files via FTP, search Gopher sites, and jump to other machines on the Internet via Telnet. In Chapter 2, I delve into the mysteries of constructing the URLs that are the heart of the Web information-linking scheme.

URLs:
What They
Are and How
to Use Them

In This Chapter

In this chapter, I discuss the various types of URLs (Uniform Resource Locators), where they come from, what they're all about, and how to create them for your own use. I include brief explanations of FTP, Gopher, telnet, and e-mail as they relate to URL construction.

Where URLs came from

What URLs are all about

Various types of URLs, based on service type

Are you itching to start writing your own HTML documents and creating a world of information on the Web? Take heart — when you've mastered the concepts in this chapter, you'll be ready to start tackling the fun stuff!

Finding Information in the Flood of Data

As our society makes the transition from products to information, we see the rapid acceleration of an age-old problem: identifying needed resources. Finding and obtaining resources has been an important theme of world history, whether it be spices, fuel, raw materials, or information. It would seem that computers today would make searching *easier*. After all, aren't computers supposed to be experts at sifting through large bodies of data to find what you seek? Well, yes and no. First, I should differentiate between data and information. *Data* is "stuff" — an all-encompassing body including every iota of digital memory and space on hard disks and backup tapes. *Information*, on the other hand, is the data that is relevant to and valuable for your specific interests. If you're interested in the Beat poets of the 1960s, for example, then information on other topics, such as municipal drainage systems or needlepoint, is clutter.

Computers have tremendously expanded the proliferation of data. As a result, separating information from the massive flood of data is one of the fundamental challenges of the information age. I can only imagine how much worse the situation will get in the next decade, as more and more data flows down the wires.

When considered in this vein, the Internet has a big problem. Because it has no central authority or organization, the Net's vast stores of data are not laid out in any meaningful or intuitive fashion. You are just as likely to find information on Beat poets on a machine run by a German embassy as you are to find it on a small liberal arts school's computer in San Francisco.

URLs to the Rescue

CERN is the high-energy physics research facility in Switzerland that created the underlying technology of the World Wide Web. When Tim Berners-Lee and his team at CERN began creating a common mechanism for uniquely identifying information in dataspace, they realized the need for a scheme that would neatly encapsulate the various parts and that could be extended to include a wide variety of Internet services. The result was the URL.

To state the case succinctly, a URL (Uniform Resource Locator) is a unique descriptor that can identify any document (plain or hypertext), graphic, Gopher menu or item, Usenet article, computer, or file archive anywhere on the Internet or your machine. That's what makes URLs so tremendously valuable, although their format seems a bit puzzling and cryptic at first.

The name *URL* can be something of a misnomer. Many times, jotting down URLs as you surf the Web only helps you find resources the *second* time, serving as a sort of memo service for your Internet travels. Resource location — finding information for the *first* time on the Internet and the World Wide Web — is a problem I explore later in this book. For now, think of URLs as business cards for specific resources on the Internet.

How to Read a URL

On the plus side, the format for specifying a URL is consistent throughout the many services that the URL encompasses, including Usenet news, Gopher, Web HTML documents, and FTP archives. As a general rule, a URL is composed of the following elements:

```
service ://    hostname: port      /      directory-path/
```

Not all of these components appear in each URL, as you will see when you learn about the different types of URLs for different services. But the preceding example is good as a general guide.

Consider the following example:

```
http://www.intuitive.com/index.html
```

In this example, the service is identified as http. (HyperText Transport Protocol, the method by which Web documents are transferred across the Internet.) By using http:, you indicate to the *client* program — the program, such as Mosaic, Navigator, MacWeb, or Explorer, that you use on your computer to browse the Web — that you'll be connecting to a Web document. The host computer that offers the information you seek is www.intuitive.com. The com (called the *zone*) tells you it is a commercial site, intuitive is the *domain* or *host*, and www is the name of the Web *server,* a particular computer. Usually, as is the case here, you don't have to specify a *port* (ports are sort of like TV channels) because most servers use standard default port numbers. The file to open is index.html.

The following URL is a slightly more complex example:

```
ftp://ftp.cts.com/pub/wallst
```

The URL identifies a file archive for the firm Wall Street Direct (I just happen to know this). You can see that the URL points to an archive by its service identifier, FTP (File Transport Protocol, meaning the way files are copied over the Net). The server and host in question is ftp.cts.com. Notice that this URL specifies that upon connecting to the FTP server, the browser program should change to the /pub/wallst directory and display the files therein.

Here's one more example:

```
news:alt.internet.services
```

The preceding URL enables a browser to read the Usenet newsgroup alt.internet.services, and you will notice that it is quite different from the other URL examples. For one thing, it doesn't specify a host. When you set up your browser program (the details differ from browser to browser), you indicate in a preferences or configuration file which host can be used to access Usenet. Usually, the host is the news server at your Internet provider. As a result, no slashes are required in the URL because the browser already has that information. URLs for news resources are therefore boiled down to the service and newsgroup name.

You can specify a variety of Internet information publishing services with URLs. The actual meanings of the URL components differ subtly, depending on which type of service is being specified. In the following sections, I examine URLs for each service in more detail.

FTP via URL

If you are familiar with the historical roots of the Internet and its predecessor networks (notably ARPANET), you already know that one of the system's earliest uses was to transfer files quickly between hosts at different sites. The standard mechanism for accomplishing file transfers was and still is FTP. But as computers have acquired friendlier interfaces, FTP has remained in the Stone Age. Many users still use clunky command-line interfaces for this vital function.

 FTP via a Web browser is much nicer.

Anonymous FTP

Millions of files are accessible throughout the Net via FTP. At a majority of hosts, you don't even need an account to download the files you seek. That's because a standard Net practice called *anonymous FTP* enables any user to log in to an FTP host using the name *anonymous*. If asked for a password, you type in your e-mail address. You can use anonymous FTP to acquire new programs for your computer.

FTP was one of the first services addressed in the URL specification developed at CERN. An FTP URL takes the following form:

```
ftp://host/directory-path
```

The URL `ftp://gatekeeper.dec.com/pub`, for example, uniquely specifies the pub directory of files available via FTP at the host gatekeeper at Digital Equipment Corporation.

In fact, the URL `ftp://gatekeeper.dec.com/pub` is specific, by omission. By not including a username and password, the URL tells you that the site is accessible by anonymous FTP.

Non-anonymous FTP

Although most Web browser FTP-ing is done anonymously, FTP URLs *can* include the username and password for a specific account. If I had the account *coolweb* on DEC's machine, and the password was *xyzxyz,* I could modify the URL to allow other people to connect to that account, as in the following example:

```
ftp://coolweb:xyzxyz@gatekeeper.dec.com/pub
```

Ports

Things can get even more complex when you start dealing with ports. FTP, like other programs on Internet servers, may be listening to ports other than the default port for its type of service.

Let me explain: Imagine that each server on the Internet is like a TV station — not broadcasting and receiving all data across all possible frequencies; but aiming at specific types of data, formatted in a standard manner, at individual frequencies or channels. On the Internet, those channels are called *ports*. If you want to watch your local ABC affiliate on TV, for example, you may know that the station comes in on channel seven and not on channel four. By the same token, if you want to connect to the mail server on a specific computer, you may know that the server has a *default port* of 25. Some sites, however, opt to change these default port numbers (don't ask why). In such cases, you need to identify the special port within the URL.

What if a site decides to offer anonymous FTP for public use but uses port 494 instead of the default FTP port? Then you have to specify that channel number in the URL, as in the following example:

```
ftp://gatekeeper.dec.com:494/pub
```

The preceding URL instructs a browser to connect to channel 494, look for the FTP server, and then move to the pub directory therein.

If you want to use your own account and password simultaneously, simply put together the URL that contains all the necessary information, as follows:

```
ftp://coolweb:xyzxyz@gatekeeper.dec.com:494/pub
```

Fortunately, you're unlikely to see anything so complex with an FTP URL. In most cases, you'll have the URL so you can look at it and see its components, even though it may be somewhat intimidating.

Using FTP URLs

The most valuable thing about FTP URLs is that, if you specify a directory, most Web browsers list the files in that directory, and with a double-click you can either transfer the files you want or move into other directories to continue browsing. If you specify a file within the URL, the browser connects to the server and transfers the file directly to your computer.

The following example is a URL containing all the information you need to obtain a copy of the HTTP specification document, should you for some reason want to read this highly complex and lengthy technical description of the transport protocol:

```
ftp://ftp.w3.org/pub/www/doc/http-spec.txt
```

Are you curious what else is in that directory? To find out, use the same URL but omit the actual filename at the end, as in the following:

```
ftp://ftp.w3.org/pub/www/doc/
```

Gopher via URL

URLs for FTP archives are rather tricky, but they're nothing compared to Gopher URLs. If you've used the Gopher Internet service at all, you already know that it's a nicely designed hierarchical menu system for browsing file and text archives, sort of like a massively extended file system. Gopher service design involves a simple dialog between the Gopher client (on your Mac) and the Gopher server (somewhere on the Net).

Be aware, however, that the descriptions of menu items in Gopher don't necessarily correspond to the Gopher internal names for the items.

Climbing a Gopher tree

I'll give you an example. By default, specifying a host within Gopher connects you to the top level of the Gopher menu, sometimes called a *tree,* on that host. (It's confusing — think of the tree as being upside down.) For the most part, Gopher menu items can be files or other menus. Choosing items from the Gopher menu either moves you down the tree or retrieves the items.

For example, if you choose the third menu item from the top level menu of the Gopher server running at gopher.ic.ac.uk, you get a new set of menu items, as shown in Figure 2-1. The top menu item is Search Gopherspace Using Veronica. Choosing get info from the Gopher client program, however, reveals that the internal Gopher identification, the actual directory for this entry, is /veronica.

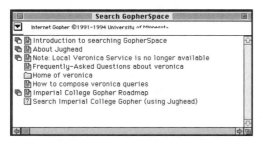

Figure 2-1: Visiting gopher.ic.ac.uk with TurboGopher.

It gets stickier. Within a Gopher URL, a single-character prefix in a Gopher address identifies the Gopher item's type. For example, 0 denotes files, and 1 denotes directories (folders). Therefore, to fully specify the directory shown as item 2 in Figure 2-1, you must preface the Gopher directory in the URL with 1/, as follows:

```
1/veronica
```

How does the numerical prefix translate into a URL? Quite simply: it's tacked onto the end of the URL in the same way that the directory path and filename information was included with the FTP URL, to wit:

```
gopher://gopher.ic.ac.uk/1/veronica
```

In case the use of uppercase and lowercase characters hasn't already tipped you off, remember that URLs are case sensitive. Type them *exactly* as you see them.

Real-life Gopher URLs

Now that you've learned more than you ever wanted to know about Gophers and URLs, you're ready to look at some actual Gopher URLs! The good news is that the majority of Gopher URLs don't look much different from their FTP cousins, as shown in the following example:

```
gopher://owl.trc.purdue.edu/
```

The preceding example is the simplest possible Gopher URL. The URL specifies the Gopher service (gopher:) and the name of the server system (owl.trc.purdue.edu/). In this case, the system is a server at Purdue University (my alma mater). Here is another example:

```
gopher://press-gopher.uchicago.edu:70/1
```

The preceding URL specifies the main information Gopher for the University of Chicago Press. Instead of using the default Gopher port, though, the site opted for port 70 (who knows why?). After the port, the URL indicates that the first thing the user will see is a directory, specified in a Gopher URL by inserting /1. When no *specific* directory is indicated in the URL, the preceding URL actually accomplishes exactly the same thing as the following slightly simpler example:

```
gopher://press-gopher.uchicago.edu:70/
```

Here is a slightly longer example:

```
gopher://boombox.micro.umn.edu/0/gopher/Macintosh-
TurboGopher/helper-applications/Anarchie-140.sit
```

That URL loads an executable file (Anarchie) that is available through the Gopher server. Anarchie is a great shareware program that enables you to easily access the Archie FTP database system and then actually grabs the files for you. Think of Archie as an intelligent assistant who finds and obtains copies of any software or file you want on the Internet. A copy of Anarchie is included on the CD-ROM.

Electronic Mail via URL

URLs for e-mail are quite simple, fortunately, and require minimal explanation. You can specify any e-mail address as a URL simply by prefacing the snippet mailto: as the service name, as in the following example:

```
mailto:taylor@intuitive.com
```

Again, make sure that you don't use spaces in the URL.

Note that you can *send* e-mail in a URL but you cannot *retrieve* it.

Some browsers, such as Mosaic, launch a separate e-mail program to handle e-mail services. Others, such as Netscape, handle e-mail directly. A box pops up and enables you to compose and send mail (albeit with little control of the final content when compared to a full-blown electronic mail package such as Eudora).

Telnet via URL

Transferring files through FTP is unquestionably valuable (hence its status as one of the original Internet services). Another capability that caused Internet use to explode is *telnet*. Telnet gives everyone on the Net the ability to log in to other computers on the Net, just as though they were connected to that machine directly. Not all Internet computers support telnet, but many do.

Telnet, you will be glad to know, is easy to specify in URLs: you simply specify the service and the host to which you want to connect. For example, to log in to the media laboratory at the Massachusetts Institute of Technology (MIT), use the following URL:

```
telnet://media.mit.edu/
```

When you use telnet URLs, your Web browser program actually tries to launch a separate, external telnet program to negotiate the telnet connection, which means that nothing happens unless you've already installed and configured a separate telnet program (such as NCSA Telnet). Mosaic, Netscape, Internet Explorer, MacWeb, and similar programs aren't designed to enable you to directly interact with the remote computer from within the browser. You can grab your own copy of NCSA Telnet by visiting the National Center for Supercomputer Applications at:
http://www.ncsa.uiuc.edu/SDG/Software/Brochure/
MacSoftDesc.html

Usenet News via URL

Working with Usenet news is somewhat tricky because you must find an existing server that will allow you access. Many systems don't give you that access to Usenet, even if you pay for an account on the system. (A list of *public* Usenet hosts — hosts that attempt to provide news free of charge to all — is available on the Net, but in my experience, only about five percent of them actually enable you to connect.)

To see the list of public Usenet sites for yourself, visit:
`http://www.phoenix.net/config/news.html`

If you are already connected to a server that offers access to Net news, you should be able to configure your browser to access it. Alternatively, check your account settings for an NNTPSERVER, a computer that can usually be used to access news from your Web browser, too.

Building a news URL is a straightforward process. Simply type news: followed by the exact name of the newsgroup. No slashes are needed (or allowed), and there's not yet a standard approach for specifying individual articles. Here are a couple of examples:

```
news:news.answers
news:comp.sys.mac.announce
```

The Heart of the Web: HTTP URLs

Although all the services (except telnet) listed earlier in this chapter are valuable and interesting when used via a Web browser, the capability to connect with other Web servers via HTTP is what *really* makes the Web revolutionary.

The general format for HTTP references is the same as in the FTP references earlier in this chapter. The following is a typical HTTP URL:

```
http://www.halcyon.com/normg/snews.html
```

That particular URL is for the *Seattle Hometown News*. You can see the secret: the URL lives within the directory of a user called normg. The format of the preceding URL should be quite familiar to you by now: the service name, a colon, the double slash, the host name, a slash, some specific options (in this case, the directory normg), and the name of a specific file with the Web standard html filename extension to denote an HTML markup file.

If you've ever used a PC running Windows 3.x, then you know that it's unable to cope with four-letter filename suffixes. Windows simply chops off the fourth character in the extension, making it .htm instead. You'll see this all over the Net. In this book, I use both the proper .html extension, and as .htm.

As it turns out, many times you don't even need to specify a filename if you'd rather not do so. The following is another example of a URL, this time for the *Palo Alto Weekly* in Palo Alto, California:

```
http://www.service.com/paw/
```

Note that the URL contains a default directory (paw). But because the URL doesn't specify a filename, the Web program is savvy enough to choose the default file — probably default.html, as configured on each server. If your system doesn't recognize default.html, then try index.html or Welcome.html, or ask your administrator for the secret filename.

If the HTTP server is on a nonstandard port, of course, that fact can be specified as follows:

```
http://bookweb.cwis.uci.edu:8042/
```

The preceding URL is for the University of California at Irvine bookstore. Instead of using the default port for an HTTP server, the site opted for port 8042. If you want to create a URL containing both the port and a specific filename, you can do so, as in the following example:

```
http://bookweb.cwis.uci.edu:8042/Anime/AMG/intro.html
```

Theoretically, you can specify an unlimited number of URL types (although you probably don't want to know that at this point!). The vast majority of the URLs that you'll see, however, are in the http, ftp, telnet, gopher, mailto, and news formats, as demonstrated in this chapter.

Translating spaces in URLs

One important issue before I am done with this chapter: *a URL cannot contain spaces.*

Repeat: *URLs cannot contain spaces.*

This "no spaces" limitation caused me much consternation and some lengthy debugging sessions when I started working with Web servers. The other limitation, of course, is that they're case-sensitive, even on machines that are otherwise case insensitive for filenames.

If you have a space in a Gopher address or menu name, for example, you have to translate each space into a special character that is understood to represent a space within a URL. You can't use the underscore character (_), however. That character may be used to mean something else in some systems, and automatically translating it into a space would, no doubt, break many things. You wouldn't want to do that.

Instead, the URL specification enables any character to be specified as — ready for this? — *a hexadecimal equivalent prefaced by a percent sign (%).* To use test server in a URL, for example, replace the space with its hexadecimal equivalent (20), resulting in `test%20server`.

Hexadecimal (base 16) numbers range not from 0 to 9, as in the decimal (base 10) system, but from 0 to 15. Actually, here are the hexadecimal numerals: 0, 1, 2, 3, 4, 5, 6, 7, 8, 9, A, B, C, D, E, F.

To compute the decimal equivalent of a hexadecimal number, multiply each number by the base raised to the appropriate power. Hex 20 therefore would be 2 * 161 + 0 * 160, or 32 decimal. (Don't worry if this doesn't make sense; you'll probably never need to figure this out. Just remember to check Table 2-1 for the most common hex equivalents.)

Table 2-1 shows the special URL forms of some common characters that you may encounter while building URL specifications. Notice especially that you need to codify any use of the percent sign itself so the Web browser program doesn't get confused. Almost perverse, eh?

Table 2-1: URL Coding for Common Characters

Character	Hex Value	Equivalent URL Coding
Space	20	%20
Tab	09	%09
Enter	10	%0A
Line feed	0D	%0D
Percent (%)	25	%25

Moving On

A solid understanding of URLs and how they're built is vital to working with the Web, adding pointers, and generally getting around. There are lots of weird variations to the basic URL, so don't be too nervous if you feel a teeny bit lost. The main point of this chapter is to give you a passing familiarity with what URLs are, how they're built, and how different types of services require different URL formats. In a few chapters, you'll learn how to tie URLs into your own Web documents; after that, the material in this chapter doubtless will crystallize and make much more sense. Chapter 3 begins the fun part of this book (indeed, the heart of the book): how to write cool Web documents!

Basic HTML

Okay, it's time to get going and learn HTML! In this chapter, you'll go from 0 to 60 in no time flat, and by the end, you'll be able to create attractive Web pages.

Basics of HTML Layout

What is HTML? At its most fundamental, HTML (HyperText Markup Language) is a set of special codes that you embed in text to add formatting and linking information. HTML is based on SGML (Standardized Generalized Markup Language). By convention, all HTML information begins with an open angle bracket (<) and ends with a close angle bracket (>). For example, <HTML>. That formatting instruction, or *tag* — or *HTML tag*, as it's also known — tells an HTML *interpreter* (browser) that the document is written and marked up in standard HTML. An example of an HTML interpreter is Microsoft's Internet Explorer, available for free on their Web site. Get your own copy at:
http://www.microsoft.com/ie

HTML, like any other markup language, inherits some problems. Suppose, for example, that you want to have the word <HTML> — including angle brackets — in a document. You need some way of preventing that word from being interpreted as an HTML tag. Later in this book, you'll learn how to include such tricky information within your documents. For now, keep an eye open for this kind of problem as you read along.

HTML and browsers

What happens if a program that interprets HTML, such as Explorer, reads a file that doesn't contain any HTML tags? Suppose that you recently created the file not-yet.html but haven't had a chance to add HTML tags. Your file looks something like this:

```
Dave's Desk
West Lafayette, Indiana
3 November, 1996

Dear Reader,

   Thank you for connecting to my Web server, but I
regret to tell you
that things aren't up and running yet!
They will be _soon_, but they aren't today.

                  Sincerely,

                  Dave Taylor
```

Looks reasonable, although some of the lines seem shorter than you're used to when you read such notes. Figure 3-1 shows what the file looks like when it's read into the Navigator browser. A quick note: if you want to immediately start creating HTML files, you can use just about any editor, from Microsoft Word to TeachText. Just make sure you save the file with either an '.html' or '.htm' suffix and that — a key thing — you save as *text only* rather than in the default format of your program.

Figure 3-1 is clearly not at all what you wanted and probably would be quite puzzling to a viewer. Notice also that, although placing an underscore before and after a word is a clue in some BBS systems that the word should be underlined (_soon_), that is *not* part of HTML, so the underscores are left untouched, whether or not they make sense to the viewer.

Netscape: not-yet.htm

Back | Forward | Home | Reload | Images | Open | Print | Find | Stop

Dave's Desk West Lafayette, Indiana 3 November, 1996 Dear Reader, Thank you for connecting to my Web server, but I regret to tell you that things aren't up and running yet! They will be _soon_, but they aren't today. Sincerely, Dave Taylor

Figure 3-1: The file not-yet.html, without any HTML, in Navigator.

What the document shown in Figure 3-1 needs is HTML tags — some information that Web browser programs can use to lay out and format the information therein. The implied formatting information contained in not-yet.html works for humans visually, but Web browsers would ignore it because it's not in HTML. In other words, to you or me, seeing a tab as the first character of a sentence is a good clue that the sentence is the beginning of a new paragraph, but as you can clearly see in Figure 3-1, that just isn't the case with World Wide Web browsers.

The example shown in Figure 3-1 may seem a little silly right now. But as you work with HTML, I'm sure you'll discover from time to time that when you think you set up a document in a certain way, it looks dramatically different from within a Web browser.

Always test your HTML documents by viewing them through one or more Web browser programs to ensure that everything looks correct.

If you open it, close it

Although many HTML tags are stand-alone units, some are *paired,* with beginning and end tags. The beginning tag is called the *open* tag, and the end tag is called the *close* tag.

The most basic of all tags is the one shown earlier: <HTML>, which indicates that the information that follows is written in HTML. The <HTML> tag is a paired tag, however, so you need to add a close tag at the end of the document, which is the same as the open tag with the addition of a slash: </HTML>. By the same token, if you begin an italicized phrase with <I> (the italics tag) you must end it with </I>. Everything between the open and close tags receives the particular attribute of that tag (the procedure of surrounding what you want to format is called *section-block notation*).

If you get confused and specify, for example, a backslash instead of a slash, as in <\HTML>, or some other variant, the browser program doesn't understand and simply ignores the close tag, and the attributes in the open tag continue past the point where you meant them to stop. In the case of the <HTML> tag, because </HTML> should appear at the end of the document, the problem probably isn't significant because there would be nothing after it to mess up. But some systems on the Net are very picky and can show some peculiar results for HTML tags that aren't closed.

 Certainly, remembering to close any tags that you open is a good habit.

Simple-minded browsers

What do you think would happen if you included quotation marks around the tags — for example, if you used "<HTML>" at the beginning of your document rather than <HTML>? If you guessed that the entire "<HTML>" including the pairs of quotes would be displayed, you're right. Let me again emphasize that the Web browsers are very simple minded in their interpretation of HTML. Anything that varies from the specific characters in the HTML language specification results in a layout other than the one you want.

Breaking at Paragraphs and Lines

The most important markup tags you will learn — and probably the tags that you'll use most often — specify that you want a *paragraph break* or a *line break*. Several variants of these tags exist. But you can create readable and useful Web documents by using only the two tags <P> and <BR>.

To specify that you want a paragraph break, use the tag <P>. (The tag is mnemonic: *P* for *paragraph*.) The following example adds some <P> tags to the not-yet.html file seen in Figure 3-1, and also wraps the file in the <HTML> and </HTML> tags:

```
<HTML>
Dave's Desk
West Lafayette, Indiana
3 November, 1996
<P>
Dear Reader,
<P>
   Thank you for connecting to my Web server, but I
```

```
regret to tell you
that things aren't up and running yet!
They will be _soon_, but they aren't today.
<P>
                    Sincerely,
<P>
                    Dave Taylor

</HTML>
```

Figure 3-2 shows what the preceding HTML text looks like in a browser.

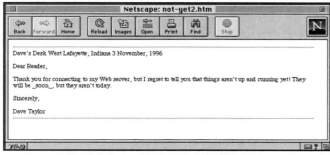

Figure 3-2: Paragraph breaks in not-yet.html.

Figure 3-2's version of the file is a huge improvement over Figure 3-1's, but some problems still exist, not the least of which is that the first few lines don't look right. In their zeal to organize the text neatly, Web browsers, by default, fill as many words into each line as they can manage. Filling the lines is okay for the main paragraph of the file, but the first few lines will be closer to what you want if you indicate that the browser should break the line between items, rather than fill it all in.

To break lines in HTML, use the *break* tag: <BR>. Like any tag, the break tag can appear anywhere in the text, including at the end of the line you want to break. Following is the HTML file when the break tag is used:

```
<HTML>
Dave's Desk<BR>
West Lafayette, Indiana<BR>

3 November, 1996<BR>
<P>
```

```
(continued)
Dear Reader, <BR>
<P>
  Thank you for connecting to my Web server, but I
regret to tell you
that things aren't up and running yet!
They will be _soon_, but they aren't today.
<P>
                    Sincerely, <BR>
<P>
                    Dave Taylor<BR>
</HTML>
```

From a stylistic perspective, you should try to have a consistent scheme for your tags, particularly because you may have to go into fairly complex files and figure out what's wrong. As a result, I suggest that you place all line breaks at the end of text lines, and all paragraph marks in lines of their own. This book uses that style throughout.

Figure 3-3 shows the output of the not-yet.html file when <BR> is used.

Figure 3-3: The file not-yet.html with <P> and <BR> tags.

One remaining problem with the layout is the fact that the signature information is intended to be shifted to the right a few inches, as in a standard business note, but in the browser it's still at the left edge of the document.

To remedy the problem, you can use the *preformatted information* tag: <PRE>. The <PRE> tag is also a paired tag, so it works across as many lines as needed, without any fuss, and must end with </PRE>. The following example changes the last few lines of the not-yet.html file to reflect the use of this tag:

```
<HTML>
Dave's Desk<BR>
West Lafayette, Indiana<BR>
3 November, 1996<BR>
<P>
Dear Reader, <BR>
<P>
   Thank you for connecting to my Web server, but I
regret to tell you
that things aren't up and running yet!
They will be _soon_, but they aren't today.
<PRE>

                    Sincerely,


                    Dave Taylor

</PRE>
</HTML>
```

After adding the <PRE> tags, you achieve the desired formatting, but now another problem has cropped up: the text in the preformatted block (the stuff between <PRE> and </PRE>) appears in a different, monospace typeface! You can see the difference in Figure 3-4 if you look closely.

Typefaces refer to a particular style of letters in a variety of sizes. A *font*, by contrast, is a typeface in a specific size and style. Helvetica is a typeface, but 12-point Helvetica italic is a font.

Figure 3-4: Format is correct, but typeface is new.

Navigator changed the typeface in Figure 3-4 because the browser assumed that the text to be preserved was a code listing or other technical information. That's just part of the <PRE> tag. So, it worked, sort of, but it's not quite what you wanted. (You can use <PRE> to your advantage in other situations, however, as you'll see later in this chapter.) For now, just leave the stuff at the left edge of the screen.

Breaking Your Document into Sections

If you take a close look at HTML, you see that it's divided into two sections: what I call the *stationery* section (the information that would be printed on the pad if the file were a physical note) and the body of the message itself. Think of the information you typically find at the top of a memo:

```
M E M O R A N D U M
To:            Date:
From:          Subject:
```

Those are the most common items of information at the beginning of a memo, and then there's usually a *rule* (a line) followed by blank space in which you write the actual content.

Similarly, for the sake of organization, HTML files commonly are broken into two sections: the *head* (or *header*) that contains the introductory page-formatting information, and the *body*. You use the paired tags <HEAD> </HEAD> and <BODY> </BODY> to surround each section. The following example shows how the not-yet.html file looks when these tags are added:

```
<HTML>
<HEAD></HEAD>
<BODY>
Dave's Desk<BR>
West Lafayette, Indiana<BR>
3 November, 1996<BR>
<P>
Dear Reader,
<P>
   Thank you for connecting to my Web server, but I
regret to tell you
that things aren't up and running yet!
They will be _soon_, but they aren't today.
```

```
<P>
                        Sincerely,
<P>
                        Dave Taylor

</BODY>
</HTML>
```

The <HEAD> </HEAD> and <BODY> </BODY> formatting information doesn't add anything to the display, I admit. Also, the document doesn't contain any introductory HTML formatting information yet. If you were to view the preceding HTML text in a Web browser, it would look identical to Figure 3-3. Later, when you start learning some of the more complex parts of HTML, you'll see why section-block notation (for example, <HEAD></HEAD>) can be a boon.

What do you think would happen if I fed the following information to a Web browser?

```
<HTML><HEAD></HEAD><BODY>
Dave's Desk<BR>West Lafayette, Indiana<BR>3 November,
1996<BR>
<P>Dear Reader,<P>Thank you for connecting to
my Web server, but I regret to tell you that
things aren't up and running yet!
They will be _soon_, but they aren't today.
<P>Sincerely,<P>Dave Taylor</BODY></HTML>
```

If you guessed that the screen output of the preceding example would look exactly like the carefully spaced material shown earlier, you're correct.

Remember that Web browsers ignore carriage returns when the document is reformatted for display. That suggests that you can save a great deal of space — and display a great deal more of your document on screen — simply by skipping all the extra returns — *but I strongly recommend against such a strategy.* Why? In a nutshell, writing your Web documents with the markup tags in logical places makes the document easier to work with later. I've written and had to debug more than a thousand HTML documents, and I can assure you that the more things are jammed together, the less sense they make a few weeks later when you have to add some information or modify the content.

Title Your Page

One of the subtle (but quite simple) things you can do to make your Web page quite cool is give it a good title with the `<TITLE>` tag. The title usually appears at the top of the window displayed on the user's computer. Go back and look at the information in the top header of Figure 3-4: there is none! Some browsers simply display the filename.

The `<TITLE>` tag enables you to define the exact title you want in the document. It is a paired tag and appears within the `<HEAD>` `</HEAD>` block of information, as follows:

```
<HEAD>
<TITLE>This is the title</TITLE>
</HEAD>
```

For the document you've been developing in this chapter, not-yet.html, a nice title would be one that reinforces the message in the file itself, as in the following example:

```
<HTML>
<HEAD>
<TITLE>Not Yet Ready for Prime Time!</TITLE>
</HEAD>
```

Figure 3-5 shows how the new title text would look within the Navigator browser. Notice particularly the change in the top window border (also known as the title bar).

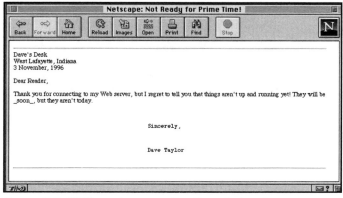

Figure 3-5: TITLE produces an attractive window frame.

The best titles should be succinct and avoid 'home page' or 'Web site' (because they're obviously just that). The title "CFMT Web Home Page" isn't very good. It's also a smart idea to avoid super long titles like "Restaurants, Shops, and other Businesses located on the main drag in Downtown Toronto."

The <TITLE> tag has one limitation: some Web browsers don't display titled windows, so the <TITLE> information isn't displayed for folks using those browsers. On the other hand, the text in <TITLE> is also used as the link info when a user saves a Web document into a *bookmark* or *hotlist* (compiled URLs for sites you've visited and want to remember). So, a meaningful <TITLE> for each page you create can be very helpful to your readers.

Common Footer Material

Just as you commonly see certain information, such as the title, in the header of a Web document, other information is commonly placed at the foot of the document. On the Web, you usually find copyright information and contact data for the creator of the page at the bottom of a document.

The tag used for such contact info is <ADDRESS>. It's a paired tag (<ADDRESS> *address information* </ADDRESS>). The following example shows the not-yet.html document with this tag added:

```
<HTML>
<HEAD>
<TITLE>Not Yet Ready for Prime Time!</TITLE>
</HEAD>
<BODY>
Dave's Desk<BR>
West Lafayette, Indiana<BR>
3 November, 1996<BR>
<P>
Dear Reader,
<P>
Thank you for connecting to my Web server, but I
regret to tell you
that things aren't up and running yet!
They will be _soon_, but they aren't today.
<P>
                        Sincerely,
```

```
(continued)
<P>
                        Dave Taylor
<ADDRESS>
Page Design by Dave Taylor (taylor@intuitive.com)
</ADDRESS>
</BODY>
</HTML>
```

Do you *have* to use the <ADDRESS> tag? Nope. Like various other items that appear in HTML pages, it can be used or skipped. (In Web pages that I create, I tend to not include address information, but many people like to have that information at the bottom of pages.) That's why I call tags like <ADDRESS> *quasi-standard* — it's useful, but not always present. As you can see in Figure 3-6, the address information is presented in italics, which is quite attractive for certain Web pages.

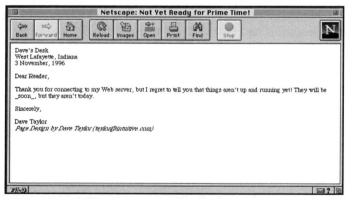

Figure 3-6: <HTML> plus <ADDRESS> information.

Defining Section Heads

The formatting information discussed so far in this chapter enables you to create attractive text. But what if your Web page should be broken into *sections* or even *subsections*? The various levels of *header-format* tags handle that situation.

Each header-format level has an open and close tag. The highest-level header-format tag is <H1>; the lowest (the smallest and least important subsection) is <H6>. To specify a top-level header, use <H1>*First Header*</H1>.

Header-format tags would be best illustrated in a different HTML page than not-yet.html, because it doesn't need headers and is already attractive. The following is the beginning of a table of contents or outline for an imaginary Web site:

```
<HTML>
<HEAD>
<TITLE>The Cool Web Movie Database</TITLE>
</HEAD>
<BODY>
Welcome to the Cool Web Movie Database. So far, we offer
information on the many brilliant films of David Lean;
soon, many more will be online.
<H1>The Early Years</H1>
<H2>In Which We Serve (1942)</H2>
<H2>This Happy Breed (1944)</H2>
<H1>Films with Sam Spiegel Productions</H1>
<H2>The Bridge on the River Kwai (1957)</H2>
<H2>Lawrence of Arabia (1962)</H2>
<H1>The Later Years</H1>
<H2>Doctor Zhivago (1965)</H2>
<H2>Ryan's Daughter (1970)</H2>
<ADDRESS>
This information maintained by Dave Taylor
</ADDRESS>
</BODY>
</HTML>
```

Figure 3-7 shows how the preceding text appears in a Web browser.

Most Web pages that you design probably won't have *quite* as many headers as the example in Figure 3-7.

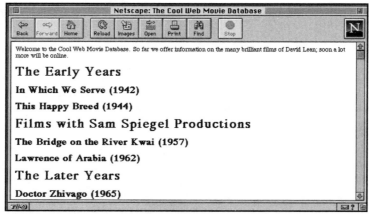

Figure 3-7: David Lean movies, outline form.

The following example adds a little more information about some of the films to show the value of different headers:

```
<H1>The Early Years</H1>
<H2>In Which We Serve (1942)</H2>
Co-directed and produced by Noel Coward, this film also
starred Noel Coward as Captain Kinross and Celia Johnson
as Mrs.
Kinross.
<H2>This Happy Breed (1944)</H2>
Based on the play by Noel Coward, this film starred Robert
Newton and again featured Celia Johnson.
<H1>Films with Sam Spiegel Productions</H1>
<H2>The Bridge on the River Kwai (1957)</H2>
Produced by Sam Spiegel, this film was the first of the
Lean blockbuster movies and featured a young Alec
Guinness, William Holden,
and a
brilliant performance from Sessue Hayakawa.
<H2>Lawrence of Arabia (1962)</H2>
One of my personal all-time favorite movies, this epic
adventure really established Lean as the creator of
sweeping
panoramas.
```

When the preceding example is viewed in a browser, the different headers appear in different size type, and information that is *not* part of the header appears in a roman (nonbold) typeface (see Figure 3-8).

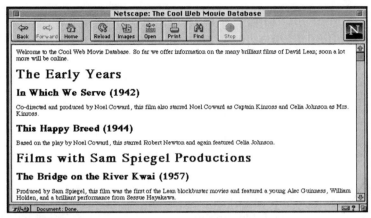

Figure 3-8: Movie information with some text.

One thing to remember about HTML is that the actual fonts, sizes, and layout of the final presentation can be altered by users based on the preferences they can set in their browsers. I contend, however, that precious few people actually alter the preference settings, so if your page looks good with the default values, you should be okay. If the default values look a little weird, as may well be the case with Explorer in particular, by all means experiment with the settings.

The Horizontal Rule

A very useful tag for readers is the *horizontal rule* tag: `<HR>`. Dropped anywhere in a Web document, it produces a skinny line across the page. The following example shows the movie information page with the `<HR>` tag added:

```
<HR>
<H1>The Early Years</H1>
<H2>In Which We Serve (1942)</H2>
Co-directed and produced by Noel Coward, this film also
starred
```

```
(continued)
Noel Coward as Captain Kinross and Celia Johnson as Mrs.
Kinross.
<H2>This Happy Breed (1944)</H2>
Based on the play by Noel Coward, this film starred Robert
Newton and
again featured Celia Johnson.
<HR>
<H1>Films with Sam Spiegel Productions</H1>
<H2>The Bridge on the River Kwai (1957)</H2>
Produced by Sam Spiegel, this was the first of the Lean
blockbuster
movies and featured a young Alec Guinness, William Holden,
and a
brilliant performance from Sessue Hayakawa.
```

You *can* overuse the horizontal rule, as well as any other formatting and design element, in a Web document. Used judiciously, though, the <HR> tag is tremendously helpful in creating cool pages. Figure 3-9 shows the browser view:

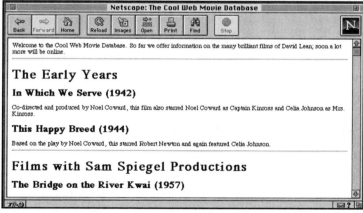

Figure 3-9: Movie database with horizontal rules.

Table 3-1 contains a summary of the HTML tags covered in this chapter.

Table 3-1:	Tags Used in this Chapter	
HTML Tag	**Close Tag**	**Meaning**
<ADDRESS>	</ADDRESS>	Address and creator information
<BODY>	</BODY>	Body of the HTML page
 	none	Line break
<HEAD>	</HEAD>	HTML formatting information
<Hn>	</Hn>	Document header level (*n = 1-6*)
<HR>	*none*	Horizontal rule
<HTML>	</HTML>	Defines a Web-formatted file
<P>	*none*	Paragraph breaks
<PRE>	</PRE>	Preformatted information
<TITLE>	</TITLE>	The title of the page

Moving On

A great deal of information was jammed into this chapter. You have learned most of the basics of HTML and are about ready to start creating your own Web pages. Already, you should be able to reproduce formatted information (like this chapter of this book, to pick the most immediate example) in an attractive format for users on the World Wide Web. The next chapter continues to explore HTML by explaining how to use boldface and italic formatting, add other types of emphasis to text, and make various other changes within sentences and paragraphs.

Text Styles

In This Chapter

In this chapter, I explore some of the nuts and bolts of text presentation and information layout.

How to boldface and italicize text

Underlining, monospace, and other text changes

Font sizes and colors

Other ways to emphasize words or phrases

By *text styles,* I mean specification of boldface, italics, and other changes that can be made in text. In Chapter 3, I showed you all the basics of HTML document layout in the proverbial fell swoop. But there's much more to creating cool Web pages.

Before you finish this chapter, you'll learn how to highlight certain words, phrases, titles, names, and other information with italicized or boldface type within the hypertext markup language. You'll also see that you can use all the HTML character formatting commands all over the place, but a better strategy is to use them only when they are most appropriate. Remember when you were given your first box of crayons, and you went wild using all the colors on each illustration that you worked on? Eventually, it dawned on you (unless you were a young Peter Max) that a *subset* of colors can be much more useful and attractive. In this chapter, you'll get a sense of *when* to emphasize words, as well as how to code the emphasis with HTML.

A Little History

Page design and layout have been around for thousands of years — since the beginning of writing as a form of communication. In Egyptian hieroglyphics, for example, vertical lines separated columns of glyphs to make them easier to read. Before the year 1000 A.D., scribes all over the world were using various techniques to present information on a page, including illumination (adding gold or silver to the ink or including other illustrations in the margins or twined around the letters), illustration, and other devices.

By the time Johannes Gutenberg introduced his printing press in the fifteenth century, with its revolutionary movable type supplanting etched- or engraved-plate printing, designers and artists were codifying various approaches to page design. A glance at the Gutenberg Bible foreshadows many aspects of modern text design, including italicized and boldface text.

Why am I rambling on about the history of page layout? Well, it's important to realize that italicized and boldface text have commonly accepted standard meanings. You don't have to follow the rules to the letter, but if your goal is to help people breeze through your Web material and quickly find what they seek, then keeping the guidelines in mind can be quite valuable.

Bold and Italic

In the examples in Chapter 3, I mentioned that some standard computer notation for underlining doesn't work. In Figure 3-1, I included the example _soon_, hoping that when read by a browser, the word would be italicized, underlined, or otherwise presented in a manner that would emphasize it.

One of the most important characteristics of any cool document layout — on the Web or in print — is the use of different fonts and various styles to help the reader navigate the material. For example, imagine this page without any spacing, paragraph breaks, headings, italics, or boldface words; it would look boring. More important, it would be more difficult to skim the page for information or to glance at it quickly to gain a sense of what is being discussed.

I like to remember the differences between type distinctions by imagining that I'm reading the material to an audience. Italicized words or phrases are those that I *emphasize* in my speech. Words or phrases in boldface I imagine to be *road signs* — items that help me skim the material and find specific spots. Apply this practice to text, and you see why section headings are in bold rather than italics: headings would be harder to find if they didn't stand out. The same reasoning applies to text size, large words stand out from smaller adjacent text.

Let's dive in and see how boldface and italic work in Web page design. Italic and boldface formatting require paired tags.

➡ The italic formatting tag is <I>, which is paired with </I>.

➡ The boldface formatting tag is <B>, and its partner is </B>.

Here's how a brief HTML passage looks with both boldface and italic text.

```
It turns out that <B>Starbucks</B>, the popular and
fast growing coffee chain, got its name from the
coffee-loving first mate in Melville's classic
tale of pursuit and revenge <I>Moby Dick< /I >,
although few people realize it.
```

Figure 4-1 shows how the preceding information looks in a Web browser. Notice that I made a slight mistake in the coding: the name of the book, *Moby Dick*, has an open italic tag, but I incorrectly added spaces within its partner, the close italic tag. As a result, the request to end the italic passage doesn't end when the title of the book is complete. Also, if you view this exact same snippet in Explorer or Navigator you'll find that each has a slightly different way of dealing with an error of this form. Another good reason to double-check your HTML in multiple browsers!

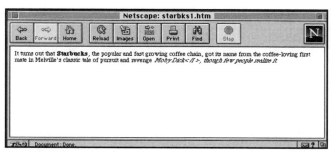

Figure 4-1: Boldface, italic, and a mistake.

You must always follow the angle bracket of an HTML formatting tag with the format code immediately; no spaces are allowed.

Underlining, Monospace, and Other Text Changes

A number of other formatting options are available within Web documents.

➡ The underline formatting tag is <U>, which is paired with </U>.

➡ The monospace tag is <TT> (TeleType), which is paired with </TT>.

➡ Superscripts are denoted by ^{and}; subscripts by _{and}.

➡ Text can be 'crossed-out' using <STRIKE>, which ends with </STRIKE>.

Monospace is so named because each letter in a monospace typeface occupies exactly the same width, even if the letter is quite narrow. Monospace type typically looks like the product of a typewriter. This is a monospace typeface. Proportional typefaces are more common. The text you are reading now is a proportional typeface. Note that it varies the width of the letters for easier reading; five occurrences of the letter *i,* for example (iiiii) isn't as long as five occurrences of *m* (mmmmm).

You may not want to use the <U> and <TT> tags too often, because of the possible problems. Mosaic, for example, doesn't understand the <TT> format, and some versions of Netscape Navigator ignore <U> formats. Also, when you create a Web document that contains *links* to other documents, the links are displayed in a different color — usually blue. However, to make links stand out more and to ensure that people with grayscale or black-and-white displays can recognize them, links also appear with an underscore. Which underlined words or phrases are links, and which are just underlined text? Figure 4-2 shows this underlining problem more clearly.

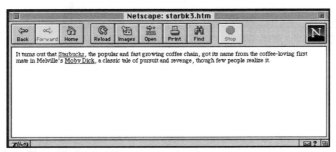

Figure 4-2: Links or underlined text?

You can't tell by looking at Figure 4-2, but the word *Starbucks* is a pointer to another document on the World Wide Web, whereas the book title, *Moby Dick*, is just an underlined word. As you can see, using underscores in Web pages can be confusing.

Monospace is often more useful than underlining, but it's not used extensively in Web pages either. For example, if you want to simulate computer input or output, you can display that text in monospace, as in the following:

```
Rather than typing <B><TT>DIR</TT></B> to find out what
files you have in your Unix account, you'll instead
want to type <B><TT>ls</TT></B>, as shown:
<PRE>
% <B>ls</B>
this that        the-other
</PRE>
```

The preceding example demonstrates that the preformatted text tag `<PRE>` produces text in monospace typeface, but it also preserves the original line breaks rather than fill the words into each line of text.

You can combine some HTML tags to produce exactly the output that you seek. In Figure 4-3, the terms *DIR* and *ls* appear in bold monospace text.

Figure 4-3: Monospace (and bold monospace) with <TT>.

If you're working with a mathematical formula or otherwise have reason to use superscripts and subscripts on your Web pages, there are two tags that offer easy formatting, as shown here:

```
<h2>If you could double the amount of water on the
planet - essentially H<sub>2</sub>O<sup>2</sup> - you'd
never have to worry about mowing the lawn again; it'd be
under the ocean!</h2>
```

The resulting format is very attractive and lends itself to slick formulae and instant math, as you can see in Figure 4-4.

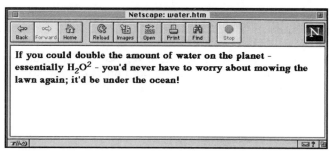

Figure 4-4: Super and Subscript format tags at work.

Note a trick here: to make the text stand out, I've enclosed the entire passage in ⟨H2⟩ header tags. It will automatically make the text larger and bold. There is an easier way, however, as you'll see later in this chapter.

Sometimes you want to show a change in text to someone visiting your page, and being able to cross out the text while still having it displayed can be quite useful. You can do that in most Web browsers with the ⟨STRIKE⟩ strikethrough tag. Here's how it would look as source:

```
<H2>If you could double the amount of water on the
planet - essentially H<SUB>2</SUB>O<SUP>2</SUP> - you'd
never have to worry about <STRIKE>mowing the lawn again;
it'd be
under the ocean!</STRIKE>buying a clothes dryer:
everything would be permanently wet!</H2>
```

The strikethrough formatting works well in this case, as you can see in Figure 4-5, because the text is fairly large (remember I'm using the ⟨H2⟩ trick to accomplish that), but if the text were smaller, the strikethrough line could make it unreadable. Be sure you carefully preview any ⟨STRIKE⟩ text before you unleash it on the world for just that reason.

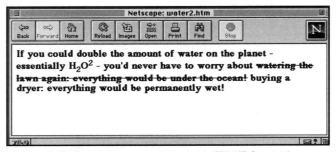

Figure 4-5: Corrections on screen with STRIKE formatting.

 Depending on the Web browser you're using, some HTML tags can be combined, and others can't. Combining bold and italics in some cases doesn't work, but either format is fine when combined with ⟨TT⟩.

Font Sizes and Colors

One of the recent additions to the hypertext markup language is also one of the most entertaining: font sizes and color changes. Font size ranges from one to seven, one being the smallest and seven being the largest. It's the opposite to the numbering of header tags, unfortunately, where header one is the largest and header six is the smallest.

All font changes are modifications to the <FONT> tag, and it's the first tag we've encountered where the tag itself includes specific attributes. HTML tags that can have attributes typically specify them as name=value pairs. The <FONT> tag is a fine example, to change the size of a passage of text, you'd use the formatting:

```
<FONT SIZE=7>some important text</FONT>.
```

In this example the words 'some important text' would be displayed at the largest possible size in the browser.

Notice that the closing tag for the <FONT> tag needn't include the attributes of the opening tag: we didn't need to use </FONT SIZE=7> to end the larger text. This is an important nuance and a great timesaver as you start to explore more complex formatting later in the book.

Font sizes can be specified exactly, as in the example above, or they can be relative size changes. To make a particular word one font size larger than the text surrounding it, here's the HTML:

```
This is a <FONT SIZE=+1>very</FONT> important issue to us.
```

The default font size in most browsers is SIZE=3, but in Microsoft Internet Explorer you can change the default size on the page by using the font size button on the toolbar (see Chapter 1 for details). Relative changes can't go below SIZE=1 or above SIZE=7, so if you have a default size of three and add ten to it, with a tag like <FONT SIZE=+10> it'll be identical in function to <FONT SIZE=7> or <FONT SIZE=+4>.

Color can be specified for a range of text in a very similar manner by using a different FONT attribute. The logical name is "color" and that's just what you can use: <FONT COLOR=blue>I'm blue</FONT> will display the specified passage of text in the specified color.

The current list of colors is aqua, black, blue, fuchsia, gray, green, lime, maroon, navy, olive, purple, red, silver, teal, white, and yellow. You can check for yourself online at:

```
http://www.microsoft.com/workshop/author/newhtml/
htmlr005.htm
```

Another strategy is to get the terrific HTML Color Picker, a Mac shareware app that helps you pick colors, at:

```
ftp://ftp.hawaii.edu/mirrors/info-mac/text/html/
html-color-picker-203.hqx
```

A wide variety of colors can be specified by name and you can have even finer resolution of color control by using RGB hexadecimal values. For basic colors, you'll find that you can work without worrying about it and get the result you want.

One final tag and we'll have an example that demonstrates all of these modifications. To change the default size of all text on a page you can use `<FONT SIZE=4>` or similar at the very top of the document, but in fact there's a specialized tag for just this purpose called `<BASEFONT>`. Its use is demonstrated below:

```
<BASEFONT SIZE=4>
<font size=7>Common Foods of the French Quarter</font><br>
You can visit <font size=+1>New Orleans</font> and have a
great time without ever leaving
the picturesque and partyin' French Quarter area,
particularly if you partake of some of these
fabulous local foods:
<UL>
<LI><FONT COLOR=RED>Beignets</FONT> - small deep-fried
donuts in powdered sugar. Best with
a steaming fresh <FONT SIZE=+1>cup of coffee</FONT>.
<LI><FONT COLOR=GREEN>Seafood Gumbo</FONT> - a stew-like
soup that's delicious.
Typically served with a side of white rice
that's best dumped into the soup directly. Skip the
chicken gumbo some
places serve too; the seafood is definitely better!
<LI><FONT COLOR=ORANGE SIZE=+2>Jambalaya</FONT> - the best
of all possible dinners. You'll just have
to order it so you can find out what it's about.
<LI><FONT SIZE=2 color=blue>Alcohol</FONT> - it's the
grease on the wheels of the visitor experience in the
French Quarter, but I'm not convinced it's as necessary
for a good time as the bars suggest . . .
</UL>
Whatever you do, make sure you have <font
```

```
size=+1>F</font><font size=+2>U</font>
<font size=+3>N</font>!
```

In this example, shown in Figure 4-6, the screen is full of fun and interesting text in a variety of sizes and colors. Note particularly that if you want to change both the size and color of a passage of text you can accomplish this by having multiple attributes in the `<FONT>` tag. That is, instead of using `<FONT COLOR=ORANGE><FONT SIZE=+2>`, you can mush them together and have a single directive `<FONT COLOR=ORANGE SIZE=+2>`.

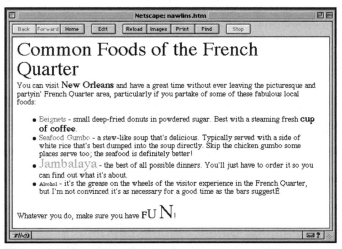

Figure 4-6: A wide variety of colors and sizes specified.

Logical Styles

The style directives discussed up to this point are easy to understand. HTML also supports *logical styles*. Logical styles enable readers (and their software) to define emphasis.

The most common logical styles are `<EM>` `</EM>` for emphasis and `<STRONG>` `</STRONG>` for stronger emphasis. Figure 4-7 shows an example of these tags.

In the example shown in Figure 4-7, the first point (shown in italics) is specified as `<EM>Things are Okay</EM>`, and the second point (shown in boldface) is specified as `<STRONG>Things are getting better!</STRONG>`.

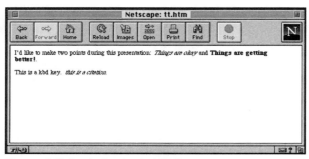

Figure 4-7: Logical styles in HTML.

There are many other logical tags that are specified in the HTML standard but are rarely used. I list them in Table 4-1 for your information — you might experiment with them to see if they meet particular formatting needs that arise.

Table 4-1:	A Variety of Logical Text Tags	
HTML Tag	Close Tag	Meaning
<CITE>	</CITE>	Bibliographic citation
<CODE>	</CODE>	Code listing
<DFN>	</DFN>	Word definition
<KBD>	</KBD>	Keyboard text (similar to CODE)
<SAMP>	</SAMP>	Sample user input
<VAR>	</VAR>	Program or other variable

Putting It All Together

Following is an example of a complex HTML document viewed within a Web browser. The example includes material covered in Chapters 3 and 4.

```
<HTML>
<HEAD>
<TITLE>Travels with Tintin</TITLE>
<BASEFONT SIZE=4>
</HEAD><BODY>
<H1><FONT COLOR=ORANGE>Travels with Tintin</FONT></H1>
Of the various reporters with whom I've traveled around
the world, including writers for <I>UPI</I>, <I>AP</I>,
```

```
and <I>Reuters</I>, the most fascinating has clearly been
<B>Tintin</B>, boy reporter from Belgium
(<TT>tintin@belgium.gov</TT>).
<P>
Probably the most enjoyable aspect of our travels was his
dog, <B>Snowy</B>, although I don't know that our hosts
would agree!
<P>
<FONT SIZE=6 COLOR=BLUE>The First Trip: Nepal</FONT>
<P>
After winning the Pulitzer for <I>Adventure with Red
Rackham's Treasure</I>, Tintin
told me he wanted a vacation. Remembering some
of his earlier adventures, he decided to visit Nepal.
Early one Sunday, I was sipping my tea and reading the
<I>Times</I> when he rang me up, asking whether I'd be
able to take a break and come along...
</BODY>
</HTML>
```

Can you guess how the preceding text will look from a browser? Check
Figure 4-8 to find out.

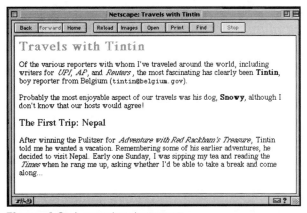

Figure 4-8: A complex document.

The document in Figure 4-8 is quite attractive, albeit with some poor
spacing around the italicized acronyms in the first sentence. Fortunately,
some of the most recent Web browsers realize that an additional space is
needed after the last italicized character, so this becomes even more

readable. Also notice the automatic blank lines around the <Hn> format that I had to add by hand with the two <P> tags later in the document when I opted to use the <FONT SIZE=5> tag to create my own section head.

A summary of the many character formatting tags learned in this chapter is contained in Table 4-2.

Table 4-2:	Tags Used in this Chapter	
HTML Tag	Close Tag	Meaning
<B>	</B>	Display text in bold
<I>	</I>	Display text in italic
<U>	</U>	Underline specified text
<TT>	</TT>	Monospace text
<BASEFONT SIZE=n>		Change base font size to 'n' (1-7)
<CITE>	</CITE>	Bibliographic citation
<CODE>	</CODE>	Code listing
<DFN>	</DFN>	Word definition
<EM>	</EM>	Logical emphasis style
<FONT>	</FONT>	Font / character modifications
<FONT COLOR=xy>	</FONT>	Change the color of type (RGB or by-name)
<FONT SIZE=n>	</FONT>	change font size to 'n' (1-7)
<KBD>	</KBD>	Keyboard text (similar to <CODE>)
<SAMP>	</SAMP>	Sample user input
<STRIKE>	</STRIKE>	Strike-through formatting
<STRONG>	</STRONG>	Logical stronger emphasis
_		Subscript
[	]	Superscript
<VAR>	</VAR>	Program or other variable

Moving On

In this chapter, I focused on formatting characters and words. In the next chapter, I focus on larger formatting issues, including how to add both numbered and bulleted lists to your HTML documents, and how to include glossaries or other definition lists.

Lists and Special Characters

In This Chapter

In this chapter, I introduce you to various types of list formats for Web pages, including ordered (numbered) and unordered (bulleted) lists. I also explain how to add special and non-English characters and comments to your Web documents.

Definition lists

Ordered (numbered) and unordered (bulleted) lists

Other approaches to lists

Special characters in HTML documents

Comments within HTML code

You'll see lots of lists on the Web. After you read this chapter, you'll be able to use the different list styles to your advantage.

Definition Lists

One of the most common elements of multipage documents is a set of definitions, references, or cross-indexes. Glossaries are classic examples; words are listed alphabetically, followed by prose definitions. In HTML, the entire section of a glossary would be contained by a *definition list,* which is contained within a pair of *definition list* tags: <DL> and </DL>. Within the pair of listings, a definition has two parts.

➡ Definition term (<DT>)

➡ Definition description (<DD>)

Here's how a definition list can be used in HTML to define some genetics terms:

```
<HTML>
<HEAD>
<TITLE>A Quick Glossary of Genetic Terms</TITLE>
</HEAD>
<BODY>

<I>Adapted from Dawkins, The Extended Phenotype</I>
<DL>
<DT>allometry
<DD>A disproportionate relationship between size of a body
part and size of the whole body.
<DT>anaphase
<DD>Phase of the cell division during which the paired
chromosomes move apart.
<DT>antigens
<DD>Foreign bodies, usually protein molecules, which
provoke the formation of antibodies.
<DT>autosome
<DD>A chromosome that is not one of the sex chromosomes.
<DT>codon
<DD>A triplet of units (nucleotides) in the genetic code,
specifying the synthesis of a single unit (amino acid) in
a protein chain.
<DT>genome
<DD>The entire collection of genes possessed by one
organism.
</DL>
</BODY>
</HTML>
```

Figure 5-1 shows how the preceding HTML code looks in a Web browser. Notice the automatic indentation and formatting.

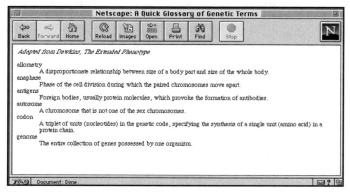

Figure 5-1: A glossary in HTML.

If you're writing a book about herbal remedies, for example, you may want to have a cross-reference of herbs for specific problems. Certain key herbs could be italicized to highlight them. The following example shows how you might want such a listing to look:

Blood Pressure

Balm, Black Haw, *Garlic*, Hawthorn

Bronchitis

Angelica, *Aniseed*, *Caraway*, Grindelia

Burns

Aloe, Chickweed, *Elder*

Obtaining the preceding format within an HTML document would require the following tag placements:

```
<DL>
<DT><B>Blood Pressure</B>
<DD>Balm, Black Haw, <I>Garlic</I>, Hawthorn.
<DT><B>Bronchitis</B>
<DD>Angelica, <I>Aniseed, Caraway</I>, Grindelia.
<DT><B>Burns</B>
<DD>Aloe, Chickweed, <I>Elder</I>.
</DL>
```

Figure 5-2 shows the result, which is, if I do say so myself, quite attractive and similar to the original design. (By this point, I hope that you can read the preceding HTML snippet and understand all the paired formatting tags. If not, you might want to nip back to Chapter 4 and study it a bit more to refresh your memory on text style formatting.)

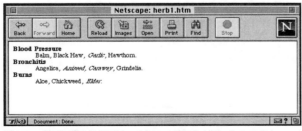

Figure 5-2: Medicinal herbs as a definition list.

The basic concept of a list is exhibited in the definition-list format: a pair of tags within which other tags have special meanings. What happens if you use <DT> and <DD> without wrapping them in a <DL></DL> pair? The result is identical to Figure 5-2: the default meanings of the <DT> and <DD> tags are consistent, whether they appear within a list or not. Which isn't to say that it's guaranteed to work correctly on *all* Web browsers just because it formatted correctly in the test program. Indeed, Mosaic formats a definition list incorrectly if it isn't surrounded by <DL></DL>.

 Always check your HTML formatting in multiple Web browsers before concluding that the formatting is correct.

Unordered (Bulleted) Lists

Definition lists are handy, but a list type that you see much more often on the World Wide Web is a bulleted list, also called an *unordered list*. Unordered lists start with <UL> and close with </UL>, and each list item is denoted by the *list item* (<LI>) tag. The format is similar to that of the definition list, as the following example shows:

```
Common Herbal remedies include:
<UL>
<LI>Blood Pressure - Balm, Black Haw, <I>Garlic</I>,
Hawthorn.
<LI>Bronchitis - Angelica, <I>Aniseed, Caraway</I>,
Grindelia.
<LI>Burns - Aloe, Chickweed, <I>Elder</I>.
</UL>
```

The result as viewed from a browser is attractive, if somewhat confusing, as Figure 5-3 shows.

Figure 5-3: A bulleted list.

More useful is a combination of the two list types. The definition list looked very cool with the additions of boldface and indentation, but the bullets next to each item in the unordered list look slick, too. The solution is to nest lists within one another, as follows:

```
Common Herbal remedies include:
<DL>
<DT><B>Blood Pressure</B>
<UL>
<LI>Balm
<LI>Black Haw
<LI><I>Garlic</I>
<LI>Hawthorn.
</UL>
<DT><B>Bronchitis</B>
<UL>
<LI>Angelica
<LI><I>Aniseed</I>
<LI>Caraway
<LI>Grindelia.
</UL>
<DT><B>Burns</B>
<UL>
<LI>Aloe
<LI>Chickweed
<LI><I>Elder</I>.
</UL>
</DL>
```

Figure 5-4 shows the result of the preceding code, which is a very cool layout.

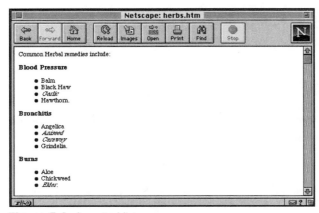

Figure 5-4: A nested list.

The output in Figure 5-4 is what you want. But is the HTML coding behind it the best possible approach? Think about it: You define terms with `<DT>` but don't actually have any definition with `<DD>`. In this case, as it turns out, the nested list just adds to the confusion. You can achieve an identical result with the following, simpler example:

```
Common Herbal remedies include:
<P>
<B>Blood Pressure</B>
<UL>
<LI>Balm
<LI>Black Haw
<LI><I>Garlic</I>
<LI>Hawthorn.
</UL>
<B>Bronchitis</B>
<UL>
<LI>Angelica
<LI><I>Aniseed</I>
<LI>Caraway
<LI>Grindelia.
</UL>
<B>Burns</B>
<UL>
<LI>Aloe
<LI>Chickweed
<LI><I>Elder</I>.
</UL>
```

The preceding example illustrates the dangers and problems in description languages such as HTML. Because you can accomplish tasks in various ways, you have to wonder: are the most obvious methods always the *best?*

As a rule of thumb, the simpler a design is, the more likely it is to work correctly.

Ordered (Numbered) Lists

What if you want to create a list, but with numbers instead of bullet points? The adage "simpler is better" suggests the formatting in the following example:

```
<H2>Enchilada Sauce</H2>
1. Heat a large saucepan, and saute the following
ingredients until soft:
<UL>
<LI>Two tablespoons virgin olive oil
<LI>Large onion, chopped
</UL>
2. Add a quart of water.<BR>
3. Sprinkle in a quarter-cup of flour.<BR>
4. Jazz it up by adding:
<UL>
<LI>Two tablespoons chili powder
<LI>Two teaspoons cumin
<LI>One teaspoon garlic powder
</UL>
5. Finally, add a teaspoon of salt, if desired.
<BR>
Whisk as sauce thickens; then simmer for 20 minutes.
```

The result is quite nice, as Figure 5-5 shows.

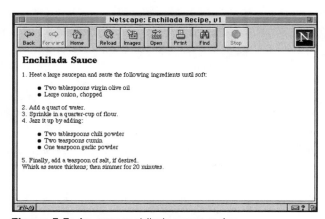

Figure 5-5: An easy enchilada sauce recipe.

Before you carry this book into the kitchen, however, I need to tell you that I got confused while I typed this recipe. The water should be added at the end, *not* in Step 2.

Now what? You certainly don't want to have to renumber all the items in the numbered list. The situation calls for the cousin of the unordered list: the *ordered list* (<OL>). The list ends with the close tag </OL>. Each item in the list has a *list item* tag (<LI>). With ordered lists, unlike definition lists, you can see that it makes quite a difference whether you use the <LI> tag without an <OL></OL> list surrounding it. The meaning of the <LI> tag depends on what kind of list it lies within.

Following is the way the recipe looks with my gaffe corrected and the HTML code rewritten to take advantage of the ordered-list tag:

```
<H2>Enchilada Sauce</H2>
<OL>
<LI>Heat a large saucepan, and saute the following
ingredients until soft:
<UL>
     <LI>Two tablespoons virgin olive oil
     <LI>Large onion, chopped
</UL>
<LI>Sprinkle in a quarter-cup of flour.
<LI>Jazz it up by adding:
<UL>
     <LI>Two tablespoons chili powder
     <LI>Two teaspoons cumin
     <LI>One teaspoon garlic powder
</UL>
<LI>Add a quart of water.
<LI>Finally, add a teaspoon of salt, if desired.
</OL>
Whisk as sauce thickens; then simmer for 20 minutes.
```

The output (see Figure 5-6) is not only correct, but is considerably better looking because Web browsers automatically indent lists of this nature. As a result, the nested-list items are indented twice.

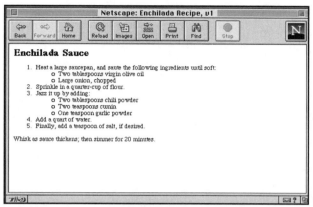

Figure 5-6: Automatic numbering and indents, too.

Other Approaches to Lists

With definition lists, ordered lists, and unordered lists, you probably can cover all your bets. One problem with these formats, however, is that the output, viewed in a Web browser, may be spaced out too much; your list may sprawl across more space than necessary. The designers of HTML tried to address the spacing problem by providing the tags <DIR> and <MENU>.

For information that can be presented in compact form, you should use the directory formatting tag (<DIR>) and its partner (</DIR>). If the list items are really succinct (as in 20 characters or fewer), you may want to try the menu format (<MENU>), which produces multicolumn displays in some of the most advanced browsers.

The following example shows how the <DIR> and <MENU> formats look in a typical HTML snippet:

```
<HTML>
<HEAD>
<TITLE>Dave's On-Line Deli</TITLE>
</HEAD><BODY>
<H2>Welcome to the Virtual World of Dave's On-Line
Deli!</H2>
Sandwich Choices:
<DIR>
```

```
(continued)
<LI>Turkey on a croissant
<LI>Ham and cheese
<LI>Veggie Delight
</DIR>
Soups of the Day:
<MENU>
<LI>Tomato
<LI>Tomato and rice
<LI>Chicken
<LI>Lentil
<LI>Barley
<LI>Gumbo
<LI>Corn chowder
<LI>Mystery Soup
</MENU>
<I>Please order at the counter...</I>
</BODY>
</HTML>
```

What will the HTML text look like in a browser? Figure 5-7 shows that Explorer displays a simple unordered list, only without bullets next to the items (an omission that makes this page look not so cool).

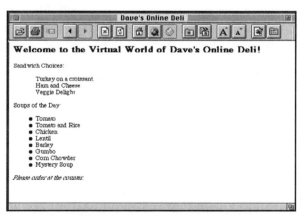

Figure 5-7: <DIR> and <MENU> items in Explorer.

If you view the same HTML document in a more sophisticated program, such as Netscape, the document is a regular unordered list with bullets (see Figure 5-8).

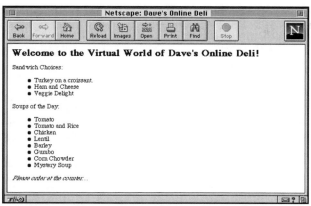

Figure 5-8: <DIR> and <MENU> items in Netscape.

To be honest, I can't find any Web browsers that correctly interpret the <MENU> and <DIR> tags. Most browsers take the formatting tag to mean that the list is just another tab-indented list, as you can see in Figures 5-7 and 5-8. Should you use these formatting options for the information in your document? It's up to you. I skip these formats in my own work. But as soon as browsers can format <MENU> items in multiple columns, I'm sure that many people will find this powerful list format to be much more interesting. I know I'll change the design of some of my Web pages.

To create multicolumn text you'll want to use a zero-border table. See Chapter 9 for details.

Special Characters in HTML Documents

If you're an alert reader, you may have noticed a typographical error in the recipe shown earlier. The recipe instructed the cook to *saute* the ingredients, yet the word should have an accent (*sauté*). Languages contain a variety of special characters that you may need to use, particularly if you plan to present material in a language other than English. Not surprisingly, you can include special characters in HTML code by using special tags, called *entities* or *entity references*.

Unlike the tags you've learned so far, special character entities aren't neatly tucked into paired brackets (<>); instead, they always begin with an ampersand (&) and end with a semicolon (;). Most entities are somewhat mnemonic, as Table 5-1 shows. You can also view a list of all special characters at the following URL:

```
http://www.sandia.gov/sci_compute/symbols.html
```

Table 5-1:	Special Characters in HTML	
Character	**HTML Code**	**Meaning**
&	&amp;	Ampersand
<	&lt;	Less than
>	&gt;	Greater than
á	&aacute;	Lowercase a with acute accent
à	&agrave;	Lowercase a with grave accent
â	&acirc;	Lowercase a with circumflex
ä	&auml;	Lowercase a with umlaut
å	&aring;	Lowercase a with ring
ç	&ccedil;	Lowercase c with cedilla
ñ	&ntilde;	Lowercase n with tilde
ø	&oslash;	Lowercase o with slash
ß	&szlig;	Lowercase sharp s symbol

Not all Web browsers can display all of these characters, particularly on Windows systems. Check them on a few browsers before you use them in your own Web page layout.

To create an uppercase version of one of the characters in Table 5-1, simply make the first letter of the formatting tag uppercase. For example, Ø produces an uppercase O with a slash through it, as in the word *CØPENHAGEN*. To produce a different vowel with a diacritical mark, change the first letter of that tag. The word *desvàn*, for example, is correctly specified in an HTML document as desvàn.

The following example contains some foreign language snippets so that you can see how these formatting tags work:

```
The following are formatted with &lt;b&gt; for
boldface and &lt;i&gt; for italics.
<P>
<B>Gibt es ein Caf&eacute; in der N&auml;he? </B><BR>
<I>Is there a caf&eacute; nearby?</I><P>
<B>Je voudrais un d&icirc;ner. </B><BR>
<I>I want to eat dinner.</I><P>
<B>Y una mesa por ma&ntilde;ana, por favor.</B><BR>
<I>And a table for tomorrow, please.</I><P>
<B>Oh! C'&egrave; una specialit&agrave; locale?</B><BR>
<I>Oh! Is there a local specialty?</I><P>
```

I don't actually speak French, German, Spanish, or Italian particularly well, but I guarantee the preceding set of questions will confuse just about any waiter in Europe. Figure 5-9 shows the result of the preceding formatting.

Figure 5-9: Language examples on the Web.

Some problems occur with the international characters supported in the basic HTML code, not the least of which is the fact that some significant elements are missing. If you want to write in Spanish, for example, you'll have to do without the upside-down question mark (ι)and the upside-down exclamation point ($\mathfrak{i}$). Many international symbols have been added over the last year, but there still are lots of holes.

Comments within HTML Code

If you have spent any time working with complex markup languages such as HTML, you know that the ability to include tracking information and other comments can help you to organize and remember your coding approach when you return to the pages later.

Fortunately, HTML supports a specific (if not peculiar) notational format for comments within your documents. Any text surrounded by the elements <!- and -> is considered to be a comment and is ignored by Web browsers, as you can see in the following example:

```
<HTML>
<!- Last modified: 21 February 1995 ->
<TITLE>Enchilada Sauce</TITLE>
<!- inspired by an old recipe I heard in Mexico,
but I must admit that it's going to be very
different, because even the flour is subtly different
in Juarez and elsewhere than in the States . . . ->
<H1>Enchilada Sauce</H1>
```

When I feed the preceding text to a Web browser, the browser displays only one line of information, as you see in Figure 5-10.

You don't *have* to use comments, but if you're starting to build a complex Web space that offers many documents, just time-stamping each file could prove to be invaluable.

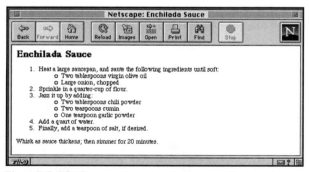

Figure 5-10: Comments galore but none displayed.

Table 5-2 contains a summary of all commands you learned in this chapter:

Table 5-2:	Tags Used in this Chapter	
Tag	**Close Tag**	**Meaning**
`<DD>`	-	Definition description
`<DIR>`	`</DIR>`	Directory listing
`<DL>`	`</DL>`	Definition list
`<DT>`	-	Definition term
`<LI>`	-	List item
`<MENU>`	`</MENU>`	List of short items (can be formatted in multiple columns by the browser software)
`<OL>`	`</OL>`	Ordered (numbered) list
`<UL>`	`</UL>`	Unordered (bulleted) list
`<!-`	`->`	Comments within HTML

Moving On

Each chapter so far expands the depth and sophistication of your HTML skills. In this chapter, you learned about the various types of lists and how you can combine them — and many formatting tags — to produce very cool results. The next chapter is lots of fun. I show you the missing link, quite literally. Building on the explanation of URL formats in Chapter 2, in Chapter 6, I talk about how to add links to other Web sites and other places on the Internet.

Adding Pointers and Hot Links

In This Chapter

In this chapter, I talk about actual HTML pointers to other Web and Internet resources, show you how to include pointers to graphics and illustrations, and build on the URL explanation found in Chapter 2.

Multiword HTML formatting tags

Pointers to other Web pages

Referencing non-Web information

Pointers to your other pages

At this point, you should feel comfortable with your HTML composition skills. You certainly know all the key facets of HTML, with three notable exceptions: adding *links* to other documents, adding *internal links,* and adding *nontext* information to your pages. In this chapter, I show you how to add links, and in Chapters 7 and 8 I cover links to internal references elsewhere in the same document and graphics.

Much of this information builds on the extensive discussion of URLs (Uniform Resource Locators) in Chapter 2. You may want to skim that chapter again to refresh your memory before you proceed.

Multiword HTML Formatting Tags

So far, every document formatting tag that you've seen has looked like a couple of letters surrounded by angle brackets. But in fact, formatting tags can contain more information than just a few letters. All tags must begin with the open angle bracket, followed immediately by the *tag element;* no spaces are allowed. Inside the tag, however, you can specify other attributes in the format *attribute-name = value.*

One of the tags that you learned about earlier — <PRE>, for preformatted text — enables you to specify the set width that you'll be using, as shown in the following example:

```
It's a hot, hot day in the park, and lots of people
are wandering around without clothes on. Here's a
text picture of what I'm talking about:
<PRE WIDTH=5>
    +------+
    | CENSORED |
    +------+
</PRE>
<I>Sorry, but until all the releases are signed,
I can't let you see this picture.</I>
```

In the preceding HTML example, I deliberately added an error: I specified that the preformatted text should be shown with the assumption that the maximum width of each line of text is five characters (WIDTH=5). The actual output makes it clear that the browser ignores this particular facet of formatting, as shown in Figure 6-1.

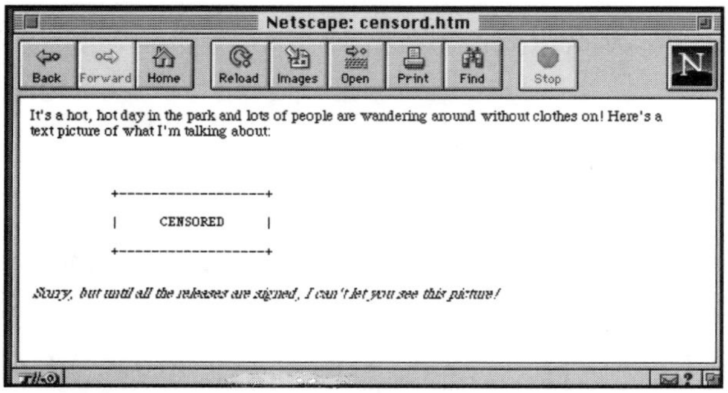

Figure 6-1: An HTML tag with attributes.

The preceding proves to be a great example of one of the challenges facing Web page designers. The formatting information that you specify in your HTML code may not be interpreted as you think it will be (as shown in Figure 6-1) or at all (as in the request for multicolumn lists by the <MENU> formatting tag).

Fortunately, most of the other HTML tags work if you specify the appropriate attributes. You can specify anything you want within an HTML formatting tag; the browser interprets only those attributes that make sense within the context of that tag. (You can have fun with this, too. How about a format tag of `<P aragraph=right-justified>`? This tag works identically to the format tag `<P>` by itself, because the attribute `aragraph` is — no big surprise — meaningless.)

 You can't have a space between the `<` and the tag name, but the elements are surrounded by spaces within.

Pointers to Other Web Pages

The basic HTML formatting tag for external references is `<A>`, the *anchor* tag (its ending partner is `</A>`). It *must* contain attributes. Without attributes, the `<A>` tag has no meaning and doesn't affect the formatting of information. The following example would result in the display of text without formatting:

```
You can now visit <A>the White House</A> online!
```

To make this link *live,* meaning to make it cause a browser to do something, you need to specify the *hypertext reference* attribute: `HREF="value"`. The *value* can be empty if you don't know the actual information, but you must specify the attribute to make the link active. You can rewrite the sentence as follows to make it a Web link:

```
You can now visit <A HREF=""> the White House</A> online!
```

The preceding line of HTML code would be displayed in a Web browser with the portion between the `<A>` references (the anchor tags) appearing in blue, underlined, or highlighted in some other fashion. The information that should be contained between the quotation marks is the URL for the Web page you want to link to. The URL for the White House, for example, is: `http://www.whitehouse.gov/`

 One classic problem that appears in HTML code is the use of curly, smart, or fancy quotes; Web servers just don't know what they mean. Double-check to ensure that the quotes in your HTML documents all have straight quotes: "like this" rather than "like this."

The following is the sentence with the correct, live hypertext link to the White House:

```
You can now visit <A HREF="http://www.whitehouse.gov/">the
White House</A> online!
```

The following is a more comprehensive example that combines various facets of HTML to build an interesting and attractive Web page:

```
<HTML>
<HEAD>
<TITLE>Visiting the White House and Other Government
Sites</TITLE>
</HEAD>
<BODY>
In cyberspace, you can virtually travel anywhere. Of the
various places
that are fun to check out, however, few are as interesting
as the home page for the <A HREF="http://www.whitehouse
.gov/">White
House</A>.
<H2>Government Sites on the Web</H2>

<UL>
<LI> <A HREF="http://www.fbi.gov/">Federal Bureau of
Investigation</A>
<LI> <A HREF="http://www.fedworld.gov/">FedWorld, a great
starting point for Government Research</A>
<LI> <A HREF="http://novel.nifl.gov/">National Institute
for Literacy@sr</A>
<LI> <A HREF="http://www.osmre.gov/">Office of Surface
Mining Reclamation and Enforcement</A>
<LI> <A HREF="http://www.sbaonline.sba.gov/">Small Business
@srAdministration</A>
<LI> <A HREF="http://www.ssa.gov/">Social Security
Administration</A>
<LI> <A HREF="http://web.fie.com/web/fed/aid/">U.S. Agency
for @srInternational Development (1)</A>
<LI> <A HREF="http://www.info.usaid.gov/">U.S. Agency for
International Development (2)</A>
</UL>
</BODY>
</HTML>
```

Figure 6-2 shows that the preceding HTML code is quite attractive when viewed in a browser. The ugliness and confusion of the URLs is neatly hidden; readers can simply click on the name of an agency to connect directly to it.

Notice in Figure 6-2 that the first link for the U.S. Agency for International Development is a complex URL with a specified path and page.

Also notice that *White House* in the prose at the beginning of the Web page is now highlighted and underlined, comprising a real Web link, too.

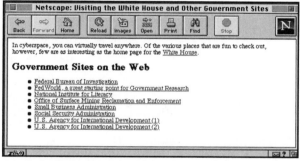

Figure 6-2: Government sites on the Web.

Understanding this section is a terrific step forward in learning HTML. After you grasp how to build anchors, you'll be able to build Web "tables of contents," starting points for exploration on the Internet, with the best of them.

But how do you point to information that *isn't* another Web document? I show you how in the next section.

Referencing Non-Web Information

To point to material that isn't a Web document, you simply use the appropriate URL, as specified in Chapter 2. If you learn, for example, that the FDIC (Federal Deposit Insurance Corporation) has a Gopher site but no Web site, and that the Gopher site is at fdic.sura.net on port 71, you could build a URL for it, as follows:

```
gopher://fdic.sura.net:71/
```

You then could drop the URL into your HTML code as a different value in an HREF attribute, as follows:

```
<A HREF="gopher://fdic.sura.net:71/">FDIC</A>
```

The following example shows how the HTML code I discussed in the preceding section looks with the addition of the FDIC and the Consumer Product Safety Commission Gopher sites:

```
<HTML>
<HEAD>
<TITLE>Visiting the White House and Other Government
Sites</TITLE>
</HEAD>
<BODY>
In cyberspace, you can virtually travel anywhere. Of the
various places
that are fun to check out, few are as interesting as the
home
page for the <A HREF="http://www.whitehouse.gov/">White
House</A>.
<H2>Government Sites on the Web</H2>
<UL>
<LI> <A HREF="http://www.fbi.gov/">Federal Bureau of
Investigation</A>
<LI> <A HREF="gopher://fdic.sura.net:71/">Federal Deposit
Insurance Corporation</A>
<LI> <A HREF="http://www.fedworld.gov/">FedWorld, a great
starting point for
government research</A>
<LI> <A HREF="http://novel.nifl.gov/">National Institute
for Literacy</A>
<LI> <A HREF="http://www.osmre.gov/">Office of Surface
Mining Reclamation and Enforcement</A>
<LI> <A HREF="http://www.sbaonline.sba.gov/">Small Business
Administration</A>
<LI> <A HREF="http://www.ssa.gov/">Social Security
Administration</A>
<LI> <A HREF="http://web.fie.com/web/fed/aid/">U.S. Agency
for International
Development (1)</A>
<LI> <A HREF="http://www.info.usaid.gov/">U.S. Agency for
International
Development (2)</A>
<LI> <A HREF="gopher://cpsc.gov/">U.S. Consumer Product
Safety Commission</A>
```

```
</UL>
</BODY>
</HTML>
```

In my Web browser, the preceding looks almost identical to the earlier version, except that it has two new items listed (see Figure 6-3). This example underscores one of the real strengths of HTML: *all anchors* (hypertext pointers), regardless of the kind of information they point to, look the same on a Web page. No funny little Gopher icons appear next to the Gopher items, no FTP icons appear next to FTP archives, and so on. The pages contain uniform sets of pointers to other spots on the Internet that contain interesting, valuable, or fun resources.

Figure 6-3: Which sites are Gopher sites?

In Figure 1-7, I showed how you can code various types of information in HTML format. I repeat that figure here as Figure 6-4.

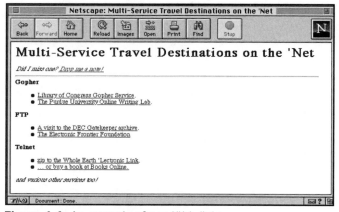

Figure 6-4: An example of non-Web links.

Now you can appreciate the figure's surprising hidden complexity, as shown in the following HTML code:

```
<HTML>
<HEAD>
<TITLE>Multi-Service Travel Destinations on the
'Net</TITLE>
</HEAD><BODY>
<H1>Multi-Service Travel Destinations on the 'Net</H1>
<I>Did I miss one? <A HREF="mailto:taylor@intuitive.com">
Drop me a note! </A></I>
<HR>
<B>Gopher</B>
<UL>
<LI><A HREF="gopher://gopher.loc.gov/">Library of Congress
Gopher Service</A>
<LI><A HREF="gopher://owl.trc.purdue.edu/">The Purdue
University Online Writing Lab</A>
</UL>
<B>FTP</B>
<UL>
<LI><A HREF="ftp://gatekeeper.dec.com/">A visit to the DEC
Gatekeeper archive</A>
<LI><A HREF="ftp://ftp.eff.org/">The Electronic Frontier
Foundation</A>
</UL>
<B>Telnet</B>
<UL>
<LI><A HREF="telnet://well.com/">zip to the Whole Earth
'Lectronic Link </A>
<LI><A HREF="telnet://books.com/">... or buy a book at
Books Online</A>
</UL>
<I>and various other services</I>
</BODY>
</HTML>
```

Of all the links demonstrated in this Web document, I think that the most notable is the mailto: link in the first line of text. Notice that the mailto: link is not presented as:

```
<A HREF="mailto:taylor@intuitive.com">Click here</A> to
send me mail.
```

Instead, the link is smoothly and transparently integrated into the prose:

```
<A HREF="mailto:taylor@intuitive.com">Drop me a
note!</A></I>
```

 Try to avoid using *Click here* and similar labels for hypertext tags; cool Web pages come from creative, meaningful, and unobtrusive integration of links into the text.

Pointers to Your Other Pages

Being able to link to external information sources and sites on the Internet is a huge boon to Web designers, but if you stopped at that and never learned any more, you'd be missing half the picture. The one piece that you still need to learn is how to reference other documents on your own server.

Although *personal* home pages often have a simple format similar to the examples in this chapter (that is, a few paragraphs about the person, perhaps a graphic or two, and a list of favorite Web), more complex and sophisticated sites have a wide range of Web documents available. These sites include the appropriate links to the other internal documents so that readers can easily jump among them.

There is an easy way and a hard way to reference internal documents (documents on your server). The hard way builds on the earlier examples: you figure out the full URL of each page and use those URLs as the hypertext reference tags. The easy way to reference another document on your server is to specify the document name only (or path and name) without any of the URL preface information. For example, if you have a starting page called home.html and a second page called resume.html in the same directory on the server, you could create the following link:

```
You're welcome to <A HREF="resume.html">read my
resume</A>.
```

(Note: Purists would use the HTML code résumé instead of resume.)

Perhaps you want to make several files accessible on your Web server, and you want some sensible way to organize them. A hierarchical directory structure can prove to be a big advantage.

If you have a variety of information about the sandwiches and soups at the virtual deli featured in Chapter 5, you could organize that information as shown in Figure 6-5.

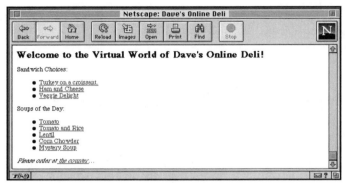

Figure 6-5: Organizing the deli menu data.

Now when people connect to the base URL (the address of the top-level menu itself), they see the formatted results of the following HTML code:

```
<HTML>
<HEAD>
<TITLE>Dave's On-Line Deli</TITLE>
</HEAD>
<BODY>
<H2>Welcome to the Virtual World of Dave's On-Line
Deli!</H2>
Sandwich Choices:
<UL>
<LI><A HREF="sandwiches/turkey.html">Turkey on a
croissant</A>
<LI><A HREF="sandwiches/ham.html">Ham and Cheese</A>
<LI><A HREF="sandwiches/veggie.html">Veggie Delight</A>
</UL>
Soups of the Day:
<UL>
<LI><A HREF="soups/tomato.html">Tomato</A>
<LI><A HREF="soups/tomato.html">Tomato and rice</A>
<LI><A HREF="soups/lentil.html">Lentil</A>
<LI><A HREF="soups/corn-chowder.html">Corn Chowder</A>
<LI><A HREF="soups/mystery.html">Mystery Soup</A>
</UL>
```

```
<I>Please order at <A HREF="order-counter.html">the
counter</A> . . .
</I>
</BODY>
</HTML>
```

The new virtual deli *home page* (which Web folks call the *root,* or the first page that visitors see when reaching a site) would be formatted as shown in Figure 6-5.

You can't see it in Figure 6-5, but the HTML code contains an error. To understand the problem — a relatively common one in complex lists — consider what happens if someone wants more information about the tomato soup instead of the tomato and rice soup. Both soup choices point to the same second page: soups/tomato.html.

If a Web user pops into the virtual deli and wants to find out more about the lentil soup, for example, he or she might click on the hypertext link Lentil. The user then would see another HTML document that provided information about the soup (and perhaps even included a picture of it). But how could you add a link back to the deli home page? Consider the following listing, paying close attention to the last few lines:

```
<HTML>
<HEAD>
<TITLE>Lentil Soup: A Cornerstone of the Virtual
Deli</TITLE>
</HEAD>
<BODY>
<H1>Lentil Soup</H1>
It will come as no surprise to regular patrons of the
Virtual Deli that our lentil soup has quickly become one
of the most popular items. With its combination of six
lentil beans, some succulent organic vegetables, and our
carefully filtered fresh spring water, a hot bowl of our
lentil soup on a cold day is unquestionably one of life's
pleasures.
<P>
We'd love to tell you the recipe, too, but we feel that
you really need to come in and try it yourself.
<P>
<B>We recommend <A HREF="../sandwiches/veggie.html"> a
veggie sandwich to accompany it.</A></B>
<HR>
<A HREF="../deli.html">Back up to the main menu.</A>
</BODY>
</HTML>
```

When visitors to the virtual deli arrive at the page created by the preceding HTML text, they have moved down a level in the server's hierarchical directory structure, but they don't know that. The URLs in the document, however, tell the story. The main menu is ../deli.html. Each "../" takes you up a level in the directory, so you could move up two levels with ../../test.html. The recommended sandwich to accompany the soup is in another directory — hence, its .. / sandwiches folder specification. See Figure 6-6 to see what the page looks like from a browser (Navigator).

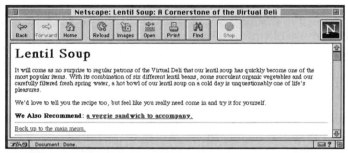

Figure 6-6: The lentil soup special.

In the previous listings, you can see the use of relative filename addresses. For example, ../deli.html pops up one level in the file system to find the deli.html page. This makes for easy HTML coding but beware that problems can easily arise if you move any of the pages around without the rest of the files.

Table 6-1:	Tags Used in this Chapter	
Tag	**Close Tag**	**Meaning**
`<A HREF=x>`	`</A>`	Link to URL 'x'

Moving On

In this chapter, you learned how to include links to other sites on the World Wide Web and throughout the Internet. You also learned how to organize a set of Web documents in manageable folders and how to specify other documents on your own server with minimal fuss. In Chapter 7, I focus on internal document references, which enable you to include a table of contents at the top of a large Web document. I also explain in Chapter 7 how to use internal document markers as hot links that enable people to jump to a specific spot in any Web document.

Internal Document References

In This Chapter

In this chapter, I show you how to add a table of contents to a large Web document and use that table as a hot link to allow people to jump to a specific spot in that same or different document on your server.

Defining Web-document jump targets

Adding jump hot links to your Web pages

Linking to jump targets in external documents

In Chapter 6, you learned about the anchor tag <A>; you also learned how to use the HREF attribute to build links to other pages on the World Wide Web. Another, equally valuable use for the <A> tag is the internal document reference, the focus of this chapter. You will find that as documents become larger, the capability to zoom (jump) to a predefined spot in a document can be invaluable.

Defining Web Document Jump Targets

I commented in Chapter 6 that the anchor tag <A> is the first of the HTML formatting tags that allows you to specify attributes. Note that rather than a format like <URL="somedoc"></URL>, which would be more consistent with the other pieces of HTML, the format of the anchor tag is <A somedoc></A>. This format is useful because some complex tags, particularly the instructions for including graphics, have dozens of variations. Imagine <IMAGELEFTBOTTOM="imagefile"> or something similar. Instead, attributes were included in the design of HTML to allow a wide variety of different formats to be easily specified.

The greatest value of these attributes in formatting tags is that you can provide a wonderful sense of consistency in the interface and presentation of information. You can have half your links lead to other pages on the Web, with three links moving the reader farther down in the document and the rest of the links leading to other pages on your own server. The links will all have the same appearance (blue and underlined in most cases) and function (causing the browser to "jump" directly to the specified information).

Up to this point, the documents shown in this book have been short, with the majority of the information confined to the first screen of information within the browser. Such an approach to Web document design results in pages that are easy to navigate. Sometimes, however, it's impossible to keep a document from stretching over several pages.

If I wanted to write this chapter as an HTML document, I could make each section a different document. Even then, however, some of those sections would be long enough that readers would be forced to scroll to find the information that they want.

A better layout is one in which the entire chapter is a single document, but the topic headers actually are links to the appropriate spots farther down in the page. Clicking on a table of contents entry like Adding jump links to your Web page, for example, would move you to that spot instantly. The challenge, of course, is to figure out when a certain length document is best as a single HTML file, and when it is best as a set of files. My rule of thumb is to move pages at logical jump points and to try and minimize load time for readers. This chapter could be a single HTML document, but the book itself would clearly be a set of documents.

The targets of internal Web document jumps are known as *anchors*. The HTML tag for an anchor point is another value for the <A> tag: <A name=value>. The *value* can be any sequence of characters, numbers, and punctuation marks, but I recommend that you stick with a strategy of mnemonic anchor names, such as *section1* or *references*. Some clients insist that all characters in the anchor be lowercased, so you may want to experiment before you build a complex document.

The following example shows how a set of tags might look within a document on Web design guidelines. The anchors are built from the author names and the years of publication, which then can be referenced as links in the rest of the document.

```
<A NAME="guidelines">
<CENTER>
<H1>WEB DESIGN GUIDELINES</H1></A>
```

```
</CENTER>
<BLOCKQUOTE>
<DL>
<A NAME="rule1">
<DT><B>Rule #1:</A>
<DD>Understand the intended users and uses of your
Web site then focus the design and layout around their
needs
and interests.</B>
</DL>
<DL>
<A NAME="rule2">
<DT><B>Rule #2:</A>
<DD>Be sparing with graphical elements.</B>
</DL>
<DL>
<A NAME="rule3">
<DT><B>Rule #3:</A>
<DD>Pages should load within no more than
thirty seconds, including all graphical elements.</B>
</DL>
<DL>
<A NAME="rule4">
<DT><B>Rule #4:</A>
<DD>Minimize color palettes.</B>
</DL>
</BLOCKQUOTE>
```

Viewed in a Web browser (see Figure 7-1), the preceding document looks like an attractive list of design rules. Because anchors are destinations on the current page rather than links to elsewhere, the text between the <A NAME> and </A> is not highlighted in any way when displayed.

What I've done in the example is not only add links to each of the reference citations but also add a link to the references section itself, which could then be easily included as part of a table of contents to the document. This would offer readers the chance to jump directly to the opening arguments, supporting arguments, conclusions, or, in this case, the references section of the document.

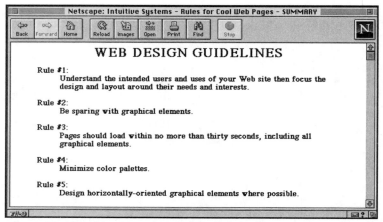

Figure 7-1: Helpful design guidelines.

Note the introduction of a new tag <CENTER> to center material horizontally on the page. I'll explore this tag a bit more in Chapter 9.

Adding Jump Links to Your Web Pages

The partner of an anchor in HTML documents is the formatting tag that defines the *jump,* or active link, within the document. It's a variant on the <A> format that you're already familiar with; the tag turns out to be another HREF hypertext reference, this time with the URL replaced by the anchor name prefaced by a pound sign (#).

For example, if the *anchor* that you want to connect is specified as <A NAME="references">, you would specify the *jump* as <A HREF="#references">go to reference info</A>.

In creating cool Web documents, the goal is to avoid phrases such as the following:

```
<A HREF="#references">Click here</A> to see the
references.
```

Instead, try to integrate the references more smoothly into the text, as follows:

```
<A HREF="#references">References and Bibliography</A>.
```

For a document on ingredients for mixed fruit drinks, for example, the HTML source might look like the following:

```
<H2>Ingredients for an Energy Blend</H2>
<UL>
<LI><A HREF="#strawberry">Strawberries</A>
<LI><A HREF="#blueberry">Blueberries</A>
<LI><A HREF="#mango">Mango</A>
<LI><A HREF="#banana">Bananas</A>
<LI><A HREF="#raspberry">Raspberries</A>
<LI><A HREF="#peach">Peaches</A>
</UL>
```

This list would be formatted nicely, as Figure 7-2 shows. The format is identical to the way the information would be presented if the links were external, perhaps even on different servers on the Web.

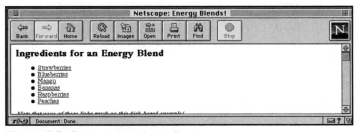

Figure 7-2: Energy blend ingredients.

For a different way to use internal references, consider the following snippet from the introductory section of the Web design document shown earlier in this chapter. Notice that an anchor also has been assigned to the section head.

```
<CENTER>
<A NAME="guidelines">
<H1>WEB DESIGN GUIDELINES</H1></A>
</CENTER>
While the number of Web pages that are available online
increases every day, the quality of these pages seems to
be declining, with more and more people (and programs, to
be fair) violating basic design guidelines. There are
a variety of reasons involved, but one that's
```

```
(continued)
common is a simple lack of experience with layout.
<P>
Some design rules might seem obscure, like
<A HREF="#rule4">minimizing the
color palette size</A>, which is
clearly specific to the World Wide Web, but
others, such as being
<A HREF="#rule2">sparing
with graphical elements</A> and
<A HREF="#rule1">focusing on the intended
user of the page</A>, are
basic rules of <I>any</I> design.
<P>
The most important idea is that <FONT COLOR=green><B>
good Web pages start with good content</B></FONT>
rather than with good form, layout or design. The
design should spring from the content and the
information therein.
```

In a browser, the information is displayed in a format that is quite pleasing to the eye and easy to navigate. All hot links and anchor information is appropriately hidden from view, or subtle enough that the reader can focus on the material itself (see Figure 7-3).

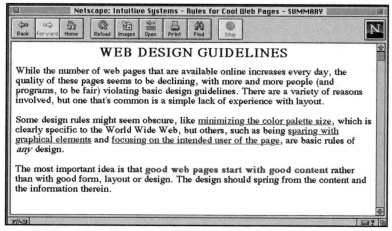

Figure 7-3: Design commentary with reference hot links.

When scholars first envisioned the need for citations in research, to defend and explain where particular views and ideas originate, what they dreamed of is surprisingly close to what we now can include in Web documents. If you are surprised by something in such a paper, or if the paper whetted your appetite for a more extensive treatment of the subject, you can click on the author citation. You then instantly move to the references section, and the appropriate citation is shifted to the top of the screen so that you can identify the information that you seek.

Figure 7-4 shows what would happen if you wanted more information on the first rule, referenced in the document with the `<A HREF="#rule1">` link.

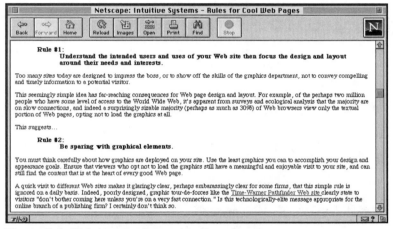

Figure 7-4: Web browser jumped to the references.

One thing to keep in mind when you specify your anchor points is the fact that the *exact* spot of the reference becomes the top of the displayed document. A sequence like the following shows the possible danger therein:

```
<H2>Bananas</H2>
<A NAME="BANANAS">The banana</A>
is one of the most exotic, yet most easily purchased,
fruits in the world.
```

The raw Web document is attractively formatted, but the resulting behavior will not be what you seek. Users who jump to the `<#BANANA>` tag will have the preceding sentence in the first line of their displays; the `<H2>` header will be one line off-screen. A much better idea is to flip the two items, as follows:

```
<A NAME="BANANAS">
<H2>Bananas</H2></A>
The banana is one of the most exotic, yet most easily
purchased, fruits in the world.
```

 Always test your Web documents before unleashing them on the world. I can't overemphasize this. Subtle problems with where your anchor tags are placed, for example, are classic mistakes found in otherwise spiffy Web pages.

Jumping into Organized Lists

Anchors and jump points also are commonly used to help readers navigate large lists of alphabetically sorted information. Consider the following simple phone book layout:

```
<TITLE>Jazz Institute Internal Phone Book</TITLE>
<H1>Jazz Institute Internal Phone Book</H1>
<P>
Section Shortcut:
<A HREF="#a-c">[A-C]</A>
<A HREF="#d-h">[D-H]</A>
<A HREF="#i-l">[I-L]</A>
<A HREF="#m-n">[M-N]</A>
<A HREF="#o-s">[O-S]</A>
<A HREF="#t-z">[T-Z]</A><BR>
<H2><A NAME="a-c">A-C</A></H2>
Benson, George (x5531)<BR>
Coleman, Ornette (x5143)<BR>
Coltrane, John (x5544)
<H2><A NAME="d-h">D-H</A></H2>
Dorsey, Tom (x9412)<BR>
Ellington, Duke (x3133)<BR>
Getz, Stan (x1222)<BR>
<H2><A NAME="i-l">I-L</A></H2>
Jackson, Milt (x0434)<BR>
Laffite, Guy (x5358) <BR>
<H2><A NAME="m-n">M-N</A></H2>
Monk, Thelonious (x3333)<BR>
Noone, Jimmie (x5123)<BR>
<H2><A NAME="o-s">O-S</A></H2>
```

```
Parker, Charlie   (x4141)<BR>
Peterson, Oscar   (x8983)<BR>
Reinhardt, Django   (x5351)<BR>
<H2><A NAME="t-z">T-Z</A></H2>
Taylor, Billy   (x3311)<BR>
Tyner, McCoy   (x4131)<BR>
Waller, Fats   (x1321)<BR>
```

Although the HTML in the preceding example is complex, Figure 7-5 shows that the result is both attractive and useful.

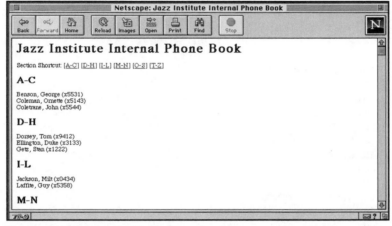

Figure 7-5: The Jazz Institute phone book.

You can start to get a feeling for how complex HTML text can become if you imagine that each entry in the phone list actually is a link to that person's home page or other material somewhere else on the Web. Every line of information displayed could be the result of four or more lines of HTML.

Linking to Jump Targets in External Documents

Now that you're familiar with the concept of jumping around within a single document, you'll be glad to hear that you can also add the #anchor notation to the end of any Web URL to make that link move directly to the specific anchor point in the document.

Suppose, for example, that the Web design guidelines page resided on a system called www.intuitive.com and that its full URL was:
http://www.intuitive.com/design-guide.html

A visit to the page reveals that a variety of anchor tags are embedded therein, including the references tag at the beginning of the references section of the paper. You could link directly to that spot from another Web page, as in the following example:

```
<CENTER>
<FONT SIZE=6><B>What Makes a Good Web Page?</B></FONT><BR>
<a href="#highlights">read the highlights</a>
</CENTER><P>
There's no consensus on what makes for good Web design
and various companies
offer their own set of guidelines for open-minded Web
developers. One of the most
succinct and easily understood is
<A HREF="http://www.intuitive.com/design-guide.html">the
Intuitive Systems Web design guidelines</A>. If you're
impatient like I am, however, you'll be glad
to know that you can skip the opening prose and
<A HREF="http://www.intuitive.com/design-
guide.html#rules">read the
guidelines therein </A>.
<P>
<A NAME="highlights">
<B>Here are the highlights</B></A><BR>
<UL>
<LI><A HREF="http://www.intuitive.com/design-
guide.html#rule1">Design for your intended users</A>
<LI><A HREF="http://www.intuitive.com/design-
guide.html#rule2">Be sparing with graphical elements</A>
<LI><A HREF="http://www.intuitive.com/design-
guide.html#rule3">Pages should
load in less than 30 seconds</A>
<LI><A HREF="http://www.intuitive.com/design-
guide.html#rule4">Minimize color palettes</A>
<LI><A HREF="http://www.intuitive.com/design-
guide.html#rule5">Prefer horizontally-oriented graphics</A>
<LI><A HREF="http://www.intuitive.com/design-
guide.html#rule6">Web sites should always
be content-centric</A>
<LI><A HREF="http://www.intuitive.com/design-
guide.html#rule7">One qualified visitor is
```

```
worth a dozen anonymous browsers</A>
<LI><A HREF="http://www.intuitive.com/design-
guide.html#rule8">Pages should
constantly be new and up-to-date.</A>
</UL>
```

The prose is displayed in a Web browser as you would expect. Figure 7-6 shows that the external reference links are displayed identically to the internal HREF, they're all underlined and in blue.

Figure 7-6: Internal or External Links? They look the same. . . .

 Pointing to external anchors can be useful for linking to large Web documents containing a great deal of information that may confuse your reader. Be careful, though; if anyone but you maintains the anchors, the names may change, the documents may be reorganized, or other changes may suddenly invalidate your links *without your even knowing it.* There's always a chance that a whole document will vanish from the Web, of course, but the chance that a link *within* a document will change is considerably higher.

 In this chapter, I introduced two useful devices for organizing and navigating large Web documents: internal anchors and links to those anchors. The same links can be accessed as part of a general Web URL, but beware: anchor names may change or move without your knowledge, thereby invalidating your connection. In the next chapter, I show you how to make your Web pages even more visually appealing by adding graphics. The chapter includes some hints on software that you can use to create graphics on your Macintosh.

Jazzing Up Web Pages

In This Chapter

In this chapter, I show you how to jazz up your Web pages with multimedia elements, and I include discussion of how to create and edit your own graphics.

Including images in Web documents

Text alternatives for nongraphical users

Image-alignment options

Stealing images off the Net

Scanned photographs

Transparent colors

Audio, video, and other media

This is the only chapter in the book that contains platform-specific information. Here you will learn about graphics editors and GIF translators for the Macintosh.

You have learned enough HTML by this point to make you dangerous: You should be able to create complex webs of information with sophisticated text formatting.

But that isn't all there is to Web design; the missing ingredient in this soup is *graphics*. The capability to place large and small images — and even to make the images hypertext references — is a crucial element of good Web page design. Not to mention that it's great fun to have Web pages with pictures, audio, and even video clips!

In this chapter, I diverge slightly from the platform-independent approach that I have taken in this book so far, and delve into some specifics of creating graphics and images for the Macintosh. Most of the examples in this chapter were created with programs that are available for both Macintosh and Windows machines, but my starting computer is a Macintosh and has been for years.

Including Images in Web Pages

Including images in a Web document is remarkably easy with the <IMG> (image) format tag. One limitation, though, is that you can use only two *graphics formats* within a document. (By "within a document" I mean that the image can be viewed within a Web browser — *inline*, as it's called in the desktop publishing and layout world.) The two formats supported by HTML are as follows:

➥ GIF: CompuServe's Graphics Interchange Format

➥ JPEG: The industry-standard Joint Photographic Expert Group format

If you have graphics in another format, for example, .TIFF, .BMP, .PCX, or .PICT, a user at the other end of the Web wire *may* be able to display those graphics, but only in a separate application that may or may not automatically be launched by the user's Web browser.

Some older Web browsers support only the GIF format, which is the de facto standard for graphics on the Web. GIF is a great thing, and the addition of support for graphics clearly has been a boon to the Web, but many of the most powerful graphics programs haven't supported the GIF format until quite recently. Why? Typical graphics programs support .PICT (for the Mac), .TIFF, .BMP, and .PCX (for Windows), and various proprietary formats, but supporting GIF requires software developers to license the encoding technologies separately, which most of those companies are loath to do.

So for your Web pages, you want your images to be in GIF format. Fortunately, a variety of freeware and shareware programs available on the Net can translate common graphics formats into GIF format. I recommend you check out GIFConverter, DeBabelizer Lite, or GraphicConverter. If you have the latest version of your graphics editor or image manipulation program, it might also have the capability to save directly into GIF format too. Check with the vendor or your local computer sales outlet to make sure.

The following are some great starting points for finding graphics software packages on the Net:

➥ Yahoo!:
   http://www.yahoo.com/Computers/Software/Graphics

➥ Yahoo!:
   http://www.yahoo.com/Computers/World_Wide_Web/Programming

➥ Yahoo!:
   http://www.yahoo.com/Computers/Internet/Archie

➥ Archie database:
   http://www.thegroup.net/AA.html

When you have a GIF file, the `<IMG>` tag is used to place that file in the text. Suppose that I have a file called black-box.gif that I want to use as the opening graphic in my Web page. The following example shows how this file might appear in an HTML document:

```
<HTML>
<HEAD>
<TITLE>The Dark Box</TITLE>
</HEAD><BODY>
<IMG SRC="black-box.gff">
<H1>Welcome to the Dark Box</H1>
There are boxes that aren't very well lit,
there are boxes that might even be
sealed, but I guarantee that you've never seen
anything quite as terrifying as
<I>The Dark Box</I>.
<P>
Dare you continue? <A HREF="blackbox2.html">yes</A> no.
</BODY>
</HTML>
```

As you can see, `<IMG>` is a formatting tag that enables you to specify different values. This tag proves to be vital as you learn more about its capabilities. The one attribute that must appear in the `<IMG>` tag is a specification of the image source file itself, in the format `SRC=filename`.

Figure 8-1 shows how the preceding HTML snippet appears when viewed in a browser.

Figure 8-1: Graphics specified but not loaded.

The small box in Figure 8-1 that contains the question mark within is in fact *not* the graphic that I wanted to include, but an indication from Navigator that an inline graphic was specified with the <IMG> tag but not *loaded*. In this case, the graphic wasn't loaded because I mistyped the name of the graphics file, specifying blackbox.gff rather than blackbox.gif. A mistake such as that is another good reason to test your Web pages extensively before letting other users visit them.

To correct the problem, I fixed the spelling. Figure 8-2 shows what the resulting Web page looks like with all the information properly loaded (more attractive than with the unloaded graphic, eh?).

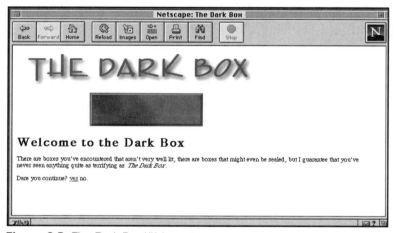

Figure 8-2: The Dark Box Web page.

You may have a fast connection to the Internet, but remember that many people are using very slow dial-up connections at 14400 baud or — horrors! — slower. Prodigy, America Online, and CompuServe users can access Web pages, but performance can be quite slow. Bigger graphics have more data to transfer to the user and therefore take longer on slower network connections. Also bear in mind that, to speed up access, many users simply skip loading the graphics unless the graphics are required to understand a page.

A popular use of graphics involves using icons instead of text tags. If I had two GIF files — yes.gif and no.gif — I could spiff up the Dark Box page as follows:

```
<HTML>
<HEAD>
<TITLE>The Dark Box</TITLE>
</HEAD><BODY>
```

```
<IMG SRC="black-box.gif">
<H1>Welcome to the Dark Box</H1>
There are boxes that aren't very well lit,
there are boxes that might even be
sealed, but I guarantee that you've never seen
anything quite as terrifying as
<I>The Dark Box</I>.
<P>
Dare you continue? <A HREF="blackbox2.html">
<IMG SRC="yes.gif"></A> <IMG SRC="no.gif">
</BODY>
</HTML>
```

The icons and graphics that are included in this image (that is, yes.gif and no.gif) are separate files in the same directory as the Web page. Figure 8-3 shows the cooler Web page with all graphics included.

A page in which graphics are a vital part of the design, however, can end up looking peculiar to a percentage of Web users because some people either cannot, or opt not to, download them when viewing Web pages. That fact makes for a design dilemma: should pages be designed to omit the graphics, include them as critical, or just as addenda?

Some Internet pundits tell you to just go wild with the graphics, because within a few months, everyone will have a fast, powerful computer and a high-speed connection. I don't agree with that. Because the GIF format, which is already compressed, still produces large graphics files, you should ensure that people who omit the images still see a meaningful page.

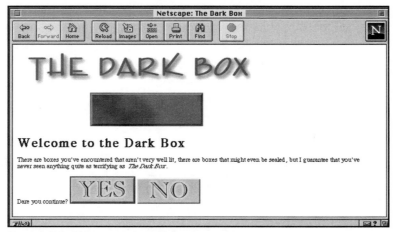

Figure 8-3: The cooler Dark Box page.

You can eliminate the blue border around a graphic image that's serving as a hyperlink by adding another attribute to the `<IMG>` tag: `BORDER=0`. If the preceding example had `<IMG SRC=yes.gif BORDER=0>` the blue border would vanish. I'll show you more about this later in the book, so stay tuned.

Text Alternatives for Text-Based Web Browsers

Although the most popular browsers — Navigator, Explorer, and Mosaic — offer lots of graphics, there is also an important Web browser called Lynx that is designed for text-only display. Lynx is found most commonly on UNIX systems where users have dial-up accounts. Even at a very slow connect speed, Lynx enables many users to navigate the Web and have fun.

With Lynx, graphics can't be included in the display. So an additional option is allowed in the HTML `<IMG>` format tag for just that situation. `ALT=text` is the magic sequence. Whatever text replaces *text* is displayed if the user can't view graphics or has turned off the automatic download of graphics, which about 10 percent of Web surfers do on a regular basis.

To understand why the `ALT=` element is necessary, see Figure 8-4, which simulates how the Dark Box page would appear in Lynx.

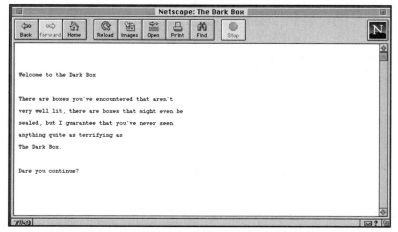

Figure 8-4: The Dark Box as a text-only display.

The user faces a problem, obviously: which of the images at the bottom represents the answer "Yes"? As it is, there's no way to tell. That is why you should always include some meaningful information in the ALT variable. The following example shows how a slight rewrite of the HTML code makes the page clear to a text-only user:

```
<HTML>
<HEAD>
<TITLE>The Dark Box</TITLE>
</HEAD><BODY>
<IMG SRC="black-box.gif" ALT="[wicked cool graphic]">
<H1>Welcome to the Dark Box</H1>
There are boxes that aren't very well lit,
there are boxes that might even be
sealed, but I guarantee that you've never seen
anything quite as terrifying as
<I>The Dark Box</I>.
<P>
Dare you continue? <A HREF="blackbox2.html">
<IMG SRC="yes.gif" ALT="<yes>"></A> <IMG SRC="no.gif"
ALT="<no>">
</BODY>
</HTML>
```

When displayed within Lynx or any other environment where the graphics aren't included, the preceding offers meaningful and helpful information that enables users to work with the page and explore the Dark Box, even when they're missing the graphic image (see Figure 8-5).

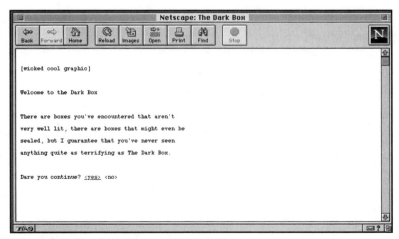

Figure 8-5: The Dark Box, text-only version.

Both Explorer and Navigator show this ALT text immediately upon loading a page, then gradually replace each placeholder with the actual graphic. Carefully planned ALT text can enhance the user experience and can even be fun.

You don't *have* to place brackets, parentheses, or anything else around the text in the ALT= section of the <IMG SRC> tag, but in my experience brackets or parentheses help users figure out the page (and make the page look better as well).

Image Alignment Options

Go back to the first section of this chapter and refer to Figure 8-3. Look carefully at the relative alignment of the text Dare you continue? with the Yes and No icons. The text is aligned with the bottoms of the icons, which looks good.

But what if you want a different alignment? Or what if you use different alignments for multiple graphics? You can specify a third attribute in the <IMG> formatting tag, ALIGN, which gives you precise control over alignment.

The three standard alignments are ALIGN=top, ALIGN=middle, and ALIGN=bottom. By default, images and adjacent material are aligned with the bottom of the image, as you can see in Figure 8-3. The following HTML snippet demonstrates the three alignment options:

```
<H1>IMG Alignment Options</H1>
<H2>ALIGN=top</H2>
Dare you continue? <A HREF="blackbox2.html">
<IMG SRC="yes.GIF" ALIGN=top></A>
(be careful! This takes courage!)
<H2>ALIGN=middle</H2>
Dare you continue? <A HREF="blackbox2.html">
<IMG SRC="yes.GIF" ALIGN=middle></A>
(be careful! This takes courage!)
<H2>ALIGN=bottom</H2>
Dare you continue? <A HREF="blackbox2.html">
<IMG SRC="yes.GIF" ALIGN=bottom></A>
(be careful! This takes courage!)
```

Figure 8-6 shows this example in a Web browser.

Figure 8-6: Image-alignment options.

The preceding example demonstrates the options for a graphic surrounded by text. However, you may want to align the Yes and No buttons at the bottom and also align the preceding text with the *centers* of the two icons. The following example shows a simple way to try and accomplish this task:

```
Dare you continue? <A HREF="blackbox2.html">
<IMG SRC="yes.GIF" ALIGN=middle></A>
<IMG SRC="no.GIF" ALIGN=bottom>
(be careful! This takes courage!)
```

Upon looking at this seemingly reasonable HTML snippet in a Web browser, I realize that the code doesn't do what I want it to do. Figure 8-7 shows the rather cheery and festive — albeit incorrect — result.

Figure 8-7: So much for aligning the icons.

The truth is that centering text on bottom-aligned graphics is beyond the capability of HTML using this approach. At best, you could make all your icons a single graphic element and then use an image map — an <ISMAP> tag — to tell your server which area corresponds to which option. (See Chapter 12 for information on ISMAP graphics.) The correct solution in this situation would be to not specify the alignment at all. The correctly formatted HTML is on the CD-ROM as yesno2.htm.

When you lay out your graphics, remember that different browsers have different screen widths and that they move elements around to fit that screen width. A classic mistake in an otherwise great looking Web page is previewing it with a relatively narrow window and thinking that it looks great. However, a user with a huge screen width would see all the graphics and text bubble up toward the top — an arrangement that ruins the overall appearance of the page.

A simple rule of thumb for images: if you don't want any material to appear after the graphics, add a <BR> tag to the end of the HTML sequence that specifies the graphic.

The three basic image alignment options refer to the alignment of information that appears subsequent to the image itself. There is an additional set of image alignment options that have shown up more recently that refer to the alignment of the image itself rather than adjacent material.

More sophisticated alignment

Although these additional image alignment options offer much more control, they also make formatting more confusing because of the difference between alignment of the image and alignment of the adjacent material.

I'll try to make sense of all the options for you by using lots of examples, because the options really *are* terrific. One thing to remember is that whatever you design with these extensions still must look attractive and interesting to the people who are using other Web browsers besides Netscape; unless you remain committed to that goal, your cool page in Netscape could easily look like a barely formatted mess in an old browser.These options are better demonstrated than discussed. The following example uses both options:

```
<B>Generic File Icon</B><BR>
<IMG SRC="generic-file.gif" ALIGN=left>
This is a generic file - that is, one that doesn't have
```

```
any application ownership information stored in the Mac
file
system or
its own resource fork. Opening these files typically
results in the use of the
<B>TeachText</B> or <B>SimpleText</B> application, if
possible, although you can fine-tune that with the new
<B>Easy Launch</B> control panel.
<P>
<B>Generic Folder Icon</B><BR>
<IMG SRC="generic-folder.gif" ALIGN=right>
This is a standard folder icon on the Macintosh. Folders
can contain just about anything, including files,
applications, and other folders. Opening a folder results
in the display
of the contents of that folder in a separate window on
the Macintosh.
```

Figure 8-8 shows how the preceding text is formatted within Internet Explorer — quite a step up from the primitive placement options shown earlier.

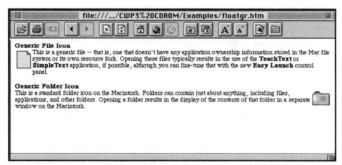

Figure 8-8: Floating graphics in Explorer.

Because older Web browsers don't recognize these alignment options, it's always valuable to nip into one of those browsers to see how things are presented to the reader. Figure 8-9 shows the same HTML code that produced Figure 8-8, but from within an older version of Navigator. Notice that the design of the HTML code, particularly the use of the boldface section title before the graphic and text, results in a dramatically different yet readable appearance.

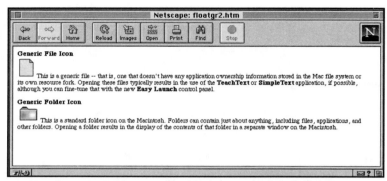

Figure 8-9: Floating graphics in an older version of Navigator.

Further options have been added to the now complex <IMG> formatting tag in the last few months. One new option enables you to specify the WIDTH and HEIGHT of the graphic when the graphic is loaded, which enables acceleration of the display of the document while the graphics are being loaded. Values are specified in pixels, as follows:

```
<IMG SRC="windows.gif" WIDTH=200 HEIGHT=350>
```

The preceding example would reserve a 200 × 350 pixel box on-screen for the graphic, which would be loaded in full after the text so that the text can be read right away. Be careful with these attributes, however, because if you actually had a 100 × 200 graphic, Navigator and Explorer would both stretch it to fit the 200 × 350 space, making it look very strange.

The BORDER variable can be used to great effect; it enables you to specify the exact width of the border around an image. The BORDER option is particularly useful if your graphic is also a hot link or anchor. The following shows an example:

```
<!- Tic-Tac-Toe ->
<CENTER>
<FONT SIZE=+3><B>Tic-Tac-Toe</B><FONT SIZE=+1><BR>
It's X's Turn... (<FONT COLOR=blue>This color</FONT>
indicates a recommended move)
<P>
<A HREF="topleft"><IMG SRC="box+x.gif" BORDER=0></A>
<A HREF="topcntr"><IMG SRC="box.gif" BORDER=0></A>
<A HREF="topright"><IMG SRC="box.gif" BORDER=0></A>
<BR>
```

```
<A HREF="left"><IMG SRC="box+o.gif" BORDER=0></A>
<A HREF="center"><IMG SRC="box+o.gif" BORDER=0></A>
<A HREF="right"><IMG SRC="box.gif" BORDER=2></A>
<BR>
<A HREF="btmleft"><IMG SRC="box+x.gif" BORDER=0></A>
<A HREF="btmcenter"><IMG SRC="box.gif" BORDER=0></A>
<A HREF="btmright"><IMG SRC="box.gif" BORDER=0></A>
</CENTER>
```

The resulting graphic is displayed in Figure 8-10. Notice that the BORDER specification enables me to indicate the recommended next move by simply placing a blue (or gray, for our figures in this book!) border around the box. This same attribute is how I turned *off* the blue border on the yes / no buttons earlier in this chapter.

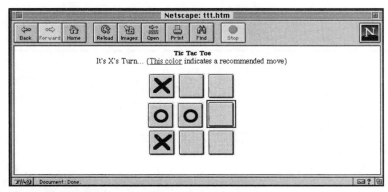

Figure 8-10: Tic-tac-toe in Netscape Navigator.

Two more attributes that I think are useful for image alignment are VSPACE and HSPACE, which control the vertical and horizontal space around each graphic. Consider an example of left and right alignment. When displayed, the text started at a different distance from the left margin, based on the width of the graphic. With HSPACE I can fix this problem by specifying a different number of pixels as a horizontal buffer between the graphics and the text adjacent, as follows:

```
<B>Generic File Icon</b><br>
<IMG SRC="generic-file.gif" ALIGN=left HSPACE=12>
This is a generic file, that is, one that doesn't have
any application ownership information stored in the
```

(continued)

```
Mac file system or its own resource fork. Opening
these files typically results in the <B>TeachText</B>
or <B>SimpleText</B> application being used, if possible,
though you can fine tune that with the new
<B>Easy Launch</B> control panel.
<P>
<B>Generic Folder Icon</B><BR>
<IMG SRC="generic-folder.gif" ALIGN=left HSPACE=10>
This is a standard folder icon on the Macintosh.
Folders can contain just about anything, including
files, applications and other folders. Opening a folder
results in the contents of that folder being displayed
in a separate window on the Macintosh.
```

Figure 8-11 demonstrates the result of the preceding text.

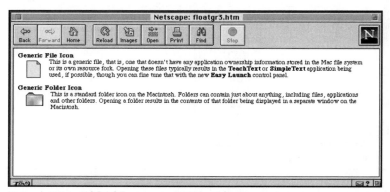

Figure 8-11: HSPACE corrects the graphic alignment.

At this point, you're learning to have some real control of the display of the document and can begin to design some cool Web pages. But I need to mention one more formatting addition before you go wild with the various options for the <IMG> tag.

If you experiment, you'll find that if you're wrapping text around a large graphic, it's difficult to move any material below the graphic.
 and <P> simply move to the next line in the wrapped area. That effect is *not* always what you want. To break the line and move back to the margin, past the graphics, use <BR CLEAR=left> to move to the left margin, <BR

CLEAR=right> to move down to a clear right margin, or <BR CLEAR=all> to move down until both margins are clear of the image.

Tossing all the additions into the mix, here's a Macintosh icon tutorial:

```
<HTML>
<HEAD>
<TITLE>An Introduction to Mac Icons</TITLE>
<BASEFONT SIZE=+2>
</HEAD><BODY>
<CENTER>
<FONT SIZE=+2><B>Intro to Macintosh Icons</B><BR>
<FONT SIZE=-1><I>Some of these are System 7.x only</I>
<FONT SIZE=-1>
</CENTER>
<P>
<B>Generic File Icon</B><BR>
<IMG SRC="generic-file.gif" ALIGN=left HSPACE=18 VSPACE=8>
This is a generic file - that is, one that doesn't have
any application ownership information stored in the Mac
file system or its own resource fork. Opening
these files typically results in the use of the
<B>TeachText</B>
or <B>SimpleText</B> application, if
possible, although you can fine-tune that with the new
<B>Easy Launch</B> control panel.
<P>
<B>Generic Folder Icon</B><BR>
<IMG SRC="generic-folder.gif" ALIGN=left HSPACE=15
VSPACE=6>
This is a standard folder icon on the Macintosh. Folders
can contain just about anything, including files,
applications, and other folders. Opening a folder results
in the display of the contents of that folder in a
separate window on the Macintosh.
<P>
<B>System Folder Icon</B><BR>
<IMG SRC="system-folder.gif" ALIGN=left HSPACE=15
VSPACE=11>
A special folder at the top level of each hard disk
on the Macintosh is the <I>System Folder</I>. This folder
contains all the files, applications, and information
needed to run and maintain the Macintosh operating
```

```
(continued)
system and all the goodies therein. The tiny Mac
icon inside the folder indicates that this
particular <I>System Folder</I> is <I>live</I> and that
the information inside was used to start
the current Macintosh.
<P>
Many files are located in the
<B>System Folder</B>, including the following:
<P>
<B>Apple Menu Icon</B><BR>
<IMG SRC="apple-menu.gif" ALIGN=left HSPACE=15 VSPACE=8>
Ever wondered where all the information that shows up on
the Apple menu (the menu you get when you click on
the <IMG SRC="apple-icon.gif"> in the top
left corner of the menu bar)? They're all just
files, folders, applications and aliases tucked into
the Apple folder itself. Open this folder some time
and compare the contents with the results of clicking
on the Apple icon itself.
</BODY>
</HTML>
```

Figure 8-12 shows the result.

Figure 8-12: The Macintosh icon tutorial.

A Few Real World Examples

This section examines some interesting graphics and layout options that people are using on the Web for their own cool designs.

The first example is the home page of Computer Literacy Bookshops of California (`http://www.clbooks.com/`). This low-key home page contains a small number of icons and offers a good demonstration of the `ALIGN=top` option. Figure 8-13 shows the top of the home page.

Figure 8-13: Computer Literacy on the Web. Copyright 1996 Computer Literacy Bookshops, Inc. All rights reserved. "Computer Literacy," "Computer Literacy Bookshops," and "clbooks.com" are service marks of Computer Literacy Bookshops, Inc.

The following HTML code is used to generate Computer Literacy's home page, something easily seen by clicking on the right mouse button then choosing View Source from the resultant pop-up menu in Explorer, or, if you're using Navigator, try View then Source:

```
<HTML>
<HEAD>
<TITLE>Computer Literacy Bookshops Home Page</TITLE>
</HEAD><BODY>
```

```
(continued)

<IMG SRC="3dmast.gif" ALT=""><P>
<H1>Computer Literacy Bookshops Home Page</H1>
Welcome! Our Web Server was designed with functionality,
not glitz, as the highest priority. Please, let us know
how we are doing and what we can do to improve our
service!
<A HREF="mailto:webmaster@clbooks.com"><I>webmaster@clbooks.
com</I></A>
<HR>
<DL>
<DT><H2><A HREF="/news/newatclb.html">
<IMG SRC="/icons/book-small.gif" ALIGN="top" ALT="[*]">
What's New at Computer Literacy?</A></H2>
<DD>Information on special free events, trade shows, new
services, and other topical information. <B>Updated
Wednesday, 15 March 1995</B>
<DT><H2><A HREF="/clbinfo/aboutclb.html">
 <IMG SRC="/icons/book-small.gif" ALIGN="top" ALT="[*]">
Store Information and Services</A></H2>
<DD>Phone numbers, fax, email address, directions to our
store locations, and a list of services Computer Literacy
provides.
<DT><H2><A HREF="/nbb/nbbindex.html">
 <IMG SRC="/icons/book-small.gif" ALIGN="top" ALT="[*]">
New Book Bulletins, Updates, and Galley Alley</A></H2>
<DD>Our latest New Book Bulletins in hypermedia format and
various related files, including an interview with Donald
Knuth, and a list of some hot forthcoming titles in Galley
Alley (sm)!
```

 Don't forget that the `<DL>` format is a *definition list* and that entries have a `<DT>` defined term and a `<DD>` definition.

The next interesting site, *PC Week,* has even fewer graphics and replaces the boring black bullet with a neat red sphere. Figure 8-14 shows the top of an early version of the now incredibly complex *PC Week* Web page, located at:

`http://www.ziff.com/~pcweek`

Following is the code used:

```
<HTML>
<HEAD>
<TITLE>PC Week</TITLE>
```

```
</HEAD>
<BODY>
<IMG ALT="PC Week"
SRC="http://www.ziff.com/~eamonn/icons/logotr1.gif">
<BR>
<H4><B><I>The National Newspaper of Corporate Computing -
World-Wide Web edition</I></B></H4><P>
<HR>
<P>
<CENTER><I>Updated July 17, 1995 7:52 AM
E.T.</I></CENTER><P>
<DL>
<H4><DT><IMG ALT="o" src="/~eamonn/icons/redball.gif"><A
HREF="http://www.ziff.com/~pcweek/daily/coop/cc0317.html">
Coop's Corner</A></H4>
<DD><I>March 17: </I>Mystery deepens in case involving
Gates' mother
<H4><DT><IMG ALT="o" src="/~eamonn/icons/redball.gif"><A
HREF="http://www.ziff.com/~pcweek/news/jul_1995/news_thay_0
316.html"> NCD to deliver all-in-one Internet front-end
ware</A></H4>
<DD>Mariner software is for users who don't want to learn
six or seven different protocols, applications
<H4><DT><IMG ALT="o" src="/~eamonn/icons/redball.gif"><A
HREF="http://www.ziff.com/~pcweek/news/jul_1995/news_tyam_0
316.html"> NeXT's Martin Yam on linking objects,
platforms</A></H4>
<DD>Predicts continued growth in Unix server market
```

Notice again the use of the tags `<CENTER>` and `</CENTER>`, used to center text on the screen in many browsers. I'll talk about it in detail in Chapter 9, so stay tuned.

An interesting decision that the designers of the *PC Week* Web site made was to show all hypertext references as *full* reference URLs rather than in the more succinct *relative* reference form. For example, the link for Coop's Corner reads

`http://www.ziff.com/~pcweek/daily/coop/cc0317.html`

but because the base address of this page is `http://www.ziff.com/~pcweek`, the link could have been written in the format `<A HREF="daily/coop/cc0317.html">` and would have been easier to work with. Frankly, the best approach is to have all local URLs specified relative to the root server, so in this case they'd use:

`/~pcweek/daily/coop/cc0317.html`

An even better reason to use the short version would be that if the entire site was renamed for any reason, there would be no need to modify each and every link in every document on the site.

Figure 8-14: PC Week on the Web. Courtesy Ziff-Davis Publishing Co. (PC Week).

A third site worth checking out, the Wentworth Gallery, has some great graphics with a straightforward alignment, an attractive interface, and it uses simple HTML code to boot. Wentworth Gallery features a variety of lithographs and other artwork, as you can see in Figure 8-15.

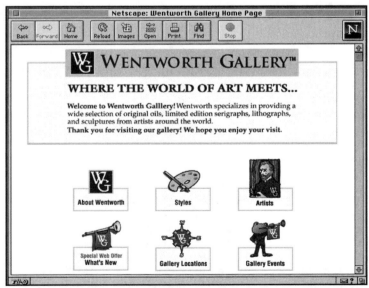

Figure 8-15: Wentworth Gallery on the Web. Illustrations by George Courage and Tony Valietti, Wentworth Gallery™ (Wentworth Gallery).

Following is the straightforward HTML that generates the page seen in Figure 8-15:

```
<HTML>
<TITLE>Wentworth Gallery Home Page</TITLE>

<BODY BGCOLOR=#FFFFFF>
<CENTER>
<IMG SRC="/wwg/admin/gifs/hmebnnr.gif">
</CENTER>
<CENTER>
<PRE>
<A HREF="/wwg/admin/aboutwwg.htm"><IMG
SRC="/wwg/admin/gifs/abwntwr.gif" BORDER=0></A>   <A
HREF="/wwg/gallery/styles.htm"><IMG
SRC="/wwg/admin/gifs/styles.gif" BORDER=0></A>   <A
HREF="/wwg/gallery/artists.htm"><IMG
SRC="/wwg/admin/gifs/artists.gif" BORDER=0></A>

<A HREF="/wwg/admin/news.htm"><IMG
SRC="/wwg/admin/gifs/whtsnew.gif" BORDER=0></A>   <A
HREF="/wwg/admin/locate.htm"><IMG
SRC="/wwg/admin/gifs/location.gif" BORDER=0></A>  <A
HREF="/wwg/admin/events.htm"><IMG
SRC="/wwg/admin/gifs/gallvnts.gif" BORDER=0></A>

<A HREF="/wwg/admin/home_sh.htm"><IMG
SRC="/wwg/admin/gifs/homshows.gif" BORDER=0></A>  <A
HREF="/wwg/admin/guests.htm"><IMG
SRC="/wwg/admin/gifs/guestrg.gif" BORDER=0></A>   <A
HREF="/wwg/admin/mail.htm"><IMG
SRC="/wwg/admin/gifs/commnts.gif" BORDER=0></A>
</PRE>
</CENTER>
<P>
<I>(c) Copyright 1996, Wentworth Gallery</I><BR>
<I>gallery@wentworth-art.com</I>
</BODY>
</HTML>
```

This is a fairly readable Web page, though it could be cleaned up by remembering that carriage returns that are buried within HTML tags don't affect the formatting. Also, the use of the preformatted block to have the spacing between graphics is a smart idea, and a great example of how you can exploit tags for specific uses. This preformatted block is valuable because the four spaces between each graphic are actually retained as four spaces, rather than compressed into a single space as would otherwise occur. The lack of an explicit <HEAD> section isn't a great problem; most Web browsers seem to be quite forgiving of omissions, but over time more and more will insist on properly formatted code.

Visit Wentworth Gallery online at:
`http://wentworth-art.com/`

Where Do You Get Images From?

Considering the number of alignment options available for graphics, it's remarkable how much variation exists among different sites on the Web. Web designers create varied appearances for their pages through the *types* of graphics they use. Where do these graphics come from? Here are a few possibilities:

➡ New images

➡ Clip art or other canned image libraries

➡ Text-manipulation programs

➡ Scanned photographs

➡ Images stolen off the Net

New images

If you're artistically inclined or want to use relatively straightforward graphics or icons, the easiest way to produce graphics for your Web pages is to create them yourself. A bewildering number of graphics applications are available for Windows, Mac, and UNIX users, at prices ranging from free to $50 to thousands of dollars for real top-notch stuff.

To give you an example, I created the opening graphic for the Dark Box (shown in Figure 8-2) from scratch in about 20 minutes. I used a commercial Mac program called Color It to produce the text and graphic and then translated the final output to GIF format with a separate shareware program called GraphicConverter.

I asked a couple of other Web designers who use cool graphics what tools they use to produce their images. Patti Siering, graphics designer for EuroGrafix, told me that she used Adobe Photoshop 3 and Strata Studio Pro 1.5.1 to produce the image in Figure 8-16.

Figure 8-16: Cool EuroGrafix image.

Another slick Web site is Traveling Software, the maker of LapLink. Web designer David Geller indicated that he used Aldus Photostyler for Windows (it's like Photoshop) to create most of the graphics on the Traveling Software page, shown in Figure 8-17.

You may want to visit a few of these sites yourself. The URL for EuroGrafix is:
`http://www.eurografix.com/eurograf/welcome.htm`
The URL for Traveling Software is:
`http://www.travsoft.com/`

Here are some of the more popular graphics packages for the Mac and those *other* platforms:

➡ **Macintosh:** Because it remains the premiere platform for graphics, you'll find that most graphics applications are available for the Mac. In addition to the "big three" — Adobe Photoshop, Aldus FreeHand, and Adobe Illustrator — Macintosh graphics programs include Drawing Table, Color It, Specular Collage, KPT Bryce, Paint Alchemy, TextureScape, Painter, Kai's Power Tools, and Alias Sketch.

➡ **Windows:** Among the many applications for developing graphics in Microsoft Windows are Illustrator, FreeHand, Painter, Fractal Design Dabbler, Canvas, Ray Dream Designer, SmartSketch, CorelDRAW!, MacroModel, AutoSketch, Kai's Power Tools, 3D Sketch, and Elastic Reality.

➡ **UNIX:** Fewer graphics programs are available for UNIX systems, but the programs that are available are quite powerful. Look for IslandDraw and IslandPaint, Photoshop, FusionArt, GINOGRAPH, Illustrator, Image Alchemy, Magic Inkwell, and Visual Reality.

Figure 8-17: Traveling Software's opening image.

Web page designer David Hendee makes graphics in Photoshop and then scales them to size. For quick loading, he reduces the pixel depth of the scaled images to the lowest setting that produces a good-looking image, often 4 bit=16 colors. To speedily handle lots of graphics, Hendee scales and finds the best pixel depth for a sample. When the test image looks okay, he uses its settings in DeBabelizer from Equilibrium to convert the entire batch of images. Navigational buttons are fine-tuned one by one; some read well at 1 bit=2 colors. For transparent backgrounds, Hendee says to make sure the background of the converted graphic is a solid color; use Photoshop's Magic Wand (uncheck the Antialias option) to adjust the background if necessary.

Clip art or canned image libraries

One result of the explosion of interest in the Web and Web page design is the wide variety of CD-ROM and floppy-based clip art and image libraries that are now available. From thousands of drawings on multi-CD-ROM libraries to hand-rendered three dimensional images on floppy, or available for a fee directly on the Net, there are lots of license-free image sources. At the same time, most of the CD-ROMs I've seen that are supposedly for Web designers are really pretty awful, quickly thrown together collections of clip art that would look great on your page if you could just figure out where it is on the disk and how to get it into your own program.

The clip art library that I'm most enamored of is the Adobe Image Club series. They're expensive, almost $100 for a set of floppy disks holding typically 35 or less images, but the quality is excellent and the results are flawless every time. If you opt to explore the clip art route, I strongly recommend you be a skeptical consumer and make sure that the interface and ease of finding specific images meets your needs. Don't forget to also check the contents of the boxed clip art 'explosion' packages; I picked up a five CD-ROM set of clip art and, most importantly, wonderful license-free photographs for $30.

Licensed material is material that you can't use without obtaining explicit permission, either by simply requesting permission or paying for it. Photographs in particular are usually licensed if they're not yours, and there's a huge business in license-free photographic archives. Most photographs you see on corporate Web pages are licensed and cannot be freely reproduced.

Text-manipulation programs

I really like funky or interesting text effects in Web pages — not just simple things such as text in boxes, but shadows, textured letters, and twisted or wavy baselines. Look at the lettering in the Dark Box image earlier, in Figure 8-3, to see the kind of thing that I think looks cool.

I manipulated the text in the Dark Box page the hard way, from within a general-purpose graphics editor. A smarter method would have been to use one of the many type-manipulation programs that are available. I have two favorites: Pixar Typestry (available for both Macs and PCs) and Broderbund TypeStyler (Mac only).

Typestry is astoundingly powerful, and offers a staggering variety of options. Figure 8-18 shows a simple graphic produced in the program (it looks much better in color).

Figure 8-18: Text graphics in Typestry.

TypeStyler is easier to use and offers a more general-purpose graphics environment but lacks the sophistication of Typestry. As Figure 8-19 shows, the program enables you to produce attractive text for Web pages.

Figure 8-19: Text graphics in TypeStyler.

If you can afford the package and have the willingness to learn the weird interface, Adobe Photoshop is an amazingly powerful image and graphics editor. With the addition of some third-party plug-in such as, ironically, The Black Box from Alien Skin Software (no relation to the example shown earlier!), you can produce stunning text graphics with just a few mouse clicks. Figure 8-20 shows an example of what can be done. Many of the graphics included with the HTML documents on the CD-ROM in the back of this book were done within Photoshop.

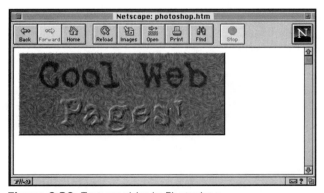

Figure 8-20: Text graphics in Photoshop.

Scanned photographs

Another way to produce graphics for your Web site is to use a scanner and work with existing art. If you're a photography buff, you probably have hundreds of original photographs from which you can glean cool additions for your site.

A few years ago, I was traveling in Paris and took a great photograph of the beautiful Sacré Coeur. A few minutes of work with a scanner made the photo instant artwork to include in my Web page, as shown in Figure 8-21.

Figure 8-21: Scanned image of Sacré Coeur.

Scanners offer further options for producing fun and interesting graphics. I also scanned the image shown in Figure 8-21 as black-and-white line art, producing the interesting abstract graphic in Figure 8-22.

If I were designing a Web site that I expected would attract users with slow connections, I could use small black-and-white representations of art, each small image, or thumbnail image, as a button that produces the full color image, to save people time waiting for data that they may not want. The HTML could look like the following:

```
<A HREF="big-image.gif"><IMG SRC="little-image.gif"
BORDER=0></A>
```

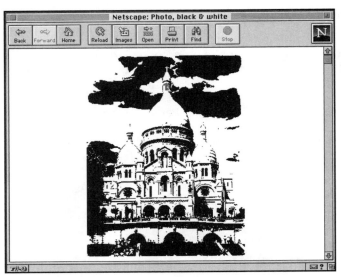

Figure 8-22: Sacré Coeur as line art.

Thumbnail versions of large graphical images are common (and appreciated by just about everyone), so if you create a page that contains many pictures, think about minimizing the data transfer with smaller versions that refer to larger images.

Another difference between the images in Figures 8-21 and 8-22 is size. Figure 8-21 works on computers that have a palette of 256 colors (standard for GIF format), meaning that each pixel of information is represented in the data file by enough data to specify which of the 256 colors is needed at each point. Eight bits are used in this case, meaning that whereas the black-and-white version simply needs to specify "on" or "off" for each pixel (1 bit), the color version needs eight times as much information to display the information correctly. Trim the color palette on an image from 256 colors to, say, 16 (that is, from 8 bits of data per pixel to 4 bits of data per pixel), and you've lopped 50 percent off the size of your graphic, often without adverse effect on the image.

Another way to work with scanners is to scan scrawls, doodles, or pictures that you create with pencils, pens, color markers, paint, pastels, or what have you, and then incorporate those objects into your Web page. Or get even more creative: scan in aluminum foil, crumpled tissues, your cat (note that this would be a "cat scan"), wood, a piece of clothing, or just about anything else.

If you're working with scanners, you already know about some of the best software tools available. I'll just note that I always use Photoshop when I'm working with color or gray scale scans. One important scanner trick if your output is for the Web: scan the images at 100 dots-per-inch (dpi) or 75 dpi or thereabouts because the additional information you can get from, say, a 2400 dpi scanner is wasted, slows down the editing process, and produces fantastically large graphics files anyway. (I've scanned in images that produced 17MB files, and that was without even trying!)

Stealing Images off the Net

There's another way to get images that doesn't involve being artistic or using a scanner: you can find interesting, attractive graphics online. Think of Net graphics as being virtual clip art (you can use real clip art, too), though don't forget that some of the images might be copyrighted. Just because MCI has a Web site (`http://www.mci.com/`) doesn't mean that you can nip over and borrow its logo without permission!

To show you what's out there, I culled some icons from a couple of icon archives on the Web. Finding these icons was a long, tedious task, because many archives contain what I consider to be just plain ugly icons, but I couldn't tell until I loaded the entire page of icons on the screen.

Copyright laws are serious, and I strongly discourage you from scanning in images from any published work that is not in the public domain. The cover of *Sports Illustrated* might be terrific this week, but if you scan it in and display it in your Web page, you're asking for some very serious trouble.

Chris Stephens at Virginia Commonwealth University offers a terrific set of icons that even load quickly. Connect to:
`http://www.cbil.vcu.edu:8080/gifs/bullet.html`
You'll see much more than the small portion of the set shown in Figure 8-23.

Another site that offers icons and graphics suitable for inclusion in your own pages is CERN, the Swiss physics lab where the World Wide Web was born (is it any wonder that CERN has all sorts of cool stuff on its server?). The URL for the CERN icon archive is:
`http://www.w3.org/pub/WWW/Icons/WWW/`
See Figure 8-24.

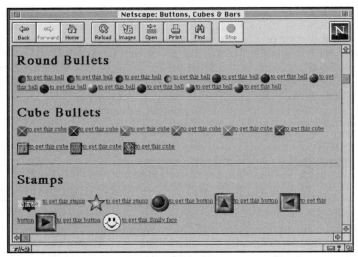

Figure 8-23: Some of the icons in the Stephens archive.

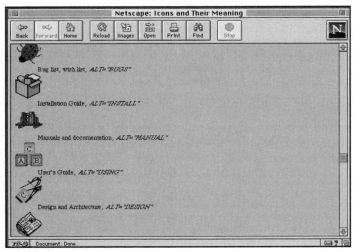

Figure 8-24: CERN icon library.

Cut out the middleman and get the master list of icon home pages by going to Yahoo! (`http://www.yahoo.com/`) and looking in `Computers / World Wide Web / Programming / Icons`.

Of course, you can just travel the Net and, when you see something you like, grab it with a screen capture program or download it directly. Different Web browsers offer different tools to accomplish this task. With Explorer, for example, simply right click on a graphic and hold the mouse button down, and suddenly there's a pop-up menu with the option of saving that graphic to the disk. If you take this route, however, be doubly sensitive to possible copyright infringement.

Transparent Colors

One subtle thing that I did with graphics in this chapter was replace the background color around the edges of the image with a *transparent color* — one that enables the background color of the window to bleed through. Transparent colors (available only with GIF format images, as far as I know) almost instantly make pages look cooler. Of course, in this book, there *are* no colors, but you've been pretending pretty well up to here, haven't you?

Figure 8-25 shows two versions of the same type of icon. The graphic on the top hasn't had its gray background set to transparent; the one on the bottom has. Some difference, eh?

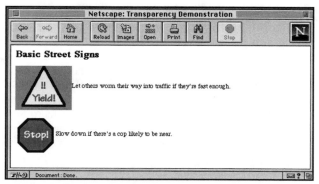

Figure 8-25: Transparent graphics.

Although few of the major graphics or type-manipulation packages support transparent GIFs (or GIFs at all, for that matter), a couple of simple shareware applications that are available on the Net enable you to choose a color for a specific graphic from the GIF color palette and set that color to be the transparent one.

On the Macintosh, the program Transparency, written by Aaron Giles, is rough and primitive but does the job admirably. You can get a copy of this program off the Net at:
`ftp://ftp.med.cornell.edu/pub/aarong/transparency/`
GraphicConverter also works with Transparency.

If you're on a Windows system, you'll want to know that the program of choice is GIFTRANS. You can obtain this program easily from the archive of the University of North Carolina at Chapel Hill; the URL is:
`ftp://sunsite.unc.edu/pub/packages/infosystems/WWW/tools/giftrans`

Documentation for GIFTRANS can be found on my Web site. Look in:
`http://www.intuitive.com/coolweb`

If you're working on a UNIX system, or if you like working within the DOS environment, you can use GIFTool, which is available at:
`http://www.homepages.com/tools/`

For a comprehensive list of utilities and all sorts of goodies, zip over to Yahoo! (`http://www.yahoo.com/`) and look in:
`Computers/ World Wide Web / Programming`

Audio, Video, and other Media

Graphics definitely add pizzazz to a Web site, but there are more media that you can use to develop your cool Web pages, including audio and video. Some significant limitations plague these add-on media, however, not the least of which is that they're large and take quite awhile to download.

Audio fragments are probably the most fun — it's great to hear voices or music coming from your computer and they're quite easy to add to your own pages. The audio recordings are usually in what's called a micro-law (or you'll see this written as mu-law) format, and can be included as a button or hot spot just like any other URL. Here's an example:

```
You're invited to listen to <A HREF="audio.au">a sample of
my latest album</A>
```

Users that clicked on the phrase *a sample of my latest album* would then download an audio file (typically 75K or larger), and then an audio player program would be launched to actually play the audio clip. A simple audio clip is also included on the CD-ROM in the back of this book. Enjoy!

Be careful when you're adding audio to your site, however; these files can grow incredibly quickly and become huge. A ten second audio clip can grow to over 150K, which could represent *quite* a long download period for people accessing the Web via slow dialup connections.

AV Macintosh have a variety of built-in audio capabilities, including recording audio directly from an attached microphone. Save the file that's produced and ensure it has a .WAV filename suffix. My personal favorite for recording and editing audio is a great shareware program called SampleEditor. You can learn about this, and many other audio tools, by checking in at Yahoo! at:

`http://www.yahoo.com/Computers/World_Wide_Web/Programming`

Movies are found in two formats, QuickTime and MPEG (Motion Picture Experts Group) format. MPEG is the format of choice for the Web, however, because it's the most universal, with MPEG players available for Mac, PC, and UNIX systems.

If you think *audio* files can expand rapidly to take up lots of space, you haven't seen anything till you try video on the Web.

The format for including an MPEG sequence is simple:

```
The latest <A HREF="video.mpg">Music Video</A> is finally
here!
```

The Web browsers see the filename suffix .MPG and know to download the file specified and launch an external video player program.

You can learn a lot more about working with MPEG and other video formats, and sneak a peek at some public domain video and animation archive sites, by popping over to Yahoo!. Check out:

`http://www.yahoo.com/Computers/Multimedia/Video`

I could say lots more about the fun and frustration of working with graphics and other media in Web pages. One thing's for sure: however people accomplish the task, you'll see a million very slick graphics, icons, buttons, separator bars, and other gizmos all over the Web. Keep a skeptical eye on your own work, though, to make sure that your neat doodads don't overtake the theme and message — the content — of your site.

Table 8-1:	Tags Used in this Chapter	
HTML Tag	**Close Tag**	**Meaning**
<IMG		Includes a graphic or other image
SRC=f		The URL or filename for the graphic
ALT=t		Alternative text to show if graphic isn't viewable
ALIGN=opt		Options for aligning graphic or material surrounding the graphic. Key alternatives are LEFT, RIGHT, TOP, MIDDLE, and BOTTOM
BORDER=n		Border around graphic surrounded by HREF, in pixels
WIDTH=n		Width of graphic — speeds up loading page in browser
HEIGHT=n		Height of graphic, in pixels. Speeds up loading page
VSPACE=n		Additional vertical space around graphic — in pixels
HSPACE=n		Additional horizontal space around graphic
<BR CLEAR=opt>		Clear to specified margin edge. Options are LEFT, RIGHT or ALL

Moving On

In my view, at least, cool Web pages are those that intelligently incorporate their graphics into the overall design and don't fall apart or become unusable (or otherwise frustrating) when users do not or cannot load the graphics, ending up with ALT=text information instead. In the next chapter, you learn about some advanced HTML options that will enable you to further control over graphics and other information.

Advanced HTML Techniques

In This Chapter

The different World Wide Web browsers understood the same HTML formatting tags until Netscape Navigator showed up late in 1994. Netscape Communications Corporation, the company that makes Navigator, added some extensions — extra formatting tags that only Netscape Navigator supported — to HTML 1.0. When the first edition of this book was released, only Navigator supported these tags. Today, however, a variety of different browsers know these tags, including both Navigator and Internet Explorer.

Centering and horizontal rules

List improvements

Background colors and graphics

Organizing information in Tables

Pages Within Pages: Frames

If you've read the whole book up to this point, you know all there is to know about HTML coding. Well, almost. In this chapter, I focus on a set of fun extensions developed by the good folk at Netscape and now widely available. As you'll learn, these extensions are terrifically useful and offer the capability to create far cooler pages than you can using only standard HTML 1.0 tags.

Centering Material and Horizontal Rules

Of the many additions to the original hypertext markup language, the one that I like most is `<CENTER>`, with its partner tag `</CENTER>`. And, using horizontal rules is also a good way to add more character to your document.

Centering text

Any information between the two tags is centered on the screen of the browser. This extension is particularly useful for opening graphics, but as you begin to design more complex pages, you probably will find other places where it can be a great help.

One situation in which using `<CENTER>` is a big win is centering the headline or title of a text HTML page. Remember the enchilada sauce recipe from Chapter 5? The following example shows how the text could be enhanced for modern browsers:

```
<HTML>
<HEAD>
<TITLE>Dave's Enchilada Sauce</TITLE>
</HEAD><BODY>
<CENTER>
<FONT SIZE=+2><B>Dave's Enchilada Sauce</B></FONT><BR>
<I>guaranteed to enhance any enchilada!</I>
</CENTER>
<OL>
<LI>Heat a large sauce pan and saut&egrave; until soft:
<UL>
<LI>Two tablespoons virgin olive oil
<LI>A large onion, chopped
</UL>
<LI>Sprinkle in a quarter cup of flour.<BR>
<LI>Jazz it up by adding:
<UL>
<LI>Two tablespoons of chili powder
<LI>Two teaspoons of cumin
<LI>One teaspoon of garlic powder
</UL>
<LI>Mix in a quart of water.
<LI>Finally, add a teaspoon of salt if desired.
</OL>
Whisk as sauce thickens, then simmer for 20 minutes.
</BODY>
</HTML>
```

Figure 9-1 shows how the preceding recipe would look in Netscape. The recipe is more visually interesting but still rather boring. As you go through this chapter, you'll learn about some enhancements that can make this text much more attractive.

Figure 9-1: Centered text in Netscape Navigator.

Before we leave the topic of centering text and other material, it's important to highlight another way to accomplish this, a way that's a bit more confusing, but fits better into the future plans for HTML: the ALIGN attribute for the paragraph tag. To center material, use <P ALIGN=center> and finish the centered material with </P>. What's nice is that you can also use <P ALIGN=right> to have material right aligned. The following shows how that might be used to great advantage:

```
<HTML>
<CENTER>
<FONT COLOR=green>this text is centered the old way</FONT>
</CENTER>
<P ALIGN=left>
this is on the left margin…
</P>
<P ALIGN=center>
<FONT COLOR=blue>this is centered the new, fancy
way…</FONT>
</P>
(<P ALIGN=right>)
and this material is tucked rightmost<BR>
so what do you think?
</P>
</HTML>
```

Figure 9-2 shows how this formats. It's colorful and quite cheery, yes?

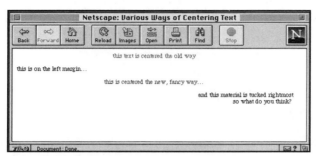

Figure 9-2: A variety of centering techniques.

Rules on the horizon

Horizontal rules, the product of the <HR> tag, are helpful, but let's be honest: a uniform line across the screen can get *boring*. The Netscape gang also thought horizontal rules were boring, so they extended the <HR> command with some additions (perhaps too many): SIZE, WIDTH, ALIGN, and NOSHADE. The first three of these options take values, the last toggles the presentation style of the rule itself.

SIZE enables you to specify the height of the horizontal line, in pixels. Want the slimmest line possible? Try using <HR SIZE=1> in your document.

A *pixel* is a single dot on a computer screen. A horizontal line that is 1 pixel high, therefore, is the thinnest line possible. Your screen probably has about 500 horizontal rows of pixels. SIZE=1 specifies a single pixel-high line.

WIDTH can be specified either in absolute pixels (a typical screen probably is 600 to 800 pixels wide) or in a percentage of the screen width. If you want a horizontal rule that is exactly 75 percent of the width of the current viewing window, you could use <HR WIDTH=75%> as your HTML sequence.

Because you can have lines that don't extend over the entire width of the browser, Netscape enables you to specify where you want a line snippet to be placed. Just as you can with the ALIGN options for images, you can specify that horizontal lines be placed LEFT, CENTER, or RIGHT. To have a line that's half the width of the browser window and centered, you would use <HR WIDTH=50% ALIGN=CENTER>.

Finally, close examination of these fancy horizontal lines shows that the lines are shaded to offer a quasi-three-dimensional appearance. If you really want a solid black bar, use the NOSHADE option.

You can combine these options in fun and interesting ways, as in the following example:

```
<CENTER><B>A Visit to the Pyramids!</B></CENTER><P>
<HR SIZE=3 WIDTH=5%>
<HR SIZE=3 WIDTH=10%>
<HR SIZE=3 WIDTH=20%>
<HR SIZE=3 WIDTH=30%>
<HR SIZE=3 WIDTH=40%>
<HR SIZE=3 WIDTH=50%>
<HR SIZE=3 WIDTH=60%>
<HR SIZE=3 WIDTH=100% NOSHADE>
```

This kind of detail can get complex, but the result can be pretty cool, as shown in Figure 9-3.

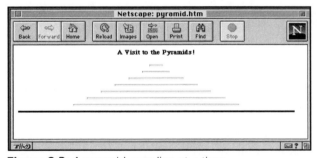

Figure 9-3: A pyramid, one line at a time.

What does the Web page in Figure 9-3 look like if you view it in a different, older browser? Figure 9-4 tells the story.

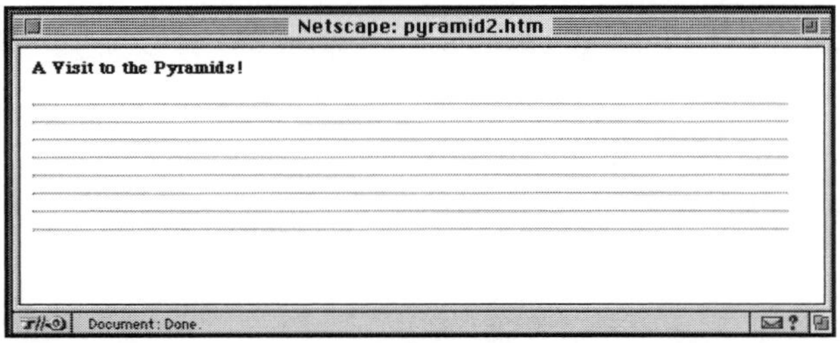

Figure 9-4: Not much of a pyramid in an older browser.

And that's the danger, in a nutshell: you may design a wickedly cool Web page with the latest extensions, but seen from other browsers, your page looks like you used the Paste command too many times (or worse).

TIP Even more cool, you can actually specify the color of a specific horizontal rule: add the attribute COLOR=*colorname*, with color names (or RGB values) as explained later in this chapter. For example: <HR COLOR=green>.

List Improvements

HTML lists have three basic extensions: one for ordered lists (<OL>), one for unordered lists (<UL>), and one for individual list items (<LI>).

Standard ordered lists have no options. You specify that you have an ordered list, and the list items are displayed with incremented numeric values: Step 1, Step 2, Step 3, and so on. If you're creating a multilevel outline or other multilevel list, however, different forms of notation for the different levels can be quite useful. You may use A to Z for the highest level, numbers for the second level, and a to z for the lowest level. That format is, of course, the typical outline format taught in English class. The following is an example of this format:

    A. Introduction

        1. Title

           a. Author

           b. Institution

           c. Working title (20 words or fewer)

        2. Justification for research

           a. What? Why?

        3. Findings

        4. Conclusions

    B. Body of Paper

        1. Previous research

        2. Research methods used

        3. Results and findings

    C. Conclusion

        1. Implications

        2. Directions for future research

    D. References

If you were to try to reproduce the preceding example within HTML, the best you could do with standard HTML notation would be to have three levels of numbered-list items, many bullet points, or no indentation at all. None of those options is what you want, naturally, and that's where the enhanced ordered-list extensions come in handy.

Ordered lists have two extensions: TYPE, which specifies the numeric type to use; and START, which begins the count at a number other than the default (default is 1). You can use five types of counting values:

➡ TYPE=A is uppercase alphabetic (A, B, C, D).

➡ TYPE=a is lowercase alphabetic (a, b, c, d).

➡ TYPE=I is uppercase Roman numerals (I, II, III, IV).

➡ TYPE=i is lowercase Roman numerals (i, ii, iii, iv).

➡ TYPE=1 (the default) is Arabic numerals (1, 2, 3, 4).

To have an ordered list begin with the fourth Roman numeral in uppercase, you could use <OL TYPE=I START=4>. The default for a list is <OL TYPE=1 START=1>.

If you've been experimenting with Explorer or Navigator, you may already have found that different levels of unordered lists produce differently shaped bullets. In fact, both of these browsers support three types of bullets — a solid disc, a circle, and a square — and you can specify which should be used for your unordered list with TYPE. For example, do you want a list in which every item is tagged with a square? <UL TYPE=square> does the trick.

Within the <LI> tag, you can specify TYPE=shape (if you're in the middle of an unordered list) or START=value (to change the current count for an ordered list). The following example shows how some of these features can be used in a Web document:

```
<B>Geometric Ramblings</B>
<OL TYPE=1>
<LI>Facets of a square:
<UL TYPE=square>
<LI>Four sides of equal length
</UL>
<LI>Interesting facts about circles:
<UL TYPE=disc>
<LI>Maximum enclosed area, shortest line
</UL>
</OL>
<CENTER>Weird, unrelated information.</CENTER>
<OL TYPE=1>
<LI VALUE=3> And much, much more!
</OL>
```

Figure 9-5 shows how the preceding HTML text would be presented to the user. Note particularly that the numbered list seems to flow without any interruption, something that would be impossible to accomplish without the Netscape addition to the ordered list.

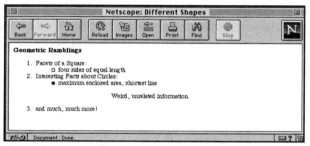

Figure 9-5: Geometric ramblings in Navigator.

Background Colors and Graphics

One cool thing that you can do for people who use current Web browsers is to specify a different background color for your page or pages. If that's not enough, you can also load an arbitrary graphic as the background to the entire page, a graphic that's either subtle (like a marbled texture) or way over the top, like a picture of your cat!

To do either of these, you need to add a variable to the <BODY> tag that should already be an integral part of your existing Web pages. Background colors are added with BGCOLOR=*colorname* or BGCOLOR=*#rgb-value* and you specify a background graphic with BACKGROUND=*filename*. It's fairly straightforward to work with background graphics, but the original color specification for a background color, unfortunately, isn't quite so simple. If you want to have complete control, your colors will need to be specified as a trio of red-green-blue numeric values, two letters for each, in hexadecimal. "Hexa-what?" I can already hear you asking. Hexadecimal is a numbering system that's base-16 rather than our regular numbering scheme of base-10 (decimal, as it's called). The number 10, for example, is 1*10 + 0, but in hexadecimal, it'd have the base-10 equivalent of 1*16 + 0 or 16.

Don't worry too much if this doesn't make too much sense to you; just grab a copy of HTML Color Picker. It's just important to know what some typical color values are, and they're shown in Table 9-1.

Table 9-1:	Hex RGB Values for Common Colors
Hex Color Value	**Common Color Name**
00 00 00	Black
FF FF FF	White
FF 00 00	Red
00 FF 00	Green
00 00 FF	Blue

You should experiment with different colors and see how they look on your system. If you're working with basic colors, however, you can use their names, thankfully. A list of some of the most common are shown in Table 9-2.

Table 9-2:	Colors Available by Name		
AQUA	BLACK	BLUE	FUCHSIA
GRAY	GREEN	LIME	MAROON
NAVY	OLIVE	PURPLE	RED
SILVER	TEAL	WHITE	YELLOW

One word of warning: if you specify a color that can't be displayed on your system, Navigator or Explorer will try to produce a similar color by 'dithering' or creating a textured background with elements of each of the two closest colors. Sounds nice, but it isn't; you end up with a pebbly background that can make your text completely unreadable. Also remember that some users who view your Web page might have a 16-color or even black-and-white display; the results can be unpredictable on those systems. I may sound like a curmudgeon, but I really recommend that you think twice before using a weird color scheme. Either use the default background color, specify 'white' as the background, or use a very subtle background graphic.

Let's have a look at a page that specifies a yellow background with BGCOLOR=yellow:

```
<HTML>
<BODY BGCOLOR=yellow>
One of the nice things about background colors is that you
can produce interesting and unusual effects with
relatively little work.
```

```
(continued)
<P>
Want to have something look exactly like a piece of paper?
 Use &lt;BGCOLOR=#FFFFFF&gt; or its equivalent,&lt;
BGCOLOR=white&gt;
<P>
Is green your favorite color? Try either
&lt;BGCOLOR=green&gt; or &lt;BGCOLOR=#00FF00&gt;
</HTML>
```

Viewing this in Netscape Navigator, as shown in Figure 9-6, affirms that the result indeed is a bright and cheery yellow background, as we'd hoped.

Here you can see another HTML trick; to have < or > show up on a Web page you have to do something special — specify the character as either the lt or gt (less than or greater than) symbol, wrapped in an ampersand and semicolon. Hence '<' and '>'. I talked about these funky special characters in Chapter 5.

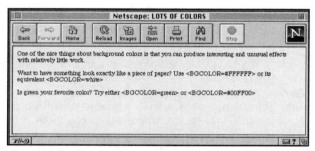

Figure 9-6: Changing to a colored background.

Graphics are similarly easy to work with, albeit a bit more dangerous, since even the most simple graphic can almost instantly obscure the text that you might have on a particular page. The following is a simple example using a graphic that you've already seen from the tic-tac-toe board, but this time as the repeating background graphic:

```
<HTML>
<BODY BACKGROUND="box.gif">
<FONT SIZE=6>
<B>One of the nice things about background colors is that
you can produce interesting and unusual effects with
```

```
relatively little work. Background graphics, however, are
much more dangerous. How easy is this to read against the
box grid background? You'll see even more wild examples as
you surf around on the Web, believe me!
</B></FONT></HTML>
```

If you look at this HTML snippet closely, you'll see that I have not only made all the text larger with the `<FONT SIZE=6>` command, but I've also enclosed the entire passage within a bold formatting tag. Nonetheless, a glance at Figure 9-7 shows that it's still difficult to read.

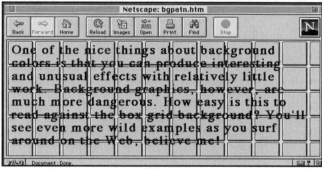

Figure 9-7: Background graphics can make pages unreadable.

The moral of this story: By all means use these fun options, just be sensitive to the potential problems and nuances you might force onto your viewers because of their own hardware or preferences.

Organizing Information in Tables

Tables are one addition to HTML that Netscape has foisted upon the Web. As a result, everyone else has added them to their browsers. Unlike the tables in your favorite word processor, however, these kinds of tables can be quite compelling, and you might find yourself naturally boxing up groups of like icons, taking a list of bullet items and making a table out of them, or who knows what! I often box the title of a Web page in a one-element table because I think it looks pretty spiffy.

Creating tables

There's a downside to tables, however. Tables are darn hard to build. You have to specify the parameters for the table, then the parameters for each row, then each cell element must be surrounded by `<TD></TD>` — table data — tags. Here's the most simple example of a table:

```
<B>Cities With Direct Access to Netcom Communications</B>
<TABLE BORDER=1>
<TR>
<TD>Austin, TX</TD>
<TD>Atlanta, GA </TD>
<TD>Chicago, IL</TD>
</TR>
</TABLE>
```

This formats with all data on the same line (that is, in the same row, denoted by `<TR> and </TR>`), as shown in Figure 9-8.

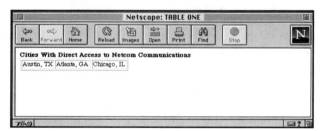

Figure 9-8: The simplest table possible.

If you want to have all the same information, but one item per row (for example, line), it instantly gets more complex by leaps and bounds:

```
<B>Cities With Direct Access to Netcom Communications</B>
<TABLE BORDER>
<TR>
<TD>Austin, TX</TD>
</TR><TR>
<TD>Atlanta, GA </TD>
</TR><TR>
<TD>Chicago, IL</TD>
</TR>
</TABLE>
```

You can see the difference in format by viewing Figure 9-9.

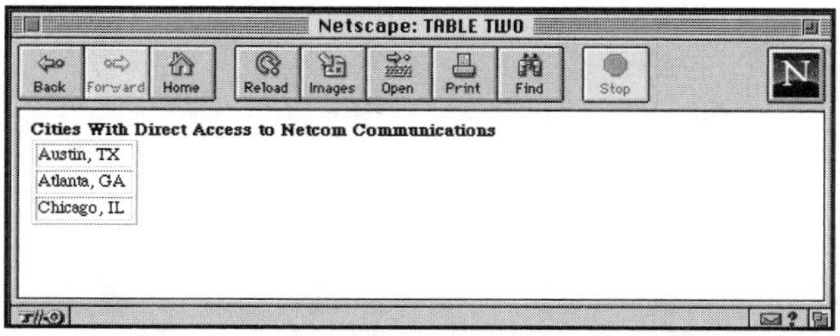

Figure 9-9: Simple table, each element on its own line.

Needless to say, this stuff can get quite complex, since you can include graphics, text, and just about anything else (including other tables!) within any element of a table. Each row can have a specific alignment specified with ALIGN= as part of the tag, and the <TABLE> tag itself has a plethora of options, including:

TABLE Tag	Meaning Therein
BORDER=n	Width of rules between cells in table
CELLSPACING=n	Spacing between individual cells
CELLPADDING=n	Space between border and contents of cell
WIDTH=n	Desired width, overrides automatic width calculations (value or percentage)

Within a table, not only can you specify the rows with <TR> and individual data elements with <TD>, but you can also specify the heading of columns with <TH> (identical to <TR>, with individual cells specified using <TD>, but defaults to bold formatting) and a caption with <CAPTION>, as in the following HTML snippet:

```
<TABLE BORDER=5 WIDTH=50%>
<CAPTION ALIGN=bottom><B>Great Shows on A&E</B></CAPTION>
<TH>Show</TH><TH>Day On A&E</TH>
<TR ALIGN=CENTER>
<TD>Sherlock Holmes</TD><TD>Monday</TD>
</TR><TR ALIGN=CENTER>
<TD>Lovejoy</TD><TD>Monday</TD>
</TR>
</TABLE>
```

Look on the CD-ROM and you can see how this formats in Navigator or Explorer.

I'll end this chapter with a complex example of a table from a page I recently designed for my own consulting business. Notice here that I'm trying to use some indenting to help illustrate the formatting in the source code, and that the top table is a one-element-only table, so I can get a raised border around the graphic. You have the following on CD-ROM, too:

```
<HTML>
<CENTER>
<TABLE BORDER=7 CELLPADDING=5 CELLSPACING=5>
  <TR ALIGN=center>
    <TD><IMG SRC="intsys.gif" ALT="Intuitive
    Systems"></TD>
  </TR>
</TABLE>
<FONT SIZE=5>— Check these pages out! —</FONT>
<TABLE BORDER=4 CELLPADDING=10 CELLSPACING=0>
  <TR ALIGN=center>
    <TD><A HREF="http://www.cybout.com/"><IMG
     SRC="cybout.gif" ALT="cybout.gif"></A></TD>
    <TD><A HREF="http://www.espan.com/"><IMG
    SRC="espan.gif" ALT="espan.gif"></A></TD>
   <TD><A HREF="http://www.thuridion.com/"><IMG
     SRC="tridion.gif" ALT="thuridion.gif"></A></TD>
  </TR>
  <TR ALIGN=center>
   <TD><A HREF="http://www.cybout.com/">Cyberian
Outpost</A></TD>
    <TD><A HREF="http://www.espan.com/">E*SPAN</A></TD>
    <TD><A
HREF="http://www.thuridion.com/">Thuridion</A></TD>
   </TR>
</TABLE>
</CENTER>
<HR>
Or see the real thing by visiting <A
HREF="http://www.intuitive.com/">Intuitive
Systems</A> on the Web.
</BODY>
</HTML>
```

The resulting formatting is quite funky and fun, as shown in Figure 9-10.

Figure 9-10: Way cool table formatting.

Humor me, just this once. Make sure when you view this page on your own system you also look at it with Internet Explorer or an older Web browser to see how it might format differently.

Advanced Table Formatting

There is one important additional table formatting capability that you can use to fine-tune tables to your specific needs; being able to specify background colors or patterns (images) to individual cells.

Colors within a specific data cell show up within the `<TD>` tag in a way that won't surprise you:

```
<TD BGCOLOR=yellow>text on yellow background</TD>
```

This would have the single cell yellow with default black text atop. Let's have a look:

```
<TABLE BORDER=4>
<TR><TD BGCOLOR=yellow>Yellow</TD><TD>Default</TD></TR>
<TR><TD BGCOLOR=teal><font color=white>against
a box</font></TD><TD>Default 2</TD></TR>
</TABLE>
```

The result of this formatting is quite attractive, as shown in Figure 9-11.

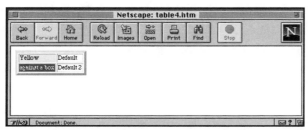

Figure 9-11: Colored table cells and fine-tuned edges.

This isn't complex enough to challenge you? You'll be delighted to know that there are lots more table-related tags added in Internet Explorer 3.0, which I'll demonstrate in the Chapter 10.

Pages within Pages: Frames

Okay, I think you're ready. Take a deep breath. It's time for us to explore something that makes tables look easy: frames. Frames were first introduced by Netscape and lots of people didn't like them. Enough sites, however, started to use the tag set, splitting a single Web page into separate *panes,* each of which is a separate Web page, that they gradually became popular on a lot of sites. Then Internet Explorer added frames capability and it all started to spiral out of control.

Meanwhile, many sites that had introduced frames versions of their home pages introduced 'no frame version' buttons for people who didn't like them, and today the original frame site, the Netscape home page, defaults to a no frame version and offers a 'frames version' button hidden on the very bottom of the page. You can draw your own conclusion as to what this means, but if you want to be an HTML expert, you'll definitely need to know how to work with frames.

The basics of frames

Unlike many of the other tags you've seen so far, frames are an all-or-nothing proposition: the page that's shown in a browser either has the frames specified in the <FRAMESET> section of the source document, or the information contained in the <NOFRAMES> default set of HTML tags and information. Here's a template:

```
<HTML>
<FRAMESET rows="75, *">
<NOFRAMES>
   <BODY BGCOLOR=white>
    <CENTER><FONT SIZE=6>You Need Frames To
Visit!</FONT></CENTER>
   </BODY>
</NOFRAMES>
   <FRAME SRC="FRAMES/TOP.HTM">
   <FRAME SRC="FRAMES/BOTTOM.HTM">
</FRAMESET>
</HTML>
```

Figure 9-12 shows what happens in a browser that understands frames:
you have the single page split into two rows, the first 75 pixels high, the
second consuming the remaining space.

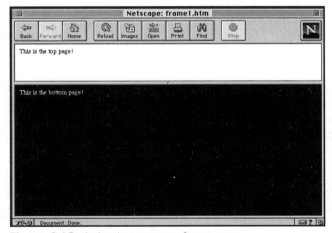

Figure 9-12: A simple two-pane frame page.

What you can't see here is that there are *three* Web pages involved in getting
this to format correctly: the basic page shown above, and two additional
pages top.htm and bottom.htm. The former contains the following:

```
<BODY BGCOLOR=white>
This is the top page!
</BODY>
```

and the file bottom.htm looks like the following:

```
<BODY BGCOLOR=black TEXT=white>
This is the bottom page!
</BODY>
```

That's the basic trick of frame documents. Instead of a single page defining all the information displayed to the visitor, the information is split into multiple pages, each given its own small piece of the data.

Specifying frame panes and sizes

Now that you're an expert with tables, it will come as no surprise to you that there are lots of options for frames, too, some of which are vitally important to understand.

The first important tag to understand is <FRAMESET>. In addition to being capable of specifying ROWS to split the Web page into horizontal panes, you can use COLS to specify vertical panes. There are three different values you can use as the value of these two attributes. A simple number specifies size in pixels, either a width or height depending on attribute. You've already seen the asterisk as a way to specify 'the rest of the space remaining,' and you can also specify a percentage of width with the *n*% notation. So here's a test for you, if you think you got all that. What's <FRAMESET COLS=30%,19,*> mean? (See the CD-ROM for an example.)

You can create complex multipane Web pages, where each pane has its autonomous behavior, by combining them in creative ways:

```
<HTML>
<FRAMESET cols="80%,*">
   <FRAMESET ROWS="30%,70%">
      <FRAME SRC="FRAMES/TOP.HTM">
      <FRAME SRC="FRAMES/BOTTOM.HTM">
   </FRAMESET>
   <FRAMESET ROWS="33%,33%,*">
      <FRAME SRC=boxx.GIF>
      <FRAME SRC=boxo.GIF>
      <FRAME SRC=boxx.GIF>
   </FRAMESET>
</FRAMESET>
</HTML>
```

In this case, what I've done is specify that there are two columns of information, one 80 percent of the width of the screen, the latter the remaining width. The first column of information is the second frameset, two rows, the first (top.htm) 30 percent of the available height, and the second (bottom.htm) the remaining 70 percent. The second skinny column of information contains three graphics evenly spaced, each 25 percent of the vertical space. The results are shown in Figure 9-13.

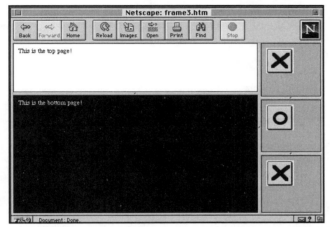

Figure 9-13: Lots of pain, err, panes, specified within a FRAMESET.

That's the gist of frames, but there's one more aspect to master before you start going wild. . . .

Frame behavior and attributes

There are a couple of different attributes that you can specify for frames, the most important of which is the NAME= attribute. Each specific frame can be given a unique name (similar to <A NAME=>) that can then be used as a way to control which window is affected by specific actions. What's the point of this? Imagine you have a table of contents of your site in a small pane that's always present, and any user clicks actually change the information shown in the *main* pane, not the small table of contents pane. That's the idea of this, and there's a partner attribute that appears in the anchor tag for any hypertext reference (A HREF). Here's an example of this at work. First, a simple frames page:

```
<HTML>
<FRAMESET cols="20%,*">
   <FRAME SRC="FRAMES/TOC.HTM">
   <FRAME SRC="FRAMES/Default.HTM" NAME=main>
</FRAMESET>
</HTML>
```

Next, the contents of the default.htm page:

```
<BODY BGCOLOR=white>
<B>It's the Animal Home Page!</B>
</BODY>
```

Finally, the all-important toc.htm page with the HREF extensions:

```
<BODY BGCOLOR=yellow>
<B>Pick An Animal</B>
<P>
<A HREF=dog.htm target=main>DOG</A>
<P>
<A HREF=cat.htm target=main>CAT</A>
<P>
<A HREF=bird.htm target=main>BIRD</A>
<P>
<A HREF=default.htm>[bad link]</A>
</BODY>
```

Figure 9-14 shows how it all looks. You'll definitely want to try this all out on the example CD-ROM to see what's going on and how it all works. In particular, notice what happens when you click on the '[bad link]' button (the one that doesn't have a target attribute) and what happens when you use the 'BACK' button on your browser.

The <FRAME> tag itself also has two attributes worth highlighting here before I let you escape this chapter. The first enables you to specify the width of a frame border: FRAMEBORDER (makes sense, eh?) with an attribute in pixels, and the second enables you to force a scroll bar or force no scroll bar, even if the pane is too small for the information therein. The following is a small sample of these attributes:

```
<HTML>
<FRAMESET cols="20%,*">
   <FRAME SRC="FRAMES/TOC.HTM" frameborder=5 scrolling=yes>
   <FRAME SRC="FRAMES/Default.HTM" NAME=main>
</FRAMESET>
</HTML>
```

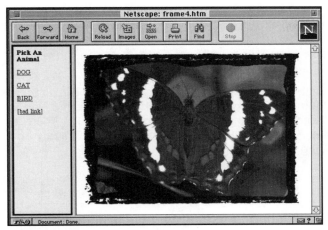

Figure 9-14: Navigational Pane works!

Compare the results, shown in Figure 9-15, with the earlier example above.

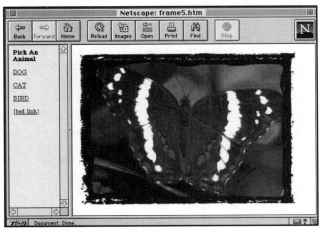

Figure 9-15: Navigational Panes with an added scroll bar.

If you're interested in learning more about the nuances of frames, there are two terrific spots on the Web to explore. For Microsoft Internet Explorer, there's lots of information at:

```
http://www.microsoft.com/workshop/author/newhtml/
```

and if you're interested in the Netscape Navigator tutorial on frames, you can find it at:

```
http://home.netscape.com/assist/net_sites/frames.html
```

Creating a multipane frames site isn't too difficult. What's tricky is to do a really good job of it, and produce a site that makes sense and actually helps people find what they want and explore your site. There are some really good examples online, fortunately, that you can study and learn from, including the following:

Winter Action	`http://www.boston.com/sports /wintact/winguide/winpoframe.htm`
clnet Central	`http://www.cnet.com/`
ACM97	`http://www.acm.org/acm97`
Carly Simon Online	`http://www.ziva.com/carly`

Whatever you do with frames, don't be intimidated by the complexity. Once you get started working with a frames-based design, you'll find it's pretty straightforward.

Table 9.3:   **Tags Used in this Chapter**

Tag	Close tag	Meaning
`<BODY BACKGROUND=`*url*`>`	`</BODY>`	Specify the background graphic for the page
`<BODY BGCOLOR=`*color*`>`	`</BODY>`	Specify the background color for the page (RGB hex value or color name, for current browsers only)
`<CENTER>`	`</CENTER>`	Center text and graphics horizontally
`<HR SIZE=`*n*`>`		Specify height of horizontal rule (in pixels)
`<HR WIDTH=`*n*`>`		Horizontal rule of specified width, pixels or percentage of window width
`<HR NOSHADE>`		Solid black horizontal rule

Tags used...

Tag	Close tag	Meaning
`<OL TYPE=n>`	`</OL>`	Ordered list, use numbering scheme based on type (a=lowercase alpha, A=uppercase alpha, I=uppercase roman, i=lowercase roman, 1=numbers)
`<OL START=n>`	`</OL>`	Ordered list, start numbering at 'n'
`<UL TYPE=n>`	`</UL>`	Unordered list, use specified shape as bullet (disc, square, circle)

Frames:

Tag	Close tag	Meaning
`<FRAMESET>`	`</FRAMESET>`	Split a page into separate panes, each with its own Web page therein
`<FRAMESET ROWS=a,b,c>`		Specify rows within a frameset, values are pixels, percentage, or '*' which denotes the remaining space
`<FRAMESET COLS=a,b,c>`		Specify columns within a frameset, values are pixels, percentage, or '*' which denotes the remaining space
`<FRAME SRC=url>`		URL of page within specified pane of frames-based layout
`NAME=name`		Mnemonic name of pane (used with the `TARGET` attribute of the `A HREF` tag)
`BORDER=n`		Size of border around pane (pixels)
`SCROLLING=n`		Add scroll bar? (values: yes,no)

Frames (continued)

Tag	Close tag	Meaning
`<NOFRAMES>`	`</NOFRAMES>`	HTML section displayed by browsers that don't understand frames

Tables:

Tag	Close tag	Meaning
`<TABLE>`	`</TABLE>`	Creates a table
`BORDER=`*n*		Size of overall table border, in pixels. Use within `<TABLE>` tag
`CELLPADDING=`*n*		Spacing between cells, in pixels. Use within `<TABLE>` tag
`CELLSPACING=`*n*		Spacing around data within each cell, in pixels. Use within `<TABLE>` tag
`WIDTH=`*n*		Width of table, pixels or percentage. Use within `<TABLE>` tag
`<TR ALIGN=n>`		Specify alignment of data cells in row (left, center, right)
`<TD ALIGN=n>`		Specify alignment of specific data cell (left, center, right)
`VALIGN=`*n*		Vertical alignment of data cell (top, middle, bottom). Use within `<TD>` or `<TR>` tag
`BGCOLOR=`*n*		Background color, RGB or color name. Use within `<TD>`, `<TR>`, or `<TABLE>` tag
`<CAPTION>`	`</CAPTION>`	Specify table caption
`ALIGN=`*n*		Alignment of caption (top, bottom). Use within `<CAPTION>` tag

Moving On

In this chapter, I gave you a whirlwind tour of the many fascinating, helpful, and occasionally confusing extensions to HTML added by the team at Netscape and now available on the latest browsers from both Netscape and Microsoft. There are some tricky formatting tag sets herein, so make sure you've had a chance to digest these before you proceed. Chapter 10 introduces some of the additional formatting tags that are supported by either Internet Explorer 3.0 or Navigator 3.0.

New Extensions in Navigator 3 and Explorer 3

In This Chapter

Microsoft's Internet Explorer 3.0, shipped with Windows 95 and released for the Macintosh late in 1996, adds a couple of very cool extensions to HTML, and also includes support for a variety of tags that previously were only understood by Netscape's Navigator.

Additional table capabilities

Embedded audio

Scrolling text in marquees

Borderless and floating frames

Watermark backgrounds

These are very cool extensions and hold the potential to make your Web pages really state of the art (and *art* is an important facet of Web page design, in case that hasn't become obvious as you've traveled through the chapters in this book).

The original vision of Web browsers was that they'd all support the same language and differ in support for the specific operating system, such as how they managed your list of favorite sites, and other incidentals. Netscape Navigator changed all that when the company released a browser late in 1994 that had its own set of extensions to the HTML language. Since then it has been somewhat of a free-for-all with each Web browser trying to outdo all the others with a few unique and interesting extensions.

It came as no surprise, therefore, when Microsoft's Internet Explorer showed up on the scene with a few unique HTML tags that only it understood. While there is a remarkable amount of overlap between the two primary browsers, there are still some areas where they differ on how to accomplish certain things, and that's what I'll be focusing on in this chapter.

Unfortunately, if you're a Mac-centric person, you'll be unhappy to learn that both Netscape and Microsoft have started to release their latest and greatest browsers for the Windows platform, then add all the functionality and capabilities for the Mac users a few months later. As I write this book, Microsoft Internet Explorer 3.0 isn't even available as an early beta for the Macintosh, but it's in final release for Windows 95. As a result, some of these screen shots are a preview of what you'll see down the road when Microsoft releases 3.0 for the Mac early in 1997.

Additional Table Capabilities (Internet Explorer Only)

In Chapter 9, you learned quite a bit about tables, but there are actually more attributes to the table tags that can help you fine-tune your presentation of information — tags that can really help you produce exactly the output you seek. You'll recall that a table is defined with the <TABLE> tag, and that each row is defined with <TR>, and each data cell therein surrounded by <TD> and </TD>.

Both Explorer and Navigator support background colors for specific cells within a table using BGCOLOR, but Internet Explorer adds to it, with the BACKGROUND attribute, allowing patterned backgrounds in table cells. Fine level control over the border color is available too, with the BORDERCOLOR attribute or, if that's not exact enough, the capability to set the two colors used in the border with BORDERCOLORLIGHT and BORDERCOLORDARK. They're all demonstrated in the following example:

```
<TABLE BORDERCOLOR=yellow BORDER=5>
  <TR>
    <TD BACKGROUND=boxx.gif><font color=teal>X Y Z<br>1 2
3</font></TD>
  </TR>
</TABLE>
<HR SIZE=9 COLOR=green>
<TABLE BORDERCOLORLIGHT=yellow BORDERCOLORDARK=red
BORDER=4>
  <TR>
    <TD><font size=+3>Some Enchanted Evenings?</font></TD>
  </TR>
</TABLE>
```

This example looks okay here in the book, as you can see in Figure 10-1, but to really see this rainbow of colors at its best, you'll want to view the file on your own computer!

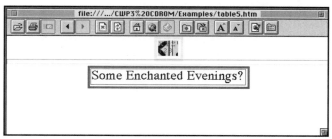

Figure 10-1: Color Options in Tables with Internet Explorer.

One thing you can see with these tables is that they tend to take up the least amount of horizontal and vertical space possible when being presented on the screen. This might not be exactly what you seek, so Internet Explorer also supports a `WIDTH` attribute to the `<TABLE>` tag, which can either specify a percentage of the screen width for the table or a specific number of pixels for the table width:

```
<TABLE BORDERCOLORLIGHT=yellow BORDERCOLORDARK=red
BORDER=4>
<TR>
<TD>
<font size=+3>Some Enchanted Evenings?</font>
</TD>
</TR>
<CAPTION>without the WIDTH attribute</CAPTION>
</TABLE>
<hr>
<TABLE BORDERCOLORLIGHT=yellow BORDERCOLORDARK=red BORDER=4
WIDTH=75%>
<TR>
<TD>
<font size=+3>Some Enchanted Evenings?</font>
</TD>
</TR>
<CAPTION>with the WIDTH attribute</CAPTION>
</TABLE>
```

Being able to force more width in the table and cells highlights the need for the `ALIGN=center` tag within the specific `<TD>` data cell specification too, as is clear in Figure 10-2.

Figure 10-2: Width specification expands tables dramatically.

There are two more tags of interest for table users within Internet Explorer, and both of them offer even finer granularity of control over the borders around the table and between the individual data cells. They're <FRAME> and <RULES>, and the values are defined as shown in Tables 10-1 and 10-2.

Table 10-1: Values of <TABLE FRAME= *attribute*>

Attribute	Meaning
VOID	Removes all outside table borders
ABOVE	Displays a border on the top side of the table frame
BELOW	Displays a border on the bottom side of the table frame
HSIDES	Displays a border on the top and bottom sides of the table frame
LHS	Displays a border on the left-hand side of the table frame
RHS	Displays a border on the right-hand side of the table frame
VSIDES	Displays a border on the left and right sides of the table frame
BOX	Displays a border on all sides of the table frame
BORDER	Displays a border on all sides of the table frame

Table 10-2

Values of `<TABLE RULES= attribute>`	
NONE	Removes all interior table borders
GROUPS	Displays horizontal borders between all table groups. Groups are specified by the `THEAD`, `TBODY`, `TFOOT`, and `COLGROUP` elements
ROWS	Displays horizontal borders between all table rows
COLS	Displays vertical borders between all table columns
ALL	Displays a border on all rows and columns

The `<FRAME>` and `<RULE>` tags combine to produce a remarkable amount of control over the borders and edges in a Web table, but they're pretty complex, too. I'll offer you the following example and encourage you to tweak the source for this example to try different combinations to see how they work:

```
<TABLE BORDER=1 FRAME=none RULES=ROWS WIDTH=60%>
<TR ALIGN=center      BGCOLOR=#DDDDFF>
<TD>January</TD>
<TD>$25,404,384.08</TD>
</TR>
<TR ALIGN=center>
<TD>February</TD>
<TD>$28,498,294.38</TD>
</TR>
<TR ALIGN=center    BGCOLOR=#DDDDFF>
<TD>March</TD>
<TD>$31,978,193.55</TD>
</TR>
<TR ALIGN=center>
<TD>April</TD>
<TD>$18,559,205.00</TD>
</TR>
</TABLE>
```

Read through that code example closely (and remember that all the important work is being done in the `<TABLE>` tag itself) and compare it to Figure 10-3 to see if this makes sense to you. Notice that the basic table is specified with a one-pixel border (`BORDER=1`), no frame (`FRAME=none`), a width that's 60 percent of the window width (`WIDTH=60%`), and horizontal rules added between rows (`RULES=ROWS`).

NOTE Remember that colors specified by hexadecimal value are in RGB — red + green + blue — order, so DDDDFF is all blue (FF) and almost all red and green (DD), a very light blue. (Of course if I specified 0000FF I'd get a pure blue, but it'd be very difficult to read black text on top. Adding some red and green lighten the color on the display.)

file:///.../CWP3%20CDROM/Examples/table7.htm	
January	$25,404,384.08
February	$28,498,294.38
March	$31,978,193.55
April	$18,559,205.00

Figure 10-3: Fine details in table design.

Embedded Audio

Everything you've learned so far is multimedia, but only unisensory. It's all visual, all layout. Computers don't have sound and the tactile feedback of a screen is pretty darn limited so far, but there is a sense that can be engaged by slick Web pages: hearing. Internet Explorer and Navigator both support not just audio links, as shown earlier in the book, but actual background or "theme" music added to your page. Unfortunately, they use different mechanisms for doing so, but you can specify both in your documents and you'll have all your bases covered. Here's a rundown on the two approaches. . . .

Internet Explorer background audio

Explorer uses an HTML tag `<BGSOUND>` that has two possible parameters: `<SRC>` enables you to specify the actual audio file, and `<LOOP>` enables you to perhaps play the audio track once or loop it for hours on end, eliciting cries of frustration and protest from otherwise calm and relaxed users.

There are three possible audio formats with this tag: .WAV or .AU audio samples, or a MIDI file, typically with the suffix .MID.

The following example:

```
<BGSOUND SRC=storm.wav LOOP=5>
```

would play the sound of a storm rumbling overhead — once loaded from the server — five times and go silent. This example is on the CD-ROM so you can try it for yourself, if you'd like!

Navigator background audio

Navigator uses the `<EMBED>` tag to accomplish the same task. It's a bit more awkward, because by default Navigator wants to pop up a small control panel for the audio player, shown at the corresponding spot on your page where the tag is present in your HTML (that is, if you imagined that instead of the `<EMBED>` tag you had an `<IMG>` tag, that's where the control panel would be included).

```
<EMBED SRC="storm.wav" width=145 height=60>
```

Seeing the width and height variables, you might think that you can set them to zero, add `AUTOSTART=true`, and have the sample play when the user visits the page without any visual display associated with the player. You can do that, and it works pretty well if you don't want the user to have any control (at which point it's acting exactly like the `<BGSOUND>` tag for Internet Explorer). Otherwise, you can specify the size of the space for the control panel by using the height and width variables. 145×60 happens to be the ideal size for the control panel in my version of Navigator, but you should experiment with different sizes.

There are a couple of other tags of interest: `<CONTROLS>` can be set to `console` or `smallconsole` to change the appearance of the player, `<VOLUME>` can be set from 1-255, with `VOLUME=255` being incredibly loud. There's also a `LOOP` attribute, with its value `true` or `false`, but in practice I couldn't get this to work. Your experience may vary, so do try it out if that's what you seek. Figure 10-4 shows the audio controls whereon I can click on play to have the audio played instantly.

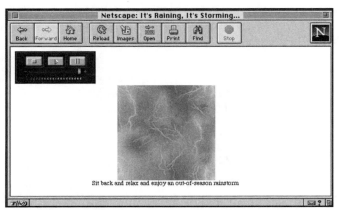

Figure 10-4: Audio control device within Navigator.

Scrolling Text in Marquees (Internet Explorer Only)

Here's a fun tag that I think adds some appreciated pizzazz to a Web page, and with remarkably little work. The `<MARQUEE>` tag defines text that is displayed to the user in an animated region within a Web page. With a little tweak, you can take what's currently a phrase or two of text that's sitting passively on your page and transform it into a cheery animated area.

This particular tag, however, is one that I won't be able to demonstrate here in the book because we don't yet have animated book pages! Therefore, as you read this, please try the examples included on the CD-ROM.

The most basic use of the `<MARQUEE>` tag is:

```
<MARQUEE>text to animate</MARQUEE>
```

Because we already know that unknown HTML tags are just ignored by browsers that don't understand them, the text to animate will be displayed passively within Navigator or any other non–Explorer browser.

The `<MARQUEE>` tag has many possible attributes — the key one being `BEHAVIOR`, which can be `scroll`, `slide`, or `alternate` — that cause text to appear one letter at a time, scroll all the way across, and vanish, then start again (the default), cause text to slide onto the screen and stop once the text touches the other margin, or bounce back and forth within the marquee, respectively. You can specify the direction from which text scrolls with DIRECTION and a value of either left or right.

The size of a <MARQUEE> space is defined by the WIDTH and HEIGHT of the box, in either pixels or a percentage of screen size. Just like a graphics image, you can also specify the space around the marquee box with HSPACE and VSPACE too. Those two are in pixels, so HSPACE=30 would give you a spare 30-pixel wide space on the left and right side of the marquee area.

The following is a relatively simple example:

```
<MARQUEE WIDTH=75%>Welcome to DeliveryTrac Online</MARQUEE>
```

This is included on CD-ROM: go try it and see what you think. If you're in Internet Explorer you'll see the text scroll from the right onto the screen, slide to the left, and vanish, just to appear on the right again. Think of it as a tiny Times Square marquee hidden in your computer! BGCOLOR enables you to specify the color of the marquee region. You can't have the background match a background image or pattern, alas, nor can you in any way modify the size or color of the text in the marquee. A refinement of the above, therefore, is:

```
<MARQUEE WIDTH=75% BGCOLOR=yellow>Welcome to DeliveryTrac
Online</MARQUEE>
```

Two more useful attributes for fine-tuning your results: SCROLLAMOUNT enables you to specify the exact number of pixels between each successive draw of the marquee text (which is most important when you have a small text region and lots of text), and SCROLLDELAY specifies the number of milliseconds, thousandths of a second, between each redraw of the marquee text.

The following is an example that combines a number of different possibilities:

```
<MARQUEE WIDTH=40% BGCOLOR=yellow BEHAVIOR=slide
    SCROLLDELAY=350>Slowly I creep onto your
screen...</MARQUEE><hr>
<MARQUEE BGCOLOR=#DDDDFF BEHAVIOR=alternate HEIGHT=10%>A
strange light blue box size within which to exist</MARQUEE>
```

Figure 10-5 shows the marquees at work a few seconds after loading the page in Internet Explorer, and Figure 10-6 shows the very same page within Netscape Navigator, which doesn't understand the <MARQUEE> tag.

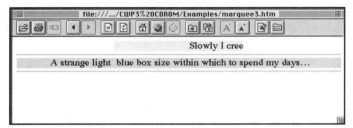

Figure 10-5: Marquees in Internet Explorer.

Figure 10-6: <Marquee> tag ignored in Netscape Navigator.

I'm quite a fan of the marquee tag when used judiciously. In particular, sliding text onto the screen from various directions offers a fun technique for assembling information in front of your visitors' eyes.

Borderless and Floating Frames

Internet Explorer played catch-up and added frame capabilities to its browser, as you found out in the discussion in Chapter 9. What's nice about its implementation of frames is that it added a new attribute to the FRAMESET statement that offers a useful additional capability: borderless frames. Meanwhile, the Netscape gang in Mountain View saw the borderless frames and said "hey, that's a neat idea," so the latest version of both browsers support borderless frames using exactly the same additional attributes.

Borderless frames

Frame borders are turned on or off with the FRAMEBORDER attribute. The default value is '1', which gives you a slight edge to each frame panel, while a value of '0' hides any border. You can also specify the spacing between frames by using the FRAMESPACING command. Use pixels as the value.

Here's the final version of my animals home page with a bit of added complexity — a new title — only the page called animals.htm has the same background color as the table of contents on the left side:

```
<HTML>
<FRAMESET rows="15%,*" frameborder=0 framespacing=0>
  <FRAME SRC="FRAMES/animals.htm">
  <FRAMESET cols="20%,*" frameborder=0 framespacing=0>
    <FRAME SRC="FRAMES/TOC.HTM">
    <FRAME SRC="FRAMES/Default.HTM" NAME=main>
  </FRAMESET>
</FRAMESET>
</HTML>
```

Figure 10-7 shows the terrific results! You should also try this on your own computer to see what's happening here.

Figure 10-7: Slick animal home page without frame borders.

While Netscape claims its version 3.0 browser supports borderless frames, your mileage may vary; I've found it sometimes works and sometimes doesn't.

Floating frames (Internet Explorer only)

At this point you probably can't imagine that there are any more types of frames or windows that you could possibly have in a Web document. Would it surprise you to find out that there's a whole other way to have a Web page appear with scroll bars, buried within another page?

The formatting tag in question is `<IFRAME>`, and it's a strange tag because all the relevant information is contained within the attributes of the main tag, but there must be a closing tag, even though there's never anything in the middle. The simplest attribute is `SRC=url`, but you can specify `ALIGN` to change the alignment of information surrounding the floating frame and give a `FRAMEBORDER` of '1' for a border or '0' for no border. You can also give the floating frame a `NAME` so that href target commands can be sent to it, and turn on and off scrolling within the frame border with `SCROLLING` assigned the value 'yes' or 'no.' For example:

```
<IFRAME FRAMEBORDER=0 SCROLLING=yes NAME="jo"
SRC="frames/default.htm">
</IFRAME>
```

A Web page with the floating frame specified above is shown in Figure 10-8.

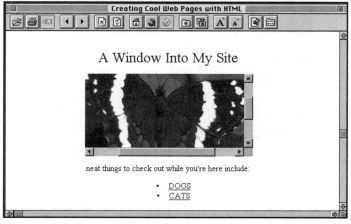

Figure 10-8: Floating frames in Explorer.

In case that isn't enough in terms of complexity, there are a couple of other options that give you further control over your floating frame: MARGINHEIGHT and MARGINWIDTH enable you to specify the exact size of the floating frame in your document (in pixels, of course), and NORESIZE enables you to freeze the size of the frame so that the user can't resize it. You might use <IFRAME NORESIZE MARGINHEIGHT=30 MARGINWIDTH=20 SRC=miniview.html> to get a small 20 × 30 floating frame containing the source to the HTML document miniview.html.

Watermark Backgrounds (Internet Explorer Only)

A few chapters ago you learned how to add the BACKGROUND attribute to a Web page so you could specify a background graphic of some sort. Internet Explorer offers an interesting, if subtle, modification to this with the attribute BGPROPERTIES with its one possible value of fixed (that is, BGPROPERTIES=fixed). If you'd like to have your material appear slightly offset from the left edge of the page, you can use LEFTMARGIN=n to specify the width of your indent (in pixels). TOPMARGIN does the same thing for the very top of a page, too.

The following is an example of all of these:

```
<HTML>
<HEAD>
<TITLE>Sample of Watermark Backgrounds</TITLE>
</HEAD>
<BODY BACKGROUND=logo.gif BGPROPERTIES=fixed LEFTMARGIN=20
TOPMARGIN=5>
Lots of text and other material would go here, of course.
</BODY>
</HTML>
```

The results are shown in Figure 10-9. Notice in particular the location of the text on the page!

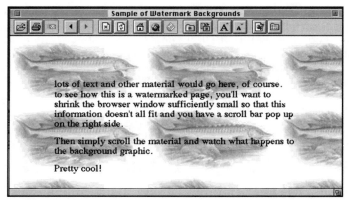

Figure 10-9: Custom body attributes in Explorer.

A Final Fun Snippet!

The following are some nifty URLs to enter into Netscape Navigator in the Open Location box to get access to internal information in the browser:

about:cache	Lists all files in disk cache
about:memory-cache	Lists all files in memory cache
about:image-cache	Lists all image files in cache
about:global	List all the places you have visited and when

There are probably similar secret URLs for Internet Explorer, but, alas, I don't know them. If you do, send me e-mail and I'll add it to the next edition!

Table 10-3:	**Tags Used in this Chapter**
Tag	**Meaning**
TABLE	Additional table attributes
BORDERCOLORLIGHT	Specify lighter of two table border colors (RGB)
BORDERCOLORDARK	Specify darker of two table border colors (RGB)
WIDTH	Width of overall table (pixels or percentage)

Table 10-3:	HTML Tags...
Tag	**Meaning**
FRAME	Where table borders should be displayed (values include ABOVE, BELOW, LHS, RHS, and BOX, see Table 10-1 for explanation)
RULES	Location of rules (lines) within tables (values are NONE, GROUPS, ROWS, COLS, or ALL)
BGSOUND	Background sound, Explorer only
SRC	URL of file containing audio information
LOOP	Iterations of audio to play
EMBED	Background sound, Navigator
SRC	URL of file containing audio information
CONTROLS	Type of controls to display (console or small console)
VOLUME	How loud to play audio (1..255, 255 is loudest)
LOOP	How many times to play audio snippet (1..infinite)
MARQUEE	Scrolling text area, Explorer only
WIDTH	Width of marquee space (pixels or percentage)
HEIGHT	Height of marquee space (pixels or percentage)
HSPACE	Additional horizontal space around marquee (pixels)
VSPACE	Additional vertical space around marquee (pixels)
SCROLLAMOUNT	Increment between each frame of marquee (pixels)
SCROLLDELAY	Milliseconds between each redraw
BEHAVIOR	How marquee will act (values are scroll, slide, or alternate)
FRAMESET	Begins a frame document

Table 10-3:	Html Tags...
Tag	**Meaning**
FRAMEBORDER	Size of border between frames (pixels)
FRAMESPACING	Spacing around border (pixels)
IFRAME	Specifies a floating frame
NORESIZE	Force the specified size regardless of window size
MARGINHEIGHT	Height of the floating frame (pixels)
MARGINWIDTH	Width of the floating frame (pixels)
SRC	URL of information to display in floating frame

Moving On

In this chapter, I gave you an overview of the new extensions to HTML added by the team at Microsoft to Internet Explorer. In Chapter 11, I explore the many search tools and Web-search databases on the World Wide Web. I also discuss how to best design HTML documents that are not only cool and interesting, but also easy to index and easy for users to find.

Needles in Haystacks

Having your own Web site is definitely worthwhile, but like an exhibit of art in a gallery, the real fun begins when people come to visit. The fundamental puzzle of the World Wide Web — and the Internet as a whole — is *how* to find information. If *you* can't find stuff, it stands to reason that others will have difficulty finding your stuff, too.

People have applied many different strategies for solving the indexing problem, ranging from creating simple databases of Web sites to which you submit information about your site, to unleashing powerful *crawler* programs that stealthily visit your site and add your information to their massive indexes.

The Cool Places to Search

Millions of documents are available on the World Wide Web, but a comparatively small number of sites offer help in finding particular information. Not simply a list of favorite links, search sites are usually concerted team efforts to index the information on the Web and thereby increase the value of the Web as a publishing medium (rather than just a spot for random surfing).

Chief among those sites is the vastly popular Yahoo! service, a database of more than 180,000 Web sites. Galaxy and the WWW Virtual Library also are important Web-server database sites. And in terms of futuristic intrigue, Lycos, AltaVista, and WebCrawler are fascinating attempts to automatically index the ever-growing World Wide Web.

Yahoo!

Of the many sites on the Web that offer comprehensive databases of other Web sites, my favorite is Yahoo!, created by Stanford grad students David Filo and Jerry Yang. Filo and Yang developed Yahoo! as a mechanism for maintaining their own ever-growing list of cool Web sites, and the site has grown so fast that their two UNIX servers couldn't keep up with the load. Today Yahoo! has spun off as a separate business on a new, faster system, and has more than 180,000 Web sites indexed. See Figure 11-1 for the Yahoo! home page. Notice that its home page immediately offers you a place to enter your search criteria too. Visit Yahoo! at
`http://www.yahoo.com/`

While Yahoo! enables you to browse through its various subjects, most people tend to immediately enter a particular keyword or category into the search box and narrow down the options right away. Figure 11-2 shows the results of a search for National Public Radio. I've had to scroll down a ways because advertising tends to eat up the very top of each page, unfortunately.

Figure 11-1: Yahoo! home page. Yahoo!™ (Yahoo!).

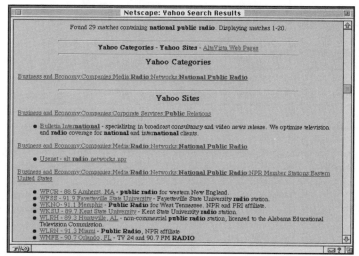

Figure 11-2: The results of a search for National Public Radio in Yahoo!. Yahoo!™ (Yahoo!).

Galaxy

The TradeWave Galaxy is a Web site quite similar to Yahoo!, albeit more rigidly organized. What I particularly like about Galaxy is that when you explore a specific area on their server the information is presented organized by the type of resource (for example, Web site, mailing list, online article), rather than blindly giving you a long list of Web sites. Figure 11-3 shows the Galaxy home page. Visit Galaxy at:
`http://www.einet.net/`

Figure 11-3: *TradeWave Galaxy.*

Figure 11-4 shows the result of choosing "consumer issues" from the information on the very first page of the Galaxy site. Notice that it automatically indicates what items are new, and then organizes the results into useful categories. As you explore some of the different search systems and index directories online, you'll find that this categorization is quite unusual.

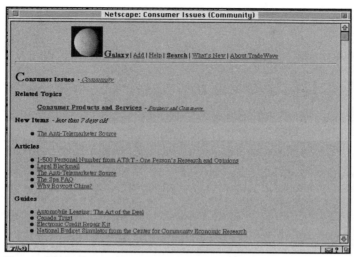

Figure 11-4: Exploring Consumer Issues in Galaxy.

The WWW Virtual Library

The WWW Virtual Library was started at CERN in 1991 by Tim Berners-Lee to keep track of the development of the World Wide Web that he had just created. Arthur Secret picked up the project in 1993, at CERN until August 1995, then on its own until December 1995, and then at the W3 Consortium since January 1996. Now the site is centrally managed by Arthur, and specific categories are managed by individuals throughout the world. Figure 11-5 shows what you see when you pop into this site. Visit the WWW Virtual Library at:

`http://www.w3.org/vl/`

The format is simple, but the result is very useful. Figure 11-6 shows the result of exploring the "games" area of the virtual library. Notice that unlike some of the other search sites we'll explore, the WWW Virtual Library includes commentary and explanation of what's listed — an invaluable addition!

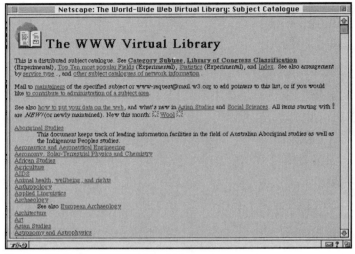

Figure 11-5: The WWW Virtual Library home page.

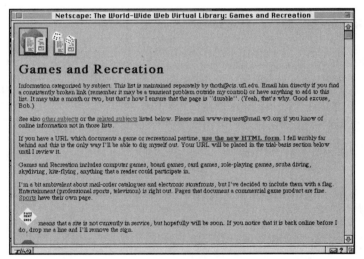

Figure 11-6: The games area in the WWW Virtual Library.

AltaVista

AltaVista is a search system developed by Digital Equipment Corp. (DEC) that exploded onto the Web scene in early 1996 and is now one of the busiest search spots. A quick look at Figure 11-7, however, shows that there's absolutely no way to browse any of the information — it's purely a search-and-see-results system. What's most impressive is the sheer volume of pages it has visited and indexed. As of my writing this chapter, the site advertises 30 million Web pages indexed, and an additional three million Usenet articles in the mix. Visit AltaVista at:
`http://www.altavista.digital.com/`

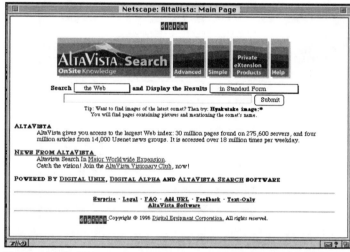

Figure 11-7: Sifting through a very large haystack with Digital's AltaVista.

There is a potential downside to the sheer volume of AltaVista and similar sites; too many matches. On Yahoo!, when I searched for national public radio, I received 28 matches. The same search on AltaVista produces almost 10,000 matches, of which the majority don't appear particularly relevant.

Huge search systems such as AltaVista have sophisticated advanced search techniques you can use, and fifteen minutes spent learning them the first time you visit is time well spent.

Lycos

Taking a very different approach to the problem, the Lycos site, first created at Carnegie-Mellon University, indexes more than fifty million Web documents by building a database of URLs and the first few lines of description from each Web page. Minimal textual information is included for the sites in the database, but the results still are surprisingly good. Figure 11-8 shows the incredibly busy Lycos home page. Visit Lycos at:
`http://lycos.com/`

Figure 11-8: Lycos home page, busy as it can be! Copyright ©1996 Lycos, Inc. All rights reserved. The Lycos™ "Catalog of the Internet" copyright 1994,1995,1996. Carnegie Mellon University. All rights reserved. Used by permission (Lycos).

To allow comparison, I search Lycos for Web sites that have something to do with frogs. Figure 11-9 shows the results of the search. Notice that there were over 1,000 matches, and notice the format of each match shown.

The results show one of the limitations of these 'robot' sites; the first two matches appear to be the same document in two different locations. What would be much more useful would be for the system to return different matches so that immediately there's a variety of different pages from which I can choose. Doesn't seem like a problem when there are a few dozen or a few hundred matches, but imagine the quality of the matches when the system finds tens-of-thousands of different pages that might be relevant!

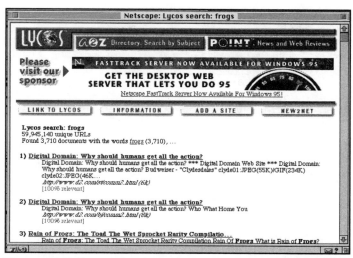

Figure 11-9: Froggy sites found in Lycos. Copyright ©1996 Lycos, Inc. All rights reserved. The Lycos™ "Catalog of the Internet" copyright 1994,1995,1996. Carnegie Mellon University. All rights reserved. Used by permission (Lycos).

The first paragraph or two of information in your Web page should describe the contents of your Web site. Be sure to include common keywords and synonyms. That's all that's being indexed here on Lycos.

WebCrawler

Similar to Lycos and AltaVista, WebCrawler wanders about the Web autonomously, indexing Web documents in its copious database, filtering them through a search and indexing program, and producing the results (with relevance ratings). I really like the visual design of WebCrawlers' home page as shown in Figure 11-10, particularly the graphic buttons along the top. Visit WebCrawler at:

```
http://webcrawler.com/
```

Figure 11-10: WebCrawler. ©1996, America Online, Inc. All rights reserved.

Registering with Web Search Sites

Clearly, the search sites I've discussed here take different approaches to indexing the Web (which means your data). So which site should you register with? All of them. Why not? All the sites are free, and lots of people will use each service to find information, which may just be your own home page. There are two primary types of Web index sites that you've seen in this overview: directories of information submitted by users (Yahoo!, TradeWave Galaxy), and crawler systems that find your actual Web pages and index them automatically (AltaVista, WebCrawler, and Lycos). To join the former, you'll need to explicitly go to the sites and fill in a form with a brief description of your page or site. The latter are easier; simply pop over to their site and add your URL to their database, or just wait a few weeks for them to stumble onto your site by themselves. Let's have a look at each type of addition more closely, then visit with SubmitIt!, a site that can send the announcement of your site to dozens of these search systems and directories for free.

Joining a directory site

It's pretty easy to join a directory site. All that's required is to go to the directory website and add your URL. Just remember, if you don't tell Yahoo!, TradeWave Galaxy, and The WWW Virtual Library about your fabulous new Web site, they won't know about it and you won't be included.

Yahoo!

To join Yahoo!, simply click on the 'add URL' button on the very top right of the banner atop all pages on Yahoo!. Your best bet is to dig around in its categorization of information until you find the category that matches your new site then click on the button, because it'll automatically add that information to help Yahoo! index you correctly. The form you'll need to fill out looks like that shown in Figure 11-11. Fill in all the blanks, and your site will be added after the administrative folks have a glance at your entry.

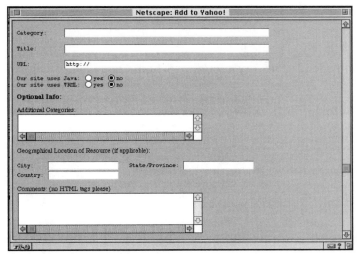

Figure 11-11: Adding your site to Yahoo!. Yahoo!™ (Yahoo!).

TradeWave Galaxy

Like Yahoo!, your best strategy for adding your site to the TradeWave Galaxy directory is to find the appropriate category on their site, then click on the 'add site' button on the very bottom of the page.

The WWW Virtual Library

Unlike the other directory sites, getting your site included in the WWW Virtual Library means that you need to identify the specific category that's most appropriate and then identify the person or people who maintains that particular area in the Virtual Library. Each area has a different editor, so be careful you choose the best fit. When you sign up, you'll probably just be sending an e-mail message to this person rather than filling in some fancy Web form, so do try to be friendly and polite, because an actual human will read your request.

Signing up for a crawler or robot site

The previous directory sites index the information you give them. There are some great benefits to those sites, but other sites that have programs — robots or crawlers — that actively seek out new Web pages are some of the most popular places to look for information online.

As I said earlier, you can go ahead and register with these sites to speed up their indexing of your pages, or you can just ignore them, knowing that eventually they'll find you anyway.

Lycos

To join the Lycos database, you need to click on the 'add a site' button almost hidden in the very center of its home page. Once you've done so, you'll see a page similar to Figure 11-12, whereon you'll want to enter the information requested, and press 'submit.' It will probably take a week or two before the robot comes to your site and finds your pages.

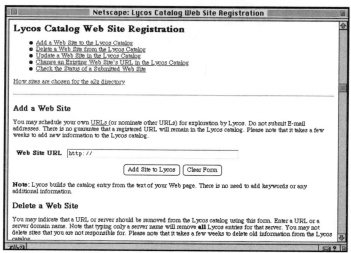

Figure 11-12: Adding your site to Lycos. Copyright ©1996 Lycos, Inc. All rights reserved. The Lycos™ "Catalog of the Internet" copyright 1994,1995,1996. Carnegie Mellon University. All rights reserved. Used by permission (Lycos).

AltaVista

On the AltaVista site, you need to choose 'add URL' from the list of options on the very bottom of the home page. Like Lycos, AltaVista will only ask you for the actual URL of the base page, and it'll take a few weeks or longer before Scooter, its crawler program, actually reaches your site.

WebCrawler

WebCrawler enables you to add your site by simply clicking on the 'add URL' button along the very top of its Web pages. You can enter more than one URL at a time, which is very helpful! Check the status of a URL in the WebCrawler database by visiting:

`http://www.webcrawler.com/WebCrawler/Status.html`

Using an announcement service

As you can tell, there are a lot of different directories and search sites on the Web, and once you've created a Web page you can easily get trapped in a world where you're spending days entering exactly the same information in different spots. Instead, why not enter it once and have it automatically sent to each of the many search sites? That's the idea behind SubmitIt!, a terrific utility created by University of Illinois student Scott Banister and now spun off as its own business.

SubmitIt!

The SubmitIt! site receives over 200,000 visitors per month and is a great example of how a simple idea can grow and become its own business, just as Yahoo! started out as a hot list page for two students. Figure 11-13 shows the SubmitIt! Home page. Visit SumbitIt! at:

`http://www.submit-it.com/`

Notice the three-column layout at SubmitIt!. If you peek at the source to this page, you'll see that they've done it with a borderless table (for example, `<TABLE BORDER=0>`).

There are three options with SubmitIt!: a free service that will announce your site to 16 different directories, including Yahoo!, InfoSeek, AltaVista, WebCrawler, and WebDirect!; SubmitIt! Gold for a business where the information will be distributed to over 200 different directories; and SubmitIt! Pro for professional Web site developers.

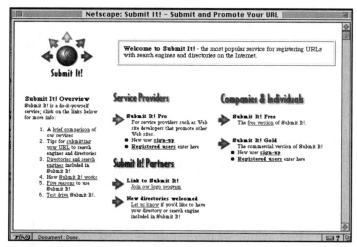

Figure 11-13: The SubmitIt! home page.

Producing Index-Friendly Web Information

Although much of the work of hooking into the Web's search systems involves filling out some forms and otherwise mailing your URL to specific addresses, you can use some design strategies to create cool and useful Web sites.

First, expect future Web-crawler-type search engines to index from the <TITLE> portion of your page in a desire to keep the amount of data manageable, so the more meaningful your title is, the more likely your site will be found when people search for you. To wit, if you're busy creating a site that explores the intricacies of coffee roasting, <TITLE>Coffee Roasting: The Quest for the Perfect Cup</TITLE> is better (and more interesting) than <TITLE>The Coffee Home Page</TITLE>.

I recommend against using the phrases *home page* and *Web* in your page's title at all.

Remember that titles are used not only by some search tools, but they are also what users see as the name of your site when they save your URL to their hotlists. A hotlist full of titles such as The Internet Mall, All About Starbucks, Digital Games Review, and Sony Consumer Electronics offers a great deal more information with less clutter than Ray-o-Vac World Wide Web Page or Stanford University Web Home Page.

Some wit and verve can help, too. Which page would *you* rather visit?

➡ Home Page for Pete Nesterenko

➡ Who Is This Pete Nesterenko Guy?

➡ My Home Page

Needless to say, the last one offers no information about the Web page and should be avoided like the plague.

Finally, don't forget to have the first paragraph of text in your home page contain a meaningful description of the contents therein; because some of the Web index systems grab the first few sentences, carefully crafting them will help ensure people find your information when they search the various spots listed in this chapter.

The <META> tag

There's an important HTML tag that can be a great help in ensuring that meaningful information about your site is included in the crawler sites; the <META> tag. It doesn't display anything, but many of the sites highlighted in this chapter will use the contents of the <META> tag as the 'abstract' or summary description of the site and its contents instead of just the first few dozen words on your page. You'd use the tag like this:

```
<META  name="description"
 content="If you're wondering what's playing at the
Stanford Theatre, we have the entire movie schedule online
in a fun and searchable format.">
<META  name="keywords" content="movie theatre, classic
movies, Palo Alto">
```

Here's how it might look as the result of a search on a system like AltaVista:

```
The Stanford Theatre

If you're wondering what's playing at the Stanford
Theatre, we have the entire movie schedule online in a fun
and searchable format.
http://www.intuitive.com/stanford - size 4k - 18 Aug 96.
```

Keeping Crawlers Away

Clearly if you're plugged in to the Internet, your pages are eventually going to be indexed by one or more of the crawler programs, or 'robots,' such as AltaVista, WebCrawler, and various others. It's fun and very useful except when you'd rather have portions of your Web site remain private or separate. To accomplish this, you need to learn about a special file called robots.txt.

The robots.txt file — and it must be called exactly that regardless of what kind of server you're working with — contains a set of commands that define the access that a robot program can have to the Web site. Unfortunately, it's a wee bit complex to write, but once you've got it right, you'll never have to touch it again.

Field entries in robots.txt

There are two fields that must be present in the robots.txt file: User-agent and Disallow. The first enables you to specify either individual robots (maybe you intensely dislike public crawler programs but like one that's part of your own company) and the second is how you specify directories to omit from the automatic indexing. Let's see a few examples of this to clarify:

```
         User-agent: *
Disallow: /
```

This is the simplest and says that everyone should just leave this site unindexed. Here the '*' for User-agent indicates that it applies to all crawler or robot programs:

```
         User-agent: Scooter
Disallow: /cgi-bin/sources
Disallow: /access_stats
Disallow: /cafeteria/dinner_menus/
```

Scooter isn't allowed to index any of the files in the cgi-bin/sources directory (a smart move), any of the access-statistics (because they probably change quite frequently) and any of the cafeteria dinner menus (because they hopefully also change quite frequently). Any other indexing program that visits the site can index everything.

Learn lots more about robots and the robots.txt file at:
`http://info.webcrawler.com/mak/projects/robots/robots.html`

Popular What's New Sites

This section gives you the scoop on what I consider to be the best and most important "what's new" pages on the Web.

What's new, too

A fun and interesting site that boasts over 500 new announcements daily. Here's a typical listing:

```
Lighthouse Getaway! (Travel & Tourism)
Bill Britten
Knoxville, TN, US
Stunning photography of over 100 lighthouses with
historical data and information on visiting the
lighthouses.
http://zuma.lib.utk.edu/lights
```

Visit What's New Too at:
`http://newtoo.manifest.com/`

WebCrawler's What's New

A low-key site that highlights some of the newest entries in the WebCrawler database. Each entry simply indicates the title of the page and its category. Visit WebCrawler's What's New at:
`http://webcrawler.com/select/nunu.new.html`

Special Internet Connections

Scott Yanoff, while a student at the University of Wisconsin in Madison, started a terrific list called Special Internet Connections. Now a Web developer for SpectraCom, Scott continues to maintain his great list of useful, valuable spots on the Internet. As part of his work, Yanoff has made available a fascinating Web spot that offers a directory of some of the coolest spots on the Web. (He was also kind enough to write the Foreword to this book.) Visit the site at:
`http://www.spectracom.com/islist/`

Figure 11-14 shows the utilitarian design of Yanoff's Special Internet Connections Web document, including a tantalizing glimpse of the many categorizations that his list features.

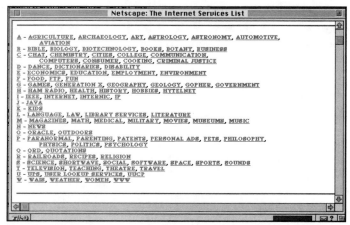

Figure 11-14: Scott Yanoff's Special Internet Connections. Spectracom, Inc. (Yanoff's list).

If you have created a site that is of public interest, Scott Yanoff will be delighted to hear from you and will consider adding you to his database. If you're creating a commercial site, though, he's most likely to forward your announcement to the Internet Mall directory (discussed later in this chapter).

The Netscape What's New Page

Netscape is one of the busiest sites on the Web, which isn't surprising given the popularity of its Navigator Web browser. What you might not realize is that Netscape has a What's New on their Web site, an area that lists some of the more interesting sites coming online with Netscape software.

Frankly, odds are Netscape isn't likely to accept your announcement of what you've done on the Web, but I still recommend it as a good place to start your own exploration. Visit Netscape's What's New Page at:
`http://www.netscape.com/home/whats-new.html`

Interesting Web Sites to Explore

Beyond lists of new sites, some spots on the Web are devoted to indexing Web sites by category and others just seem to have their own unique spin on the information available online. Here are some of the best ones.

Apollo Advertising

A very different approach to presenting information online is the Apollo Advertising site, located in England. Notice in Figure 11-15 the size of the world graphic and the very attractive APOLLO graphic at the top of the page. The prose at this site (including frequent typographical errors) is frustrating, but Apollo Advertising still can be a terrific spot to advertise your new Web site. Visit Apollo Advertising at `http://apollo.co.uk/`

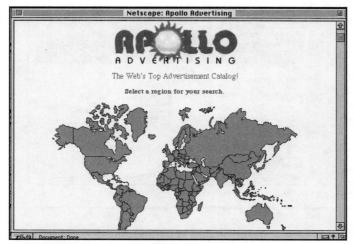

Figure 11-15: Apollo Advertising.

If you scroll below the map of the world, you see a list of countries. That list is invaluable for people with slower connections who opt not to preload all graphics before working with a Web page.

TIP Don't forget that some users may not load the graphics. Always make sure your design tries to take that fact into account.

City.Net

This site in Portland, Oregon, has another spin on things: It seeks to organize information by locale. The idea is neat, and the graphics are quite attractive, as shown in Figure 11-16. Still, a nagging voice in my head keeps asking why the geographic location of a Web site should be relevant in cyberspace. Visit City.Net at `http://www.city.net/`

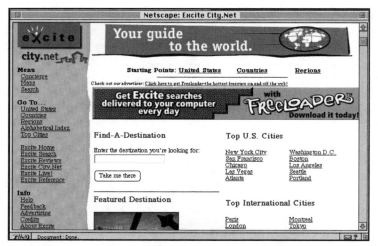

Figure 11-16: City.Net.

If the information at your new site is geographical in nature — a photo tour of a local national park, a list of favorite cafes in your city, or what have you — City.Net may be a great place to add your information.

Inter-Links

To demonstrate that you don't need to be a computer expert to maintain a cool and valuable Web site, Inter-Links was created and is run by Rob Kabacoff, Ph.D., of the Center for Psychological Studies at Nova Southeastern University in Fort Lauderdale, Florida. Inter-Links is a

straightforward index to information sites on the Web, and it also illustrates something else: A Web site can offer a great deal of useful information without being particularly cool. (I expect that, by now, you could write a page such as this with your eyes closed.) Visit Inter-Links at:
`http://www.nova.edu/Inter-Links/`

The InterNIC Directory of Directories

The Internet may appear to be an amazing anarchy, but there *is* a place with some semblance of order, a slight method to the madness. What little control that exists originates at Internet Network Information Center, known informally as the InterNIC. InterNIC subcontracts with different vendors. The directory information is run by AT&T.

This site has a ton of great stuff, but AT&T dropped the ball in the grand scheme because the directory, believe it or not, doesn't have any links to other sites! If you find a directory that sounds interesting, you have to either print out that page or write down the URL that you want, just to type it again in your browser — not a very cool arrangement, in my opinion. Still, this site is an important one, and you'll want to include your information here if possible. Visit InterNIC at:
`http://ds.internic.net/ds/dsdirofdirs.html`

The Internet Mall

A site that's near and dear to my heart is the Internet Mall, shown in Figure 11-17. It is the only commercial directory on the Internet that focuses exclusively on companies that actually sell products or services. It's also a favorite of mine because, in fact, I run the Internet Mall! If you have a business venture that's just joined the Web, you definitely should let me know so I can add you. Currently there are over 18,000 shops listed. Visit the Internet Mall at:
`http://www.internet-mall.com/`

The Living City

A Canadian company called CADVision maintains a very nice, totally different type of Web hot-spot index called The Living City. The Living City is a great example of the weird and funky things you can do within the Web environment. Visit The Living City at:
`http://www.cadvision.com/top.html`

Figure 11-17: The Living City.

Getting around within The Living City is easy. I recommend that the Internet Hierarchy be your first stop; it provides yet another hierarchical index to the thousands of sites on the Web and beyond. Figuring out how to get your Web page listed at The Living City, however, is somewhat difficult. The best strategy seems to be sending an e-mail message to city@cadvision.com, indicating the name of your site, its URL, and any other information that you want to have included.

Fee-Based Advertising Spots

Plenty of Web sites charge you money for a listing and/or require you to join their organization in order to get a link from their page to yours. Are these spots worth it? You'll have to decide for yourself. If you're a small entrepreneur, you probably won't be able to ante up the fees.

Many fee-based sites do, however, offer interesting approaches to Web page design.

If you cast your net a bit wider, you'll also quickly find that there are lots of places where you can buy a banner advertisement for your service or product in order to generate more traffic to your site. Prices for banners can range from the very inexpensive ($40 a month) to amazingly expensive ($10,000 or more for a single month). For the most part, these are sold based on the traffic levels, similar to magazine advertisements. If you want to have a million people see your graphic banner, then you'll be paying something on the order of $0.03 per person, or $30,000 for that advertisement.

Number of viewers isn't the only important criterion, however, so don't be swayed by thoughts of tons of folk visiting your Web page. The most important criterion is *who* will see your advertisement? The demographic, or quality of each viewer is what I think is critical to an advertising buy decision. Some sites sell you eyeballs, thousands upon thousands of people seeing your advertisement every day, whether it's relevant to them or they even care. Other sites offer a smarter deal; everyone who sees your ad banner is already interested in your area.

An example of this is how advertisements are sold in the Internet Mall. If you are a Realtor in Orlando, Florida, for example, you don't want to pay for people to see your advertisement if they're seeking information on vacation spots in Orlando. If they're actively looking for Realtors or real estate in the state of Florida, however, that's someone you're definitely interested in visiting your site.

Ultimately, the organization of the site where you're buying an advertising spot is most important, and something you need to examine carefully. If you're selling party T-shirts online, do you really want to pay to display your advert to someone who just searched for 'cotton plantation' or is looking for party music?

Cooperative Advertising with the Link Exchange

Sometimes it seems like there are as many approaches to advertising your site as there are stars in the sky. Most of them are online versions of other media, like e-zines that are online versions of newsletters and low-budget magazines, or online yellow pages or other phone directory systems.

Occasionally something really new comes along, and the Internet Link Exchange is just that, with its ingenious approach to advertising sites cooperatively. You can join the Internet Link Exchange for free, all you need to do is be willing to point to an ILE advertising CGI program from within your own Web page. The code they ask you to use looks like this:

```
<!— BEGIN INTERNET LINK EXCHANGE CODE —>
<a href="http://ad.linkexchange.com/X007/gotoad.map"
target="_top">
<img width=440 height=40 border=1 ismap alt="Internet Link
Exchange"
```

```
src="http://ad.linkexchange.com/X007/logoshowad?free"></a>
<br>
<font size=1>
<a href="http://www.linkexchange.com/" target="_top">
Member of the Internet Link Exchange</a>
</font>
<br>
<!- END INTERNET LINK EXCHANGE CODE  ->
```

The idea is deceptively simple; anyone who comes to your Web page sees a small advertisement for another site in the ILE network (or the exchange itself) as a banner ad on your Web page. Each time you display an advert on your page, you get a credit with ILE. As you accumulate credits, the banner advertisement for your page shows up on other ILE-member sites. If you have a very busy Web site you've developed, you could easily build up lots of viewing credits and end up with advertisements for your site throughout the Internet, bringing thousands more directly to you.

If you're looking for easy ways to add traffic to your site, I encourage you to go check out the Internet Link Exchange and some of the imitators online.

 Currently, ILE is displaying an incredible 60 million banner ads per month. Check them out for yourself at:
http://www.linkexchange.com/

An Important Mailing List

Although most of the places to announce your Web site are, naturally, on the World Wide Web, there is one mailing list to which you should not only send your announcement, but you should also read. That list is the invaluable Net-Happenings mailing list, run by the InterNIC (Internet Network Information Center).

You can subscribe to Net-Happenings by sending e-mail to majordomo@is.internic.net with subscribe net-happenings in the body of the message. To submit your new-site announcement, send a note directly to net-happenings@is.internic.net. Here's a typical announcement, about a Web site devoted to documenting a rather astounding event:

```
MISC> First Verified Walk Round the Earth

*** From Net-Happenings Moderator ***

Date: Fri, 23 Aug 1996 00:25:07 -0500
From: earthwalker1@earthlink.net

http://home.earthlink.net/~earthwalker1/

Circumambulation!  Waseca, Minnesota to Waseca, Minnesota
on foot around the earth with  exception of the oceans. An
awesome    historical journey. One of mankind's most
amazing    historical adventure Odysseys. Many small steps
that   became one giant feat for mankind. The first time
that   man circled the land mass of the earth on foot.
Featured  in the 1991 Guinness Book of Records.
```

Depending on your Internet habits and tastes, a better strategy may be to check out the Net-Happenings Usenet newsgroup using your favorite newsreader program. On Usenet, the group is called comp.internet.net-happenings. You can also get to this group's Web site by visiting the URL: `http://www.mid.net/NET/`

The Best Way

The best way to publicize your new Web site is to become active in the Internet community, and to be sure to include your site address in all your documents, advertisements, and in any other materials you use to interact with your peers, friends, and customers. Find the cool Web sites in your area of interest and ask them to include pointers to your information. Almost all sites will do that for free, particularly if you agree to list them at your site, too.

One important tag that you learned in this chapter is worth highlighting: `<META>`, which lets you specify exactly how other sites will index your Web pages. Careful use of this can prove very helpful to people seeking you online.

There are a million different destinations on the Web, and many might be of interest to you and your business. I offer you a set of valuable starting points in this chapter, but it doesn't replace the need to explore and find sites that exactly match your own interests and field. In Chapter 12, I give you a taste of some of the more advanced (and complicated) capabilities of HTML and the Web, including image maps, Java, ActiveX, and the Virtual Reality Modeling Language.

Cool Stuff
to Add

In This Chapter

In the early days of the Web, life was fairly simple for the inveterate Web page designer. There were perhaps thirty or so tags that needed to be understood to create powerful and visually exciting sites that offered compelling content. The vision of the original creators was enough impetus for things to get rolling, but in the last year the Web has taken on a life of its own. In this chapter, I'll explore some of these interesting new areas that you've heard about but might not fully understand, including Java, ActiveX, VRML, and more.

Image maps

Client-side image maps

Animated GIFs

Multiple resolution graphics

JavaScript

Visual Basic Script

Java

ActiveX

VRML

Shockwave, RealAudio, and plug-ins galore!

These extensions offer the potential to make your Web pages really state-of-the-art (and *art* is an important facet of Web page design, in case that hasn't become obvious as you've traveled through the chapters in this book).

Now that you've spent a fair amount of your time getting to understand the innards of the hypertext markup language, you probably are figuring that it's infinitely extensible, and that people who write browsers can pretty much add whatever they want. In a sense that's true, but at its most fundamental, HTML is still based on a page and document layout description language called SGML (Standardized General Markup Language). HTML offers some remarkable capabilities, but there are definite edges, areas where it just doesn't work. Designers have therefore rushed in with new scripting and programming languages to further expand the capabilities of the Web. Any one of these additions is worthy of its own book — and many are covered in detail in other books in the *Creating Cool Web* series from IDG Books Worldwide — but it's useful to have a peek at them here, too.

Before I take you to this brave new world, however, there are a few topics that haven't been discussed yet but that you'll want to know before hanging your "Web Page Expert" shingle on your door, and that's how I'll start this chapter.

Image Mapped Graphics

In the last few chapters, you learned about several sites on the Web that eschew mundane bulleted lists in favor of sexy, all-encompassing graphics. When you click on a particular spot on the graphic, the server somehow knows where you clicked and moves you to the appropriate linked page.

This impressive trick is performed through the use of an ISMAP extension to the <IMG> tag and a companion .MAP file that specifies all the known regions in the picture (the 'button' areas) and associates them with specific URLs. The <ISMAP> tag indicates that the image you're including is a 'mapped' image; clicking on different spots on the image produces different results.

Creating image maps

A very simple example consists of three parts: the graphic, a few lines of HTML to specify which graphic file to use as the image map, and the MAP document. For example, a map of Arizona could enable users to choose between Phoenix and Tucson as a travel destination by clicking on the appropriate city on the map.

Following is the HTML. Notice the ISMAP addition to the arizona.gif image instruction.

```
<CENTER>
<IMG SRC="arizona-head.gif"><BR>
<A HREF="http://mysite.com/arizona.map">
<IMG ISMAP SRC="arizona.gif" BORDER=0></A><BR>
Where would you like to go on vacation?
</CENTER>
```

When displayed, the preceding snippet produces the graphic shown in
Figure 12-1. Notice that the map is displayed as a typical GIF image,
without any special border or other indication that it is, in fact, an image
map or anything other than a regular included graphic, until you click on a
region of the map. Having an entire image as a single active area, however,
results in the standard colored border, which I turned off using the
BORDER=0 attribute.

Figure 12-1: A clickable image map.

The next step in creating our Arizona travel overview map is to identify the
areas on the graphic that are the center of the desired hot spots, specific
points on the image that are to have specific actions. I loaded the map into
a simple graphics editor and, by moving the mouse pointer to the city
spots for Tucson and Phoenix, I ascertained that they are x,y coordinates
158,208 (Tucson) and 123,160 (Phoenix). The coordinate 0,0 is the upper
left-hand corner of the image.

In case you forgot your geometry, the x,y coordinate system is one where the x-axis is horizontal, from left to right, and the y-axis is vertical, from top to bottom. The very top left corner of the graphic on the Web is 0,0, and 100,0 will be 100 pixels to the right on the very top edge; whereas 0,100 would be down the left edge of the graphic.

The regions are shown in Figure 12-2.

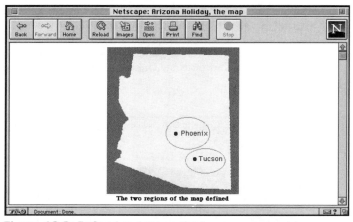

Figure 12-2: Defined regions on the image map graphic.

Next, I decide which geometric figure I want to use to define the limits of the hot spot. I'll opt for the circles shown in Table 12-1, because they enable me to easily define a region around each of the two cities identified. Other choices could have been rectangles, points, or polygons, as shown.

Table 12-1: Shapes Available for ISMAP Files

Name	Coordinates Needed in .MAP File on Server
Circle	Center-point radius or, for NCSA image maps, center, edge point
Poly	List of vertices, maximum 100, that define an irregular enclosed space
Rect	Upper-left lower-right
Point	A single spot on the map, coordinates are x,y

Here's where things get a bit more puzzling. The specific format of the .MAP file, the file that defines all the active clickable regions on the image, depends on the kind of Web server that's running on the server machine that hosts your Web pages. Up to this point, you've learned about HTML tags that work differently with different browsers, but this is the first example (in this book) of one that varies by the program at the other end, the server.

There are two choices of Web server from which everything else has sprung: CERN or NCSA. CERN, as you'll recall, is the Swiss organization that invented the World Wide Web, and NCSA is the group that developed the popular Mosaic Web browser. Because I happen to be using a CERN-style Web server to present the Arizona Travel information Web pages, I have to use the CERN format definitions. Ask your administrator if you don't know, or try NCSA format and if it doesn't work, switch to CERN.

 NCSA is the National Center for Supercomputer Applications at the University of Illinois, Urbana-Champaign.

CERN servers use the first style listed in Table 12-1 of specifying the circle in the table. I need to indicate the center point and radius for each circular hot spot I want. CERN-style .MAP files also use the general layout method/coordinates/URL, with points surrounded by parenthesis. All of this is shown in the actual image.map file shown below:

```
default countryside.html
circle (123,160) 20 phoenix.html
circle (158,208) 20 tucson.html
```

The two circles defined will let users click near the cities of Phoenix or Tucson and learn more about those specific places. That's the second and third line above. The Phoenix entry is exemplary: the region defined for this action within the graphic image (arizona.gif) is a circle centered at 123,160, it has a 20 pixel radius, and any clicks within it result in the user being transferred to the URL phoenix.html. Because users might well click outside of the two spots I've defined, I also added a default action with the 'default' specification; users who click on any area that is not covered by the two circles will be connected to the countryside.html page.

By contrast, if I were using an NCSA server, my map file would look somewhat different, because NCSA changes the order of fields to method/URL/coordinates and omits the parentheses around map points. Consider the changes to the specification for the circular hot spots:

```
default http://mysite.com/countryside.html
circle phoenix.html 123,160 123,180
circle tucson.html 158,208 158,228
```

The NCSA circle method in this example also requires a change in how you envision the hot spot. Instead of the logical center+radius approach used with the CERN .MAP format, NCSA wants two points identified: one at the center of the circle, and the other somewhere along its edge. That's why these change. Personally, I prefer the CERN format for .MAP files, because it's a lot easier to identify the center of a circle and then indicate how big it should be, but servers work with one or the other so you can't pick your favorites.

Although defining and calculating all the points in complex ISMAP graphics may be tedious, the result can be tremendously effective, as you saw in the attractive opening graphics of many of the sites featured in Chapter 10. I'm partial to the opening map of the Internet Mall site (see Figure 12-3).

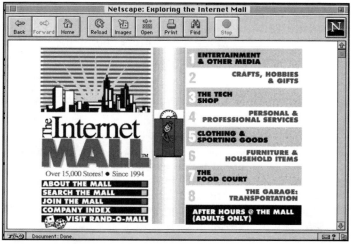

Figure 12-3: The Internet Mall opening image.

The NCSA-server format ISMAP data underlying that Internet Mall map file is complex. If you take a deep breath and look at the data line by line, however, the following example makes a lot of sense:

```
default index.html
rect about.htm 8,248 203,265
rect searchfor.html 10,267 203,278
rect howtojoin.htm 10,282 206,295
rect index.htm 11,297 203,311
rect apps/rand-o-mall.cgi 10,313 202,328
rect firstfloor.html 269,7 475,42
rect second-floor.html 271,43 474,80
rect third-floor.html 269,80 477,115
rect fourth-floor.html 266,114 478,152
rect fifth-floor.html 269,152 476,188
rect sixth-floor.html 267,188 479,224
rect seventh-floor.html 266,222 479,258
rect garage.html 268,258 479,295
rect adult.html 270,294 481,329
rect elevator.html 210,119 261,207
circle http://www.city.net/  104,87 104,13
```

The MAP specification is saved as a separate file with the .map suffix, exactly as shown here. Recall that the HREF for the surrounding image map shown earlier points to the .MAP file, not a specific HTML document.

There's a secret button that you can see from reading the map data: users who click on the city skyline on the top left will be whisked away to: http://www.city.net/

Seeing the complexity of the preceding map file, you can understand why specific tools that help you create ISMAP data files are wonderful, time-saving things. Even better, you can obtain a variety of different ISMAP assistants for free on the Internet, whether you're on a Macintosh, a UNIX workstation, or a PC running Windows. The best place to start your exploration is on Yahoo! at: http://www.yahoo.com/Computers/World_Wide_Web/Programming/Imagemaps

You can find lots of useful Mac Internet software in one place by going to the Mac Helper site at: http://www.wp.com/mwaters/machelp.html

Building an image map with WebMap

Let's have a quick look at how I might build an image map for a photograph of two friends of mine, as shown in Figure 12-4. I will be using WebMap, a program that can help you create image maps.

Figure 12-4: Cameo photograph about to become an image map.

Take a closer look at Figure 12-4, because the image is actually shown while being viewed within the WebMap program itself. Notice on the right the floating palette of image map shapes with which I can specify regions on the graphic.

I click on the rectangle tool and define two regions, enabling visitors to click on either face to get to a page about each of them. Figure 12-5 shows how WebMap looks after I've defined the two rectangular regions.

Figure 12-5: Regions defined in WebMap.

From this point it's easy — under the File menu there's an option for Export Text... which enables me to define NCSA or CERN format and create a map file. The resultant .map file, ready to go on my server and give me an attractive image map, is shown here:

```
#
# Created by WebMap 2.0b9
# Sunday, October 20, 1996 at 1:47 PM
# Format: NCSA
#

rect paul.html 132,27 205,208
rect marie.html 49,56 132,204
default default.html
```

You can get the latest version of this useful shareware Mac application off the Net, at:
`http://www.city.net/cnx/software/webmap.html`

Client-side Image Mapping

Image maps are very useful for complex Web site design, but there's a problem with it — you need to know what kind of server you have and write your mapping coordinates to fit (and if you change host providers, you may need to redo your image maps). There's another way you can have active regions on a document; client-side image mapping. Consider the graphic shown in Figure 12-6.

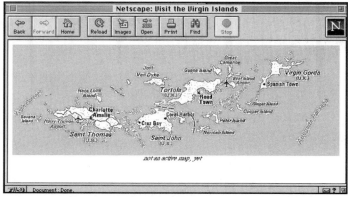

Figure 12-6: A graphic with different regions to click upon.

Until the client-side image mapping extension, all the definition of regions and calculation of which area you'd typed and what should happen took place on the remote server, but only if the server enabled that particular page to include image maps. (Some servers are configured to ignore image maps for performance reasons. You'd know, because clicking on an image map would result in you seeing the MAP file rather than being taken to the page associated with the specific region.) By moving the processing to the client side, the Mac or PC that the visitor has on their own desk, it means that you're freeing up remote server resources and gaining greater control over the map itself. It's a great improvement in my opinion!

To build a client-side image map, let's first define a set of regions on the Virgin Island map that we'd like to have as active spots on the graphic. Figure 12-7 shows this as a series of rectangular regions.

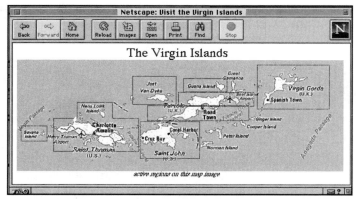

Figure 12-7: Defined hot spots on the map.

Armed with that, and with a little help from one of the many image map editors available as shareware on the Net, I produce a .MAP datafile in CERN format:

```
default default.htm
rect (9,120) (56,149) savanna.htm
rect (67,106) (220,168) stthomas.htm
rect (109,76) (173,107) Hans.htm
rect (208,28) (287,81) vandyke.htm
rect (431,7) (561,89) gorda.htm
rect (299,32) (378,57) guana.htm
rect (222,112) (329,181) stjohn.htm
rect (235,82) (417,111) tortola.htm
rect (290,57) (426,84) tortola.htm
```

For a client-side map, we need to tweak the above data that's designed for a CERN-type server. CERN format is probably a smidgen closer than NCSA to what you need for the client-side tags, so if you use an image map editor that can give you CERN data, you'll be closer to what you'll ultimately need.

To define client-side image regions, each of the lines above is respun so that each field is an attribute within the <AREA> HTML tag.

Here's how the CERN data is rewritten within an HTML file so that we can have a client-side map:

```
<HTML>
<HEAD>
<TITLE>Visit the Virgin Islands</TITLE>
</HEAD>
<BODY>
<CENTER>
<FONT SIZE=6>The Virgin Islands</FONT><BR>
<IMG SRC="virgin.gif" USEMAP="#map1"><BR>
<b>Where would you like to go?</B>
</CENTER>
<MAP NAME="map1">
<AREA SHAPE="rect" COORDS="9,120, 56,149"
HREF="savanna.htm">
<AREA SHAPE="rect" COORDS="67,106, 220,168"
HREF="stthomas.htm">
<AREA SHAPE="rect" COORDS="109,76, 173,107"
HREF="hans.htm">
<AREA SHAPE="rect" COORDS="208,28, 287,81"
HREF="vandyke.htm">
<AREA SHAPE="rect" COORDS="431,7, 561,89" HREF="gorda.htm">
<AREA SHAPE="rect" COORDS="299,32, 378,57"
HREF="guana.htm">
<AREA SHAPE="rect" COORDS="222,112, 329,181"
HREF="stjohns.htm">
<AREA SHAPE="rect" COORDS="235,82, 417,111"
HREF="tortola.htm">
<AREA SHAPE="rect" COORDS="290,57, 426,84"
HREF="tortola.htm">
<AREA SHAPE="rect" COORDS="0,0, 600,200"
HREF="default.htm">
</MAP>
</BODY>
</HTML>
```

There's lots to see here, so let's take it in order. First off, notice the new option to the `<IMG>` formatting tag: `USEMAP=internal-reference-name`. Just like the internal anchors you learned about earlier, the reference to the map data must have a $#$ as the first character, and the actual target omits that symbol. Here I'm leaving the option of having multiple maps on this page by naming this "map1."

Below this is the fun stuff: the tag that defines the region of a defined map (`<MAP>`) and the specific regions defined for each spot within the image (`<AREA>`). Still with me?

Here's how a specific rectangular region translated from CERN to AREA format. The region for Guana Island started out in CERN format defined as:

```
rect (299,32) (378,57) guana.htm
```

but because HTML wants name=value parameters, I had to change that format to one where the shape of the region is defined, the coordinates for that region (with a space between the coordinate pairs for rectangles), then the URL connected with the specified region. That is:

```
<AREA SHAPE="rect" COORDS="299,32, 378,57"
HREF="guana.htm">
```

Outside of this conversion of the CERN format to tags, the biggest change you can see in the changes for a client-side image map is that there's no *default* area (like the countryside area of my Arizona map) in a client-side map. Instead, I simply defined a region that was the size of the image (0,0 to 600,200, in pixels from the top left of the image) and specified that its action should be to go to the URL `default.htm`. By definition, the list of map coordinates is only perused until the spot you've clicked on is found, so having two identical regions specified in the `<MAP>` tag would mean that you'd never get to the second choice.

On server-side image maps, you can choose from a wide palette of different geometric shapes, and client-side maps are no different, as shown in Table 12-2.

 The Microsoft Web site has some excellent further documentation on client-side maps and their other extensions to HTML. Check it out at:
`http://www.microsoft.com/workshop/author`

Table 12-2: Shapes Available for Client-side .MAP Files

SHAPENAME	Meaning	Parameters Required
RECT	Rectangle	Takes four coordinates: x1, y1, x2, and y2
RECTANGLE	Rectangle	Takes four coordinates: x1, y1, x2, and y2
CIRC	Circle	Takes three coordinates: centerx, centery, and radius
CIRCLE	Circle	Takes three coordinates: centerx, centery, and radius
POLY	Polygon	Takes three or more pairs of coordinates denoting a polygonal region
POLYGON	Polygon	Takes three or more pairs of coordinates denoting a polygonal region

Animated GIFs

We've got image maps out of the way so let's start looking at some fun additions that you're doubtlessly seeing daily on your Web visits without knowing exactly how they're working. The first capability that has taken the Web by storm is animated GIF graphics formats.

GIF format, as you'll recall, is the basic graphics format used by most pages on the Web. It enables the designer to create a single graphic, large or small, which is displayed on the page. But what if, just like an old movie, you could have a sequence of graphics, and instead of displaying just a single still picture the browser would continually cycle between the images saved to produce the illusion of motion?

That's exactly what animated GIFs are all about, and their use can range from a whirring disk or star to bouncing letters, even to the Microsoft Internet Explorer logo itself.

To create an animated GIF you need one thing; patience. I created the dancing "jazz" GIF included on the CD-ROM by creating a single graphic, then duplicating it four times, and each time moving the letters around a bit. Then I used the animated Macintosh GIF program, GIFBuilder, to bring in each of the images as an individual frame of the resultant animation. Check out the results and see what you think!

Note that because you can specify the delay time between images, you can also have completely different graphics on each image, using it as a sort of slide show.

What's really nice about animated GIFs is that they're included on your pages just like any other GIF file, using the `<IMG>` tag. No special modifications are required.

There's another approach to animation that's worth mentioning here, too; progressive JPEGs. The idea is that they combine animation with the greater color quality of the JPEG format, but the reality is that it's extremely rare to see animation that isn't an animated GIF. Netscape has some information on progressive JPEGs on its site, at:
`http://home.netscape.com/comprod/products/navigator/versio n_2.0/progressive_jpeg/progressive_faq.html`

Multiple Resolution Graphics (Netscape Navigator Only)

A neat trick that Netscape Navigator enables you to do but Internet Explorer ignores is having two versions of a graphic sent to the user, a low resolution, smaller image that loads quickly, and a higher resolution full color image that *replaces* the coarse or low color image when received. The idea is that you can have a rough version of your graphic that downloads quickly, letting users immediately start working with your page and having some idea of the included images. If the viewer remains on the page, the higher quality version of the images gradually replaces the low resolution ones and the final page is very attractive and highly functional.

To accomplish this, Navigator understands a new attribute in the `<IMG>` tag: `LOWSRC`. If seen, the lowsrc graphic will be loaded into the page first, then the default higher resolution image will replace it. Here's an example:
`<IMG SRC="photo-hires.JPG" LOWSRC="photo-lores.GIF" HEIGHT=300 WIDTH=150>`

In this case I have two versions of my graphic, a black-and-white GIF image that's about 15K, and a full color JPEG version that's just under 60K. This example is explored on the CD-ROM.

A second way to work with low res/hi res is to take advantage of the auto-scaling feature of Navigator. You'll recall that earlier I warned you that specifying a HEIGHT and WIDTH different from the actual size of the image causes the browser to automatically blow up the image to fit, regardless of how attractive it looked. Now you can use it to your advantage: the LOWSRC image could be a thumbnail version of the larger image, but if you specify the exact size of the larger image, the browser will show a very fuzzy version and then replace it with the clean version. Figures 12-8 and 12-9 show how this might look as a two-step process.

Figure 12-8: Low res image, sized to fit the large area.

It's simple to use this tag instead of the standard <IMG> tag, but remember that so far only the Netscape Navigator browser understands the LOWSRC attribute.

Figure 12-9: The hi res image replaces the low res image.

JavaScript

Here's a common point of confusion, not only for people who use the Net, but those of us who write about it. JavaScript is a relatively simple scripting language for defining the behavior of Web pages. It's *not* the same as the much more complex Java programming language, which offers a robust and sophisticated environment for creating lots of applications.

JavaScript is not dissimilar to HyperTalk scripts for HyperCard, or BAT batch files that you might be familiar with from DOS or UNIX shell scripts. Typically just a few lines long, they can specify responses to actions or events like the page being opened, the mouse moving to a specific spot, or a field in a form being cleared. The structure of the language itself is a bit weird, alas, so let's just jump in and have a look!

Here's a JavaScript example that pops up a message:

```
<HTML>
<HEAD>
<SCRIPT LANGUAGE="JavaScript">
<!- sample JavaScript
alert('When you are ready to see this page...
```

```
// end of script ->
</SCRIPT>
</HEAD>
<BODY BGCOLOR=white>
This is all we have in the body of the message.
</BODY>
</HTML>
```

Notice here that the script is wrapped in <SCRIPT> and </SCRIPT>, and that it's all buried in a comment so browsers that don't understand JavaScript won't get confused by the script itself. Browsers that understand JavaScript cheat and actually examine the lines within comments (after seeing a <SCRIPT> tag) to pick up any scripting instructions therein. Figure 12-10 shows what happens when you first visit this page.

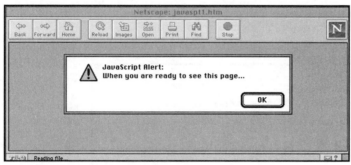

Figure 12-10: JavaScript pop-up dialog box.

The following is another example, this time one that changes what's displayed on the status line of your browser based on where you move your mouse:

```
<HTML>
<BODY BGCOLOR=white>
<BASEFONT SIZE=4>
<CENTER>
<FONT SIZE=6>Embedded JavaScript events:
<B>onMouseOver</B></FONT><BR>
<I>move your mouse onto the two lines below<BR>
and watch the status window on the very bottom of your
browser</I>
</CENTER>
```

```
(continued)
<P>
<A HREF="javaspt2.htm"
   onMouseOver="self.status='you have no status, but you
DO have bananas!';return true">
drag your mouse over me</A>
<P>
<A HREF="javaspt2.htm"
   onMouseOver="self.status='no, you got no bananas
either!';return true">
or better yet, drag your mouse over me!</A>
</BODY>
</HTML>
```

There are lots of different events that can be scripted with JavaScript. In the example above, things happen when you move your mouse over either of the two hyperlinks, as shown in Figure 12-11.

Figure 12-11: Notice the status bar message.

It turns out that there are a number of scriptable events in JavaScript, as shown in Table 12-3.

JavaScript is a simple language to use, but it will still take some time to master. There are some terrific online tutorials that can help you, including the JavaScript Authoring site at Netscape:
`http://home.netscape.com/eng/mozilla/2.0/handbook/javascript`
Or you can find a wealth of information and example scripts by popping over to Yahoo! at:
`http://search.yahoo.com/bin/search?p=javascript`

Table 12-3:	Scriptable Events in JavaScript	
Event	**Occurs when . . .**	**Event Handler**
blur	User removes input focus from page element	onBlur
click	User clicks on form element or link	onClick
change	User changes value of text, text area, or select element	onChange
focus	User gives form element input focus	onFocus
load	User loads the page in the browser	onLoad
mouseover	User moves mouse pointer over a link or anchor	onMouseOver
select	User selects form element's input field	onSelect
submit	User submits a form	onSubmit
unload	User exits the page	onUnload

You might also want to check out Danny Goodman's *JavaScript Bible, Second Edition* from IDG Books Worldwide; it's a complete guide to writing useful JavaScript routines for your Web pages.

Visual Basic Script (Microsoft Internet Explorer Only)

JavaScript is powerful, but is unlike any language that most programmers and users have ever learned.

Visual Basic Script, on the other hand, is a language based on the one all the adventurous hobbyists and students learned when they were first starting out with computers.

Microsoft offers Visual Basic Script — VBScript — as an alternative to JavaScript for Internet Explorer. The following is an example of how a simple VBScript program might look:

```
<HTML>
<BODY BGCOLOR=white>
<SCRIPT LANGUAGE="VBScript" EVENT="OnClick" FOR="Button1">
<!-
    MsgBox "You clicked on the button and up popped me!"
->
</SCRIPT>
<CENTER>
<FORM>
<INPUT NAME="Button1" TYPE="BUTTON"
       VALUE="Roses are red, beloved by the bee..."><BR>
<I>click on the button</I>
</FORM>
</CENTER>
</BODY>
</HTML>
```

How the script appears in the HTML document is very similar to JavaScript, but the language itself is easier to work with, in my opinion. Try this page in your own browser, and when you click on the button you should see a dialog box pop up identical to Figure 12-12.

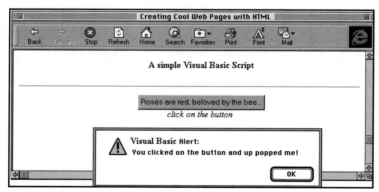

Figure 12-12: Dialog boxes with VBScript.

You can learn lots more about Visual Basic Script by visiting the terrific VBScript Central at:
http://www.inquiry.com/vbscentral/
Or you can check out the information Microsoft has at:
http://www.microsoft.com/VBASIC/

Figure 12-12 is an interpretation of what a VBScript-enabled Internet Explorer will look like on the Macintosh.

Java

In terms of sheer enthusiasm in the press and incessant commentary from pundits everywhere, no new technology has been introduced on the Net that has been as widely heralded as Java, a new programming language from Sun Microsystems. If you read your favorite magazine you were probably told that Java would save the world, cure cancer, and did I mention lower the prime lending rate and wash your car?

The reality is somewhat different. Java is a complex object-oriented programming language based on a powerful language called C++, which itself was a modified version of the C programming language so beloved by UNIX folk. C was originally developed to write UNIX device drivers so it shares many characteristics with the most primitive of languages, assembler. Add a layer of object-oriented capabilities and you've got C++. Tweak it further for the Net and you have Java, a difficult language that's not necessarily for novice programmers who just want to add cool effects to their Web pages.

The good news is that there are a wide variety of different Java development environments (like WebBurst) available, and they make creating Java applets (little programs) quite a bit easier. Even better, you can *use* Java applets without even having much of a clue about Java itself.

Let's start, nonetheless, by having a look at a simple Java program:

```
class HelloWorld {

  public static void main (String args[]) {

    System.out.println("Hello World!");

  }
}
```

That is what's involved in getting the program to say "hello world" within a Web page. You can't send this script directly in your HTML page, however, you need to actually translate it into a Java applet binary through compiling it; to work with Java you must have some sort of development environment. But, that's beyond the scope of this book!

 Don't worry if this example seems incomprehensible. Java is a complex programming language, like any other human language, and it can't be explained in just a few pages. Your best bet is to find one of the many good books introducing Java.

Referencing Java applets

If you can't include the Java source or compiled binary in your HTML code, you might be wondering just how you do actually include Java applets on your page. The answer is the `<APPLET>` tag, which has a variety of parameters, the most important of which is the CODE parameter, which specifies the exact name of the applet desired. At its simplest:

```
<APPLET code="DrawStringApplet.class" width=100
height=100></APPLET>
```

The preceding example defines a 100 × 100 box that shows the results of the DrawStringApplet when loaded and run.

You can pass parameters to applets with the `<PARAM>` tag:

```
<BODY>
This is the applet:
<P>
<APPLET code="DrawStringApplet.class" width=200 height=200>
<PARAM name="String" value="Hi there!">
</APPLET>
</BODY>
</HTML>
```

Here the parameter string includes the text "Hi there!" that I used as a value for the text string parameter.

Online Java Applets

You can add all sorts of Java applets to your own Web pages by just adding the appropriate reference to your pages, and perhaps customizing them with values for the built-in parameters. There are dozens upon dozens of nifty applets online, many of which live at Sun's Java division Web site, Javasoft, at:

http://www.javasoft.com/java.sun.com/applets/applets.html

Many more live at Gamelan's online Java library at:
`http://www.gamelan.com/`
There's also an online magazine just about Java that is not only very good, but is run by a bunch of friends of mine: *JavaWorld*, which you can visit at:
`http://www.javaworld.com/`

I encourage you to explore some of these resources online!

 There's a fabulous Java programming tutorial written by Elliotte Rusty Harold at:
`http://sunsite.unc.edu/javafaq/javatutorial.html`

ActiveX (Microsoft Internet Explorer Only)

If Java is going to save the world, then ActiveX is going to save us from Java, or something like that. ActiveX is Microsoft's contribution to the programming languages on the Net discussion, and it offers many of the same capabilities and complexities. The big difference: Java works with both Navigator and Explorer, but ActiveX is only for the Microsoft browser at this point. In the near future, Netscape will be supporting ActiveX, but current plans are only for the Windows platform.

 Not necessarily: NCompass Labs has just introduced a first beta release of NCompass, a plug-in for Netscape Navigator that enables it to understand ActiveX Controls. Find out more at:
`http://www.ncompasslabs.com/`

If you've been keeping track, ActiveX evolved from Microsoft's OLE technology by way of the OCX implementation. If it's Greek to you, don't worry, it's Greek to me too!

ActiveX functions as a *wrapper* called an ActiveX Control. The code being included interacts with the wrapper (ActiveX), and the wrapper interacts with the browser directly. Using this technique, just about any code can run within the browser space, from word processors and spreadsheets to simple games and animation.

Each ActiveX Control has a unique class ID and is included as an `<OBJECT>` tag, with parameters specified in the `<PARAM>` tag, remarkably similar to JavaScript:

```
<OBJECT ID="ClientLayout"
    CLASSID="CLSID:812AE312-8B8E-11CF-93C8-00AA00C08FDF">
        <PARAM NAME="ALXPATH" REF VALUE="Client.alx">
    </OBJECT>
```

There are a couple of sites to learn more about ActiveX, thank goodness, because it's easy to include but difficult to understand.
`http://www.microsoft.com/sitebuilder.`
ZDNet also has a nice resource online, at:
`http://www.zdnet.com/activexfiles/`
CMP has one at:
`http://www.activextra.com/`

VRML

So far, everything we've done with Web pages has happened in two dimensions: things either move horizontally or vertically. Indeed, because a computer screen is only two dimensional, that makes sense. But you need merely glance at Myst or Doom to realize that simulating a three dimensional world on a computer screen isn't too hard, and if it can be done, it can be done on the Web (although the files might take awhile to download)!

That's where VRML (Virtual Reality Modeling Language) comes into the picture. VRML is a simple language that enables you to create complex and sophisticated three dimensional worlds that users can navigate through using any of a variety of VRML viewer applications or plug-ins.

The current version of VRML is quite simple and looks somewhat like Java. Here's a snippet that defines a single green globe in space:

```
Material {
   diffusedColor      0.2    1    0.2      # red, green and
blue values, 0-1
}
Sphere {
   radius 10
}
```

Once you start using a VRML development environment you can really create some amazing worlds, and there are people on the Net who have done some fabulous work. Figure 12-13 shows one such example, a snapshot of the VRML version of San Diego by ultimately cool Planet 9 Multimedia. Visit Planet 9 at:
`http://www.planet9.com/`

Figure 12-13: VRML virtual New Orleans, a space to fly through.

Netscape Navigator includes a nice viewer application called Live3D that enables you to work with VRML worlds while within the browser: it's included in the full release of their latest (3.0) release. There are a variety of other companies also offering VRML utilities, including Virtus at:
www.virtus.com.
And Microsoft at:
www.microsoft.com

Check out *VRMLSite* magazine online for lots of fun stuff and pointers to more information on how to create 3-D environments, including tutorials and pointers to various software tools and utilities. Visit the site at:
http://www.vrmlsite.com/

Shockwave, RealAudio, and Plug-ins Galore!

Much of what's been covered in this chapter are specific pieces of a general architecture shared by both Navigator and Explorer called *plug-ins*, small helper applications that can manage a region of a Web page you're viewing. There are over a hundred different plug-ins available from a wide variety of sources, and they range from a MIDI player from Yamaha (the musical keyboard people) to a 3D world exploration plug-in from Sony, to the RealAudio audio player to Macromedia's Shockwave. The best way to find out about plug-ins is to visit the Netscape plug-in information page by clicking on About Plug-ins from the Navigator HELP menu.

Two plug-ins are worth special mention before I wrap up this chapter: RealAudio and Shockwave.

RealAudio

If you experimented with the audio clips I included to demonstrate the background audio capabilities in Chapter 10, you already know that the way it works is you request the audio, wait for the entire audio file to load, and then start to hear the music. That works all right for tiny music samples of 10–50K, but if you have more audio the size of the file produces a delay that is unacceptable, where it might take five minutes or longer before any audio is played.

The solution is RealAudio, a 'streaming' audio player, where once it has received a few seconds worth of the sound file it actually plays the audio it has received so far, like a tape deck playing the sounds as a tape rolls by. A great idea, and one that makes audio on the Web a reality. Even better, both Netscape and Microsoft have licensed and included the RealAudio plug-in with their latest browsers, so you can simply click on a RealAudio stream and tune in to a cyberspace radio program. Most excellent. One caveat; to create your own RealAudio files for others to enjoy, you need to buy the RealAudio encoding software from the company.

There's a short list of some fun RealAudio servers on the CD-ROM. If you have a Net connection, I encourage you to visit a few and see what you think!

 Visit the RealAudio home page at `http://www.realaudio.com/` for lots of samples, and don't miss National Public Radio on the Web while you're there.

Shockwave

The other terrific must-have plug-in is Shockwave. It evolved from a terrific multimedia authoring program called Director, from Macromedia. If you've ever seen a demo program running on a computer at a trade show or computer store, or even explored an interactive CD-ROM catalog, you've probably been using a Director script. With its ability to simultaneously work with audio, animation, video, text, and user input, it's a powerful package. When the Web craze hit, the folks at Macromedia started thinking about extending Director so that its datafiles could be used directly on the Net, and that's Shockwave in a nutshell.

Most sites that are using Shockwave today are creating fancy animations with synchronized sound (which is harder to do than you'd think!), but in the future I think there's going to be some amazing Shockwave files floating around on the Net.

You can learn more about Shockwave, get the Shockwave plug-in, and view lots of examples and demonstrations of the technology on the Macromedia Web site at:

`http://www.macromedia.com/`

Moving On

In this chapter, I gave you an overview of the many extensions to HTML and scripting capabilities offered through plug-ins and additions to the top Web browsers. In Chapter 13, I explore how to create interactive Web pages and obtain information from the viewer through forms and common gateway interface (CGI) programming.

Forms and the Common Gateway Interface

In This Chapter

In this chapter, I provide an introduction to forms and database queries and include a quick overview of programming your Web pages and making smart sites, whether you're using a PC, Mac, or renting space on a UNIX server.

The CGI inside your Web server

Smart Web pages using CGI scripts

An introduction to HTML forms

Receiving information from forms

I'm going to be honest with you right up front: getting back-end CGI scripts to work on your Web server is the most difficult part of sophisticated Web site design. It's programming in a weird language that's much more difficult to learn than HTML. For this book I'll be showing the simple examples as UNIX shell scripts (because odds are very good that the server upon which all your pages will reside will be running UNIX, and because it's very clear what's going on) and more complex examples in Perl, a popular multiplatform language. You can, however, write your scripts in just about any language, and in fact most of my long, ugly CGI scripts are written in the C programming language. But that's even more confusing. The long and short of it; take a deep breath and let's go!

The CGI Inside Your Web Server

You've now seen that you can have fun creating slick looking Web pages and complex sites, adding animation, frames, and lots of other sophisticated markup. What's missing from the picture, so far, is any sort of interaction between the user and the Web server. Whether it's showing the current time, asking for feedback, or even presenting the latest news or stock ticker values dynamically, it is all done from the server end rather than within the HTML document itself.

Understanding CGI

To understand how CGI works, let's take a brief step back to the most basic of Web concepts. All Web browsers talk with Web servers using a language (well, protocol, to be exact) called http, the hypertext transport protocol. At its simplest, http simply defines the interaction between the browser and server, which can be boiled down to "I want" from the browser and "here is" or "don't have" from the server. It looks like Figure 13-1.

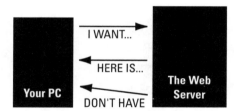

Figure 13-1: The handshake between the browser and server.

Forget all the fancy stuff of the last 12 chapters. The simple dialog shown in Figure 13-1 is what the Web, and indeed the Internet, is really all about. Your Mac asks a server somewhere on the Net for a particular file, picture, resource, or what-have-you, and is responding either "here it is" or "I don't have it." In fact when you have an HTML document that includes graphics, each graphic is requested from the server through its own dialog of a similar nature. That's why you see the source to some pages before you get all the graphics, because it ends up looking like the following:

```
I want 'test.htm'
here is 'test.htm'
oh, now I want 'opening.gif'
here is 'opening.gif'
and I want 'photo.jpeg'
```

```
here is 'photo.jpeg'
and I want 'logo.gif'
here is 'logo.gif'
and finally I also want 'lastpict.gif'
uh oh, I don't have 'lastpict.gif' Error 440: file not
found
```

While this may seem tremendously tedious — and it is — it's also a great design because it's so easily extended into other areas. What happens, for example, if instead of the 'I want' request, the browser asked 'please run the following program and send me the output'?

That capability is what programming Web servers is built around, and the environment on the server within which you can communicate with the browser is called the Common Gateway Interface, or CGI. By creating CGI scripts or programs, you can have graphics, or even entire Web pages, produced automatically by programs running on the remote server. By working within the CGI environment, in the programming language of your choice, you can replace any Web page or graphic with a program that performs calculations, looks up information in a database, checks the weather, reads a remote sensor, or whatever you'd like, then returns the results of that action to the user as a Web page.

On many servers you can tell what's a CGI script by the .cgi suffix, but really any file or graphic can actually be a program, the output of which is sent to the user. The best news is that it's invisible to the Web visitor. They just wander through your site, seeing page after page, and if some pages are the result of running scripts, the visitors will probably never know.

The world's simplest CGI example

Let's dive right in and have a look at a CGI script that might replace a static Web page with something more dynamic: "hello world," written as a UNIX shell script, which is very similar to a Windows batch file.

```
echo "Content-type: text/html"
echo ""
echo "<HTML><BODY>"
echo "<H1>Hi Mystery Web Visitor</H1>"
echo "</BODY></HTML>"
```

The 'echo' command outputs whatever you specify to 'standard output,' which is usually the screen of the user connected to the system. In this case, because it's being run as a CGI script, standard output is the remote Web server, which means that the output will be sent to the remote Web browser. As you can see, the program hello.cgi is required to return an actual HTML document, though the program itself can be in any language or format because it's run on the remote server. That is, the *output* of the CGI script or program must be a sequence of HTML tags, prefaced by the `Content-type: text/html` line. This is so everything is transparent to the user: they request a Web document and it comes back all neatly formatted and ready to be displayed by the browser.

There's an important thing to notice on the very first line of this example script: the very first line of any CGI script must identify the particular type of information being sent back to the browser. In this case it's HTML text, and the formal description for that is `Content-type: text/html`. That line must be followed by a blank line and then, finally, the actual HTML code can appear. Functionally, this program is identical to a Web page that simply had:

```
<HTML>
<BODY>
<H1> Hi Mystery Web Visitor </H1>
</BODY></HTML>
```

So why go through the bother? Because these scripts can output *anything* your heart desires. Let's look at a slightly more sophisticated example, this one that uses the `date` command on the server:

```
echo "Content-type: text/html"
echo ""
echo "<HTML><BODY>"
echo "<H1>Oh Mystery Web Visitor, the time is...</H1>"
date
echo "</BODY></HTML>"
```

Figure 13-2 shows how that script would look to a user visiting my Web site and requesting date.cgi:.

There's a lot you can do with this approach to Web page design, but CGI offers a considerably richer environment for developing sophisticated sites, an environment where you can make decisions about what kind of HTML to output based on the browser that's in use, where the user's located, and much more.

Figure 13-2: The local time, on the server.

Smart Web Pages Using CGI Scripts

Every http transaction (the 'I want'/ 'here is' pair) actually includes a set of environment characteristics — a set of variables that define the browser, computer, and much more — that are sent along from the browser to the server and are accessible from the CGI script.

Creating a CGI environment

To see environment characteristics mentioned above is simple; a CGI script that uses the UNIX printenv (print environment) command will do the trick:

```
echo "Content-type: text/html"
echo ""
echo "<HTML><BODY>"
echo "<H1>Your environment is:</H1>"
echo "<PRE>"
printenv
echo "</PRE>"
echo "</BODY></HTML>"
```

When this is run from within Microsoft Explorer, the results are as shown in Figure 13-3.

Figure 13-3: My CGI environment for writing scripts.

Notice particularly the two variables REMOTE_HOST and HTTP_USER_AGENT. The former identifies the hostname of the browser — here you can see that my computer is called ws1.hostname.com — and the latter identifies the specific browser in use. In this case you can also see a bit of a trick that Microsoft's Internet Explorer performs: it identifies itself as Netscape 2.0, but then correctly identifies itself as IE 2.1. (It's a historical artifact: when Microsoft first released its browser, sites were written to recognize Navigator, but Explorer was unknown and was treated as a dumb browser with few advanced HTML capabilities, except IE had the capabilities. Their solution? Pretend they're Navigator.)

The code name for Navigator is Mozilla.

If I request the very same Web CGI script from Navigator, the output is very different, as shown in Figure 13-4.

Figure 13-4: My CGI environment in Navigator.

The differences are interesting, but note that the two key variables, REMOTE_HOST and HTTP_USER_AGENT, are identical. Table 13-1 shows some common values for the user agent.

Table 13-1:	HTTP_User_Agent Values
Lynx/2-4-2 libwww/2.14	
Mozilla/0.96 Beta (Windows)	
Mozilla/2.0 (compatible; MSIE 3.0; Windows 95)	
Mozilla/2.0 (compatible; MSIE 2.1; Mac_PowerPC)	
Mozilla/3.0b7Gold (Win 95; I)	
Mozilla/3.0 (Macintosh; I; PPC)	
NCSA Mosaic for the X Window System/2.4 libwww/2.12 modified	
NetCruiser/V2.00	
PRODIGY-WB/1.3e	
Spyglass Mosaic/1.0 libwww/2.15_Spyglass	

Armed with this information, you can now write a simple script that outputs different HTML based on what kind of Web browser the viewer is using. In this case, let's offer different messages based on whether my visitor is using Internet Explorer or Navigato244r. To do this, I'll need to look for the sequence MSIE (Microsoft Internet Explorer) in the user agent string, which is done in UNIX with the grep command. Grep is a command that easily enables you to find lines that match the pattern in specified file or stream of information. Here's the new script:

```
echo "Content-type: text/html"
echo ""

x="`echo $HTTP_USER_AGENT | grep MSIE `"

echo "<center>"
echo "Welcome to my Web site<P>"

if [ "$x" = "" ] ; then
  echo This page enhanced for Netscape Navigator
else
  echo This page enhanced for Microsoft Internet Explorer
fi

echo "</center>"
```

The idea here is that I'm asking UNIX to search the user agent value for MSIE: if there's a match then the variable x will contain the USER-AGENT. If not, it'll be blank and will match "", the null string. Figure 13-5 shows what this program outputs from Navigator.

Figure 13-5: A page enhanced for both browsers!

Try this online:
http://www.intuitive.com/coolweb/apps/browser.cgi

Sending and reading data

There's another variable in the environment set that's very important for interactive pages, something that so far hasn't had any value. The string, or sequence of characters, is QUERY_STRING.

If you've gotten this far in the book, I think it's safe for me to assume that you've spent some time traveling about on the Web. I also bet you've been to Yahoo! or another site where it asked for some data, then gave you a page of information based on what you specified. There are two ways to accomplish this transfer of information from the browser to the server, as I'll explain in a bit, but for now let's focus on the URL itself.

Go to Yahoo! (http://www.yahoo.com) and enter a word or phrase for it to search. When you get the search results, you'll see a page of matches as you'd expect. Most importantly, however, you'll also see a slightly weird URL. If I search for "akron" the URL shown in the Address box of the browser is:

```
http://search.yahoo.com/bin/search?p=akron
```

This is reasonably consistent with what I explained way back in Chapter 2 about URLs: the basic URL here is

`http://search.yahoo.com/bin/search`

but there's a new twist. The '?' indicates that there's information to send to the remote system, and the p=akron is actually the value sent to the server from the client. For the CGI program on the server, the QUERY_STRING variable will *contain the exact information specified after the question mark.*

Now, let's try another script, one that actually will assume that you're going to enter a special URL (for now) that includes some information following the '?' symbol:

```
echo "Content-type: text/html"
echo ""

echo "<BODY BGCOLOR=white>"
echo "You sent me $QUERY_STRING"
echo "</BODY>"
```

This script is actually available live on the Web, as query.cgi, so if I invoke it as exactly that, but append "?A-Yummy-Cookie," the results will be as shown in Figure 13-6. Note particularly the Location: box under the strip of buttons in the screen shot.

Figure 13-6: Information sent via the query-string value.

You can try this script online:
`http://www.intuitive.com/coolweb/apps/query.cgi`

There are some neat things you can do now that you know this query-string URL format. Perhaps you're working on a Web site that's all about the gorilla. Now you can add a link to your Web page that would automatically search Yahoo! for gorillas without the user entering that string:

```
<A HREF=http://www.yahoo.com/bin/search?p=gorilla>More
Gorilla Info</A>
```

Overall, however, it'd be a whole lot easier if you could actually ask the user for information and then process it once you've been told something. That's the exact purpose of HTML forms.

An Introduction to HTML Forms

Forms enable you to build Web pages that enable users to actually enter information and send it back to the server site. The forms can range from a single text box for entering a search string, like you see on Yahoo!, to a complex multipart worksheet that offers powerful search or submission capabilities.

Two basic types of forms exist in HTML — GET and POST — and they revolve around the way the information is sent to the CGI script back at the server. I'll explain the difference in the next section, but for now let's look at the design and specification of forms themselves.

HTML forms are surrounded by the FORM tag, which is used as: <FORM ACTION=url METHOD=method> and </FORM> tags. The URL specified with the ACTION attribute points to the remote file or application used for digesting the information, and the METHOD *method* is either GET or POST.

In a nutshell, GET works best for small amounts of data; the information in the form is tucked into a URL that's returned to the Web server just like you saw in the previous examples. By contrast, a POST form sends the information back as an actual data stream, allowing for considerably more information from the user.

Inside the <FORM> your Web page can contain any standard HTML formatting information, graphics, links to other pages, and a bunch of new tags specific to forms. The various new tags enable you to define the many different elements of your form, as shown in Table 13-2.

The sheer number of different attributes within the <INPUT> tag can be confusing, but the way to understand the overloaded <INPUT> tag is to realize that although the entire form system was supposed to be included within <INPUT> specifiers, SELECT and TEXTAREA just didn't fit in.

Table 13-2: FORM Tags and Options in HTML

Tag	Meaning
`<INPUT>`	Text or other data-input field
`TYPE =`	type of INPUT entry field
`NAME =`	symbolic name of field value
`VALUE =`	default content of text field
`CHECKED =`	button/box checked by default
`SIZE =`	number of characters in text field
`MAXLENGTH =`	maximum characters accepted
`<SELECT>`	Grouped check boxes
`<TEXTAREA>`	Multiline text-entry field

Current Web browsers support nine different `<INPUT>` types, each of which produces a different type of output. The following are user input types:

➥ `TEXT` is the default, with `SIZE` used to specify the default size of the box that is created, in character units. A `SIZE=30` specifier would produce a 30-character wide text box.

➥ `PASSWORD` is a text field with the user input displayed as asterisks or bullets for security. `MAXLENGTH` can be used to specify the maximum number of characters entered in the password.

➥ `CHECKBOX` offers a single (ungrouped) check box; `CHECKED` enables you to specify whether the box should be checked by default. `VALUE` specifies the text associated with the check box.

➥ `HIDDEN` lets you send information to the program processing the user input without the user actually seeing it on their display; particularly useful if the page with the HTML form is also generated by a CGI script.

➥ `FILE` gives you a way to let users actually submit files to the server. They can either type in the filename or click on the 'browse...' button to select it from their computer.

➥ `RADIO` displays a toggle button; different radio buttons with the same `NAME=` value are grouped automatically, so that only one button in the group can be selected.

Note that the `type=file` is still experimental, difficult to program on the server end, and only supported by Navigator. You can find out more about this funky tag by popping over to `ftp://ds.internic.net/rfc/rfc1867.txt` and reading the official specification.

The following are the most important `<INPUT>` types:

➡ `SUBMIT` produces a push button in the form that, when clicked, submits the entire form content to the remote server.

➡ `IMAGE` is identical to `SUBMIT` but instead of a button, it enables you to specify a graphical image for the submission or 'enter' button.

➡ `RESET` enables users to clear the contents of all fields in the form.

`<SELECT>` is a pop-up menu of choices, with a `</SELECT>` partner tag and `<OPTION>` denoting each of the items therein. You must specify a `NAME` that uniquely identifies the overall selection within the `<SELECT>` tag itself. In fact, all form tags must have their `NAME` specified and all names must be unique. You'll see why when we consider how information is sent to the server.

You can also specify a `SIZE` with the `<SELECT>` tag, indicating how many items should be displayed at once, and `MULTIPLE`, indicating that it's okay for users to select more than one option. If a default value exists, add `SELECTED` to the `<OPTION>` tag (as in `<OPTION SELECTED>`) to indicate that value.

Let's have a look at that before we look at the other `<FORM>` tags.

A pop-up menu of Web pages

Here's a useful trick that's used all over the Web, from the Microsoft home page to my own company's page. It's a pop-up menu of page titles as a shortcut to navigating the site. There are two parts to this; the HTML source that's included on the page with the shortcuts, and the CGI script on the server that receives the request and turns it into a request for a specific Web page.

First off, the necessary items for the Web page itself:

```
<FORM METHOD="GET" ACTION="relayto.cgi">
<B>Some Fun Web Pages:</B>
<SELECT NAME="url">
<OPTION VALUE="http://www.intuitive.com/">Intuitive Systems
<OPTION VALUE="http://www.internet-mall.com/">The Internet
Mall
```

```
<OPTION VALUE="http://www.yahoo.com/">Yahoo!
<OPTION VALUE="http://www.altavista.digital.com">Alta Vista
<OPTION VALUE="http://www.cnet.com/">C|Net
</SELECT>
<INPUT TYPE=submit value="Go!">
</FORM>
```

This formats to a simple pop-up box as shown in Figure 13-7.

Figure 13-7: Pop-up menu with my favorite Web sites listed.

The other half of this is the CGI script on the server end. In this case it'll take advantage of a trick — if instead of using the `Content-type:` identifier you specify `Location:url` then it tells the browser to immediately connect to that site instead. Here's the entire server script, relayto.cgi:

```
if [ "$QUERY_STRING" = "" ] ; then
   echo "Content-type: text/html"
   echo ""
   echo "402 Relayto needs a valid URL"
else
   url="`echo $QUERY_STRING | sed
's/%3A/:/g;s/%2F/\//g;s/url=//'`"
   echo Location: $url
   echo ""
fi
```

It's remarkably simple, given the slick functionality it enables you to add to your Web site. The only slight confusion is the line that unwraps the URL from the query string, and that's because when the information is sent from the browser to the server, the http protocol specifies that certain characters must be sent in a safe form. The : of the URL is encoded as %3A and the / as %2F. The *sed* command helps us translate these sequences back into the original characters, and also strips out the url= portion of the QUERY_STRING.

You can play with this tag in other ways too; you might have a script called testme.htm on your server that has one line

```
echo "Location: http://www.idgbooks.com/"
```

and any time someone visits testme.htm they'd immediately pop over to the IDG Books Worldwide site.

More form tags

The other unusual tag you can include in a form is `<TEXTAREA>`, which enables you to create large spaces for users to type in their information. It has several options, starting with the mandatory `<NAME>` tag that denotes the symbolic name of the field. You also can specify ROWS and COLS to indicate the size of the resulting text field with units in characters, and WRAP means that the text the user enters should automatically wrap when they get to the right margin. `<TEXTAREA>` also is a paired tag, partnered by `</TEXTAREA>`. Any text between the two tags is displayed as the default information in the text box.

A simple HTML form might be one for users to enter messages for you:

```
<FORM ACTION=query.cgi method=get>
<B>Please let us know what you think of our new Web
site!</B>
<p>
<TEXTAREA NAME=feedback wrap rows=5 cols=60>It's
great!</TEXTAREA>
<P>
<INPUT TYPE=submit value="send it in"><INPUT TYPE=reset
value="clear what I've typed">
</FORM>
```

The resultant display is shown in Figure 13-8. Bring this example up on your system from the CD-ROM and try entering different information to see how it's wrapped for the transmission to the server.

These examples are all pretty simple so far, but forms can be quite complex. Consider the following HTML text and the way it's displayed. This form could be used as the beginning of a Web order-counter form for Dave's Virtual Online Deli:

Netscape: email.htm

| Back | Forward | Home | | Reload | Images | Open | Print | Find | | Stop | | N |

Please let us know what you think of our new Web site!

It's great!

[send it in] [clear what I've typed]

Document : Done.

Figure 13-8: A simple user input form.

```
<FORM ACTION="process-form.cgi" METHOD=POST>
<B>Dave's Virtual Deli - The Order Menu</B>
<HR>
Your name? <INPUT TYPE=text NAME="name" SIZE=30>
<BR>
Secret code: <INPUT TYPE=password NAME="password">
<HR>
<B>What kind of sandwich? </B>
<SELECT NAME="Sandwich">
<OPTION>(none)
<OPTION>Turkey on a croissant
<OPTION>Ham and cheese on wheat
<OPTION>Veggie on nine-grain
</SELECT>
<BR>
<B>Any soup? </B>
<SELECT NAME="Soup">
<OPTION>(none)
<OPTION>Tomato and rice
<OPTION>Cream of asparagus
<OPTION>Lentil Madness
</SELECT>
<P>
How you'll pay:
<INPUT TYPE=radio NAME="payment" VALUE="visa">Visa
<INPUT TYPE=radio NAME="payment"
VALUE="mastercard">MasterCard
<INPUT TYPE=radio NAME="payment" VALUE="account"
CHECKED>Account
<INPUT TYPE=radio NAME="payment" VALUE="dishes">Wash dishes
<HR>
<INPUT TYPE=checkbox NAME="firstorder" VALUE="firstorder">
First time ordering from the Virtual Deli?<BR>
<INPUT TYPE=image SRC="submit.gif">
<INPUT TYPE=reset NAME="reset" VALUE="clear">
</FORM>
```

Figure 13-9 shows the preceding form with some of the information filled out by a hungry user. The secret code value would be displayed in bullets, even though the user entered an actual password, and the pop-up menu for sandwich and soup types is automatically included by the browser itself. The user could opt to pay by washing dishes, having seen that the default option was to put the bill on his account (as specified by the CHECKED option in the HTML).

Figure 13-9: The Virtual Deli order form.

Note the SRC attribute for the TYPE=image alternative to the 'submit' button in the example above!

Before I leave the fun and interesting area of forms entry, I'll provide one more example. If you want to have a single entry box for search capability, you can use the HTML shortcut <ISINDEX>, which produces a single input box at the top, prefaced by the default text This is a searchable index. Enter search keywords:, and surrounded by horizontal rules, as follows:

```
You've found the Oxford English Dictionary online!
<ISINDEX>
You can browse this or look up a term directly.
```

This HTML snippet produces the screen shown in Figure 13-10. This isn't necessarily preferable to the more complex form items, because you have little control of layout, submission form name, and similar items. In some applications, however, the ease of generation can be quite valuable.

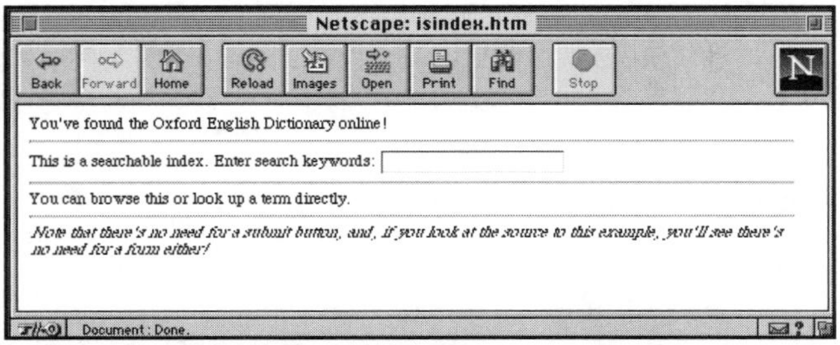

Figure 13-10: <ISINDEX> adds an instant input box.

Just as valuable, <ISINDEX> is an example of a single text-input field that enables most browsers to map the Return or Enter key to the SUBMIT option. Instead of having to click on the 'submit' button (which, remember, can have any text you'd like by specifying that in the <INPUT TYPE=submit VALUE=your text> tag or you can even replace it with a graphic by using the type=image option), typing the information and pressing Return or Enter submits the information from the form to the remote Web server. If you don't like the default prompt, use the attribute prompt="your prompt" to change it.

Receiving Information from Forms

Forms are standard HTML for the most part. Whether your server is a Windows NT box, a UNIX mainframe, or a Macintosh, the tags needed to define an input form are identical. When the time comes to consider how to process the information that users are submitting, however, you get into some sticky, system-dependent questions. With image maps, you saw that the format of the map file depends on the type of server that you're running. CERN and NCSA servers have different expectations for the information in the map file.

The interface behind forms is even more complex, because the very environment that you work with when processing the form depends heavily on the operating system used on the server. Scripting a gateway (hence the *common gateway interface*, or *CGI*, moniker for these scripts) is dramatically different on a UNIX system than on a Windows machine or a Macintosh — not to mention Windows NT, Amiga, and other types of servers.

The biggest difference involves what programming languages and tools are available. On a UNIX system, it's quite simple to create a shell script, Perl script, or even a C program or two to process and act on input. Shell scripts aren't a possibility on a Mac server, however, so AppleScript or MacPerl are used instead. Fortunately, the Perl-interpreted programming language is also available on PCs, and that's what I recommend that you use if you have a PC server.

Perl is an interpreted programming language designed for working with text and text files. The language, created by Larry Wall, is intended to be practical rather than beautiful which is its major shortcoming: it can be a bit cryptic if you're not used to reading C-like programs.

Find out more about Perl: The Perl home page is at:
`http://www.perl.com/`
there's also a terrific Perl FAQ at:
`ftp://ftp.cis.ufl.edu/pub/perl/faq/FAQ`
You can also get a complete Perl interpreter for your Mac. MacPerl is available at:
`ftp://ftp.cs.colorado.edu/pub/perl/CPAN/ports/mac/`

As I said earlier, the FORM method has two options: GET and POST. Now I can explain the difference between these two. When a GET method is used, the information is appended to the URL and handed, as such, to the script. All information shows up encoded and stored in the QUERY_STRING environment variable. POST causes the information to be sent to the server as a data stream rather than a single environment variable. Because of this, POST is much better when significant amounts of information are to be transmitted.

To keep the scope of this explanation manageable, I'll stick with the GET method to illustrate how the forms shown earlier would be sent to the CGI server script. First, the deli order would be built and submitted as follows:

```
name=Umberto+Eco&password=foucault&Sandwich=Veggie+on+nine-
grain&Soup=Lentil+Madness&payment=visa&firstorder=
firstorder&x=86&y=34
```

The + encodes spaces to keep the URL legal and each field=value pair is separated by an ampersand. (Remember, spaces and carriage returns aren't allowed in any URL.) Also, you can see that the password was shielded from prying eyes when the user entered the information, but when this information is sent to the server, it's sent as clear text. It would be up to the server script to unravel this tangle of information and process it.

The output of any CGI script is more HTML than is displayed on the user's screen after the user has submitted the form and it's processed by the server. A rough template of a script, therefore, might be like the following example:

```
replace all '+' with ' '
replace all '&' with a return
send request to kitchen
and return the following to the user:
<HTML>
```

```
<TITLE>It's Cookin'!</TITLE>
Thank you for your order. We're now busy preparing
the meal that you selected. We invite
you to stop by the <B>Virtual Deli</B> in about
15 minutes to pick up your food.
<HR>
<A HREF="deli.html">Back to the Deli</A>
</HTML>
```

Of course, processing the information is more complex. Following is a portable Perl CGI script that processes the virtual deli form information and echoes back a few of the key items to confirm the order:

```
print "Content-type: text/html\n\n";

print "<HTML>\n";
print "<BODY BGCOLOR=white>\n";

$buffer = $ENV{'QUERY_STRING'};    # grab info from
QUERY_STRING

# Split the name-value pairs into a dynamically allocated
array
@info = split(/&/, $buffer);

foreach $pair (@info) {
  ($name, $value) = split(/=/, $pair);
  # extract the % encoded info and "+" -> " " mapping
  $value =~ tr/+/ /;
  $value =~ s/%([a-fA-F0-9][a-fA-F0-9])/pack("C",
hex($1))/eg;
  # save it in DATA array information
  $DATA{$name} = $value;
}

# now we can echo back their order to confirm

print "<H2>$DATA{'name'}</H2>";
print "You ordered: ";
print "<B>$DATA{'Soup'}</B> and
<B>$DATA{'Sandwich'}</B>.<P>\n";
print "You'll be paying for your order with
$DATA{'payment'}";
print "<P>\n";
print "<HR><A HREF=\"home.html\">let's go home</A>\n";
print "</BODY></HTML>\n"
```

Notice that the variables I'm using for the output have names that are identical to those in the original HTML form (that is, the payment information field was identified as NAME=payment, and when unpacked, the variable was referenced in the Perl script as $DATA{'payment'} once it was unpacked and stored in the Perl DATA space). HTML formatting tags can also be embedded in print statements, as you can see. Figure 13-11 shows the result of sending a filled-in form to this data processing CGI script.

Figure 13-11: *Thanks for your order!*

You could change the above script to get the data from a METHOD=POST form by replacing the line $buffer = $ENV{'QUERY_STRING'} with the Perl instruction to read from the input stream: read(STDIN, $buffer, $ENV{'CONTENT_LENGTH'});

To see all the different options for CGI processing tools organized by platform, hop over to:
http://www.yahoo.com/Computers/World_Wide_Web/Programming
Quite a few helper programs are available, too, thank goodness, but don't be worried if this seems complex — it is. The good news is that many of the larger Web page hosting companies, or Internet Service Providers in the lingo, offer a set of useful CGI scripts that you can use without having to do any custom programming.

One final tip: when you're debugging your forms, you can utilize a program I've written called echoback which will show you exactly what would be sent to a CGI script from the page, regardless of whether it's a GET or POST form. Point your Web page to:
http://www.intuitive.com/apps/echoback.cgi

Moving On

In this chapter, I gave you a wealth of ideas about how to create interactive Web pages and obtain information from the viewer through forms and CGI programming. Chapter 14 answers a question that might have been bugging you since you started reading: "What about all these fancy HTML editor programs?"

Automatic HTML Generation

At this juncture you might well be saying to yourself, "that's all very well and good, but my gosh! There's gotta be some software out there to help with this process!" In fact, Internet-related software seems to be one of the hottest spots in the software marketplace with big companies like Adobe, Netscape, and Claris competing with little firms, including SoftQuad and Bare Bones Software.

Adobe PageMill and SiteMill

Netscape Navigator Gold

Claris HomePage

Gonet goLive

Bare Bones Software BBEdit

Miracle Software Web Weaver

And a cast of thousands . . .

I'll be honest with you right up front: none of these programs alleviate the need for a basic understanding of the hypertext markup language and how it works. While most of the top sites on the Web are created by people digging around in the HTML and tweaking things to their exact specifications, there are unquestionably a few programs that can prove a dramatic and important aid in creating documents for the World Wide Web.

The Internet is a fluid environment, and programs written for Web page design are changing on a weekly basis. As a result, I've tried herein to highlight some of the strengths of each of these programs while minimizing any discussion of weaknesses or design problems, because odds are good they'll be fixed by the time you read this chapter. Focus on the screen shots here and the basic concept of how you work with the program to develop a Web site.

Adobe PageMill and SiteMill

Adobe has always been a powerhouse with desktop publishing tools and utilities, starting years ago with its introduction of the PostScript language for precisely defining information on a printed page. Since then, the firm has become a mainstay in the industry with excellent products like PhotoShop and Illustrator. When the first wave of interest in the Web appeared, Adobe acquired a small firm and repackaged its slick little Web page editor as Adobe PageMill. Now on its second major release, PageMill is still in many ways the definitive WYSIWYG Web page layout program. The companion program, SiteMill, is much more useful in my view; it offers you an easy way to manage an entire project comprised of lots of HTML files, graphics, and more. It can also automatically cross-check all references to ensure that there aren't any broken links on your site.

Even with its powerful set of capabilities, PageMill exhibits many of the problems inherent when relying on software programs to build your Web pages, as you can see in Figure 14-1; while Navigator supports specification of font by name (`<font face="Courier">` for example), PageMill doesn't recognize the tag and displays it as an unknown tag. It also doesn't understand color by name and offers only the most minimal help for creating tables or editing the source to your Web page. All HTML extensions for Microsoft Internet Explorer program are unknown to PageMill, including HTML 3.2 standard style sheets, the fun marquee tag, and inline frames.

It's not so much that these specific problems are bad, they'll probably be fixed by the time you read this, but that it's a demonstration of how page editing packages seem to be perpetually one generation behind the best browser applications available.

SiteMill is less susceptible to changes in HTML or Web specifications, because it's a site manager rather than a page editor. It enables you to view an entire site, a set of documents, graphics, and off-site links in a pretty cool way, at least if you're a fan of lists. Figure 14-2 shows how SiteMill offers an interesting view of the CoolWeb HTML samples on the CD-ROM. The top window is the list of files in the project and buttons that pop-up lists of 'points to' and 'has pointer from' items in the files; the bottom window offers a succinct summary of all external references.

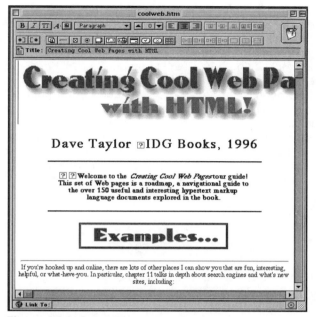

Figure 14-1: PageMill examines the CoolWeb Home Page.

Figure 14-2: SiteMill offers an overview of your site.

Working with SiteMill is a bit of a drag, because there's really no single overview window or graphical representation of the site. Instead you are forced to dig through various different lists, clicking on 'points to' and 'has pointer from' buttons to reveal lists and more. Because SiteMill is intimately attached to PageMill (if you buy SiteMill you get PageMill free), it's awkward to really exploit the full capabilities of the program: if you double-click on a URL to open that page, PageMill enables you to edit it, but is likely to rewrite your HTML source when it saves the file. And it may rewrite it incorrectly, or at least with a very different appearance. Bad karma, and potentially enough for you not to work with the program at all. Even with these limitations, SiteMill is the best bet for a Mac project and site management tool, and as it evolves along with PageMill, it will remain a good bet for future tool users. Check out the PageMill and SiteMill spot at: `http://www.adobe.com/`

Netscape Navigator Gold

Philosophically, the computer industry has shown an amusing oscillation between having one big program that solves all your problems and having lots of little programs that work together intelligently, offering you solutions to your problems, but in a way that's easier to upgrade. Until the monster Web browsers came onto the scene, the Internet business was definitely deep into the modular zone, with separate programs for reading and sending e-mail, for reading Usenet newsgroups, for using Gopher, for connecting to remote sites via telnet, for downloading files from a remote server, and for editing information locally. The Web revolution has changed that, and both Microsoft and Netscape are again offering massive applications that purport to solve all your problems at once. Navigator can not only show you Web pages, but also gopher sites, FTP sites, your e-mail, and it even enables you to read Usenet news. It should therefore come as no surprise that the Gold edition of Navigator also includes a built-in HTML page editor.

To switch from the browser to the Navigator editing environment with the current page you're viewing, you need merely click on the 'pencil' button on the toolbar. You can choose any HTML file by using Open file in editor from the File menu. To create a new page, choose New document from the File menu. The editor looks a lot like Navigator, as you can see in Figure 14-3. Even the links that you've visited in the browser are shown in a different color in the editor — something no other HTML editor does — which is a helpful way to ensure that the links you're working with point to the pages you've just visited.

One cool feature of Navigator Gold is that you can instantly be editing a local copy of *any* Web page, so if you're cruisin' the Net and see a page that looks interesting or unusual, you can easily peer inside with a single click on the 'pencil' button.

Figure 14-3: Cool Web as viewed in Navigator Gold's Edit view.

This editing environment is quite good for understanding font specifications, background colors by name, and more. The program itself still has some serious deficiencies, particularly when it comes to editing a page with form elements. Notice the number of broken HTML graphics shown in Figure 14-4 when I tried to work with the Virtual Deli order form as shown in Chapter 13.

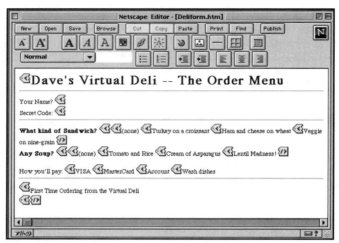

Figure 14-4: Broken links from FORM elements.

Navigator Gold is also only a page editor. There's no assistance for creating frame-based sites, nor is there any way to verify links, look at an entire set of pages at once, or any other more advanced features. You can't even directly edit the HTML source without launching SimpleText or another external program. Nonetheless, you can get Navigator Gold free from the Netscape Web site, and the program includes access to lots of page templates for you to examine. You can visit the Navigator Gold Authors Guide online at:

```
http://home.netscape.com/eng/mozilla/3.0/handbook/authoring
/navgold.htm
```

Claris HomePage

Claris HomePage is an extremely capable Web page development program that offers support for frames, tables, a wide variety of HTML extensions, image map creation, and much more. A great feature of HomePage is that you can directly edit the HTML source of the page you're developing without launching another program.

HomePage lets you set various page attributes, such as background color or pattern, although it lacks controls to make these attributes the defaults on all pages in a site. (This problem may be solved long term with HTML's new cascading style sheets, as discussed in Chapter 15.) HomePage has a built-in browser to preview pages you're developing, but it doesn't work with frame-enabled pages.

One frustrating decision that Claris and other Mac HTML developers made is that Netscape Navigator is the only browser worth tracking for HTML extensions. Web pages are designed for the larger online community, and Microsoft Internet Explorer is an excellent and popular solution for Windows users. Almost all the extensions unique to Explorer are ignored by HomePage, however, leaving Mac Web page developers with a distinct disadvantage when compared to their competition based on the PC platform.

I'd like to see Claris add a multipage project feature where people working on a site can either have a master set of style attributes or a master style document for that project. This would enable site developers to automatically assign background colors, headers, footers, and other common material automatically to any page created for a specific project. HTML authors would find the feature a tremendous time-saver.

Even with these limitations, Claris Home Page is the best Web page editor I've seen yet on the Macintosh. Being able to easily edit and tweak the HTML source code while having an attractive WYSIWYG editing environment is valuable.

What's also not included with this Web page editor is a way to step beyond just the page that you're editing and get a bigger picture of what's going on with your site, nor are there any validation utilities to check links or verify the continued existence of other sites on the Web. It also doesn't support font-by-name or any of the new style sheet extensions.

Figure 14-5 shows Claris HomePage enabling me to edit the zero-border frames page from Chapter 12, with the actual editable default.htm page in the background.

If you want to build complex pages, HomePage offers some valuable features, but its lack of site management tools might prove frustrating as the complexity of your projects increases. That's where I think Adobe SiteMill is so helpful. It's a good starting point. Visit HomePage's home page at:

`http://www.claris.com/products/clarispage/clarispage.html`

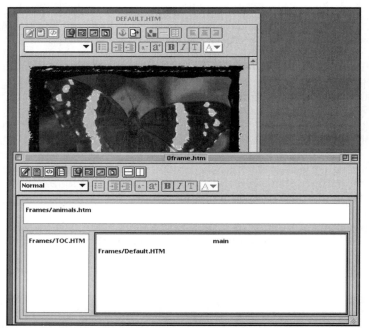

Figure 14-5: A framed page in HomePage.

Gonet golive

Based on the metaphor of a work space and toolbar, the oddly named golive Web page editor adds a floating gallery of files, graphics, and URLs. It also has some major drawbacks in the version I looked at for this chapter (version 1.1), problems that cause me to suggest that you think carefully before deciding it might be your HTML editing solution.

Golive helps you develop Web pages with a rich set of HTML capabilities, including frames, with all its tag formats based on what gonet describes as the language understood by Netscape's Navigator 3.0 browser release. There are a number of tags actually supported by Navigator that aren't understood by golive, however, most importantly including tables, basefont, and the <TT> proportional tag. Just about all the fun Microsoft Internet Explorer extensions are unknown to the program.

Pages can include HTML that golive doesn't understand; all unknown tags are shown in red, in "raw html" format. The program supports Java and Quicktime3D, but only in simple ways; common style for scripts in HTML files has them wrapped in comments but golive hides all HTML comments so you don't even know there's a script associated with the `<SCRIPT>` tag.

While the thought of a purely visual Web page editing environment is compelling, HTML is evolving so quickly that design tools must support both quick layout prototyping and direct viewing and editing of the underlying HTML. Golive offers a half-baked outline viewer as a separate program for this capability, but you can't switch from WYSIWYG (what you see is what you get, hopefully) to outline view, and worse, the outline program tends to ignore large chunks of HTML test files, showing them as text rather than with the structured outline tags. By the time you read this, however, I expect that it will have a new source-level editor available.

While primarily an HTML page editor, golive also has support for projects that are comprised of multiple files, text, and graphics. With a multifile project, however, the program doesn't check inter-file links, but whether the files reside within the same folder. An almost useless feature when compared to Adobe SiteMill's verification capability, which is extremely useful.

When working in frames, golive offers considerable support, but surprisingly neglects a 'select' option for letting the developer find specific HTML documents to assign each of the frames. On the other hand, being able to double-click on a frame and have the associated HTML document opened is very useful. You can see how it displays a frames-based site in Figure 14-6.

Golive includes a lot of great ideas and the graphics and design of the application are terrific. A valuable and robust HTML editor comes from easy support for the variety of tasks a designer must tackle, and the combination of lacking support for tables, the awkward grafting of a source editing capability, and the lack of support for Internet Explorer tags leads us to look eagerly for the next release. Check them out online at: `http://www.gonet.com/`

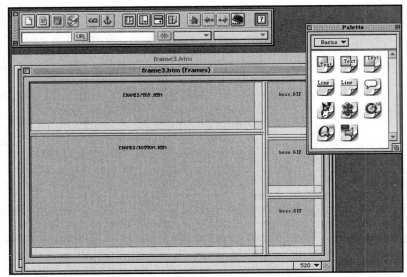

Figure 14-6: A frames-based development project in golive.

Miracle Software World Wide Web Weaver

This program is worth checking out, particularly since the company also has a pretty darn good shareware HTML editor (HTML Weaver) that is the foundation of the commercial World Wide Web Weaver. Even better, you can download a fully functional demo version of the program from their Web site to try it yourself.

Unlike the other editors I've shown you so far, WWW Weaver is really a fancy source-level editor that enables you to develop your Web pages quickly in an environment that makes it easy to see what's going on. As you can see in Figure 14-7, pages are broken into a head, body, and foot section and all HTML tags are displayed in a different color to the actual text on the page.

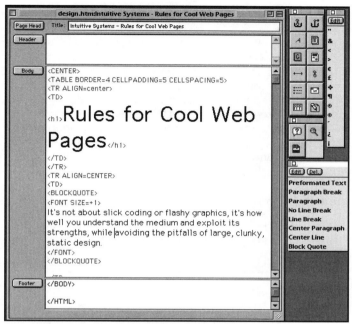

Figure 14-7: A colorful view of your Web page.

WWW Weaver includes support for tables and knows quite a bit about the modern HTML tags. The latest version also includes support for frames, but you're left in the dust if you want to do any sort of advanced scripting in JavaScript, VBScript, or similar. One huge problem is graphics aren't displayed in the editor, and the `<IMG>` tag isn't set off with a different color. In fact, there's no way to specify that different tags should be displayed in different colors, which would be a very useful addition.

On the plus side, WWW Weaver includes a very powerful search and replace capability, and the capability to import or export for DOS/Windows and UNIX text files (they have different end-of-line characters than a Mac). All text attributes are shown on-screen, leading to a what-you-see-is-vaguely-what-you-get editing style. You can also very easily create your own floating palettes containing your favorite HTML tags and use the program's scrapbook to retain useful HTML snippets from page to page.

All in all, World Wide Web Weaver is worth checking out as a text-based HTML editor, but if you really want the Mac powerhouse of source level editing, BBEdit is a strong competitor. Visit Miracle Software online at: http://webster.northnet.org/

Bare Bones Software BBEdit

Like World Wide Web Weaver, BBEdit is a source-level HTML editor without any WYSIWYG capabilities. Like WWW Weaver, BBEdit shows you HTML files with the tags colored so you can see what's going on. That's where the comparison ends, because BBEdit is a tremendously powerful application that can be customized a million different ways. The floating palettes offer instant access to dozens of different HTML tags, and you can very easily add your own tags or write your own scripts in the BBEdit scripting language. For example, maybe you'd like to select a headline in your document, and then with the click of a button have it turned into an anchor for an internal document reference; that'd be an easy task for BBEdit scripting.

The basic view of an HTML document is show in Figure 14-8.

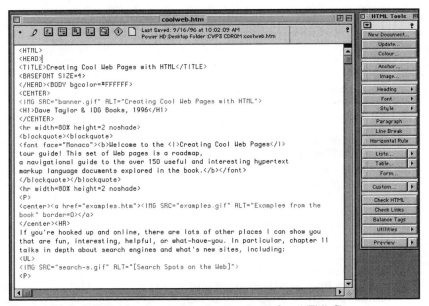

Figure 14-8: BBEdit gives you a bare-bones view of an HTML file.

Notice the floating palette of HTML commands on the top right. Take a close look, actually, since there are some tremendous capabilities represented, not the least of which is the capability to check the HTML syntax of the document to ensure it's accurate. A quick check of one of my own HTML documents reveals a variety of problems, as shown in Figure 14-9. Note how I clicked on an error and had the offending snippet shown in the lower pane of the window.

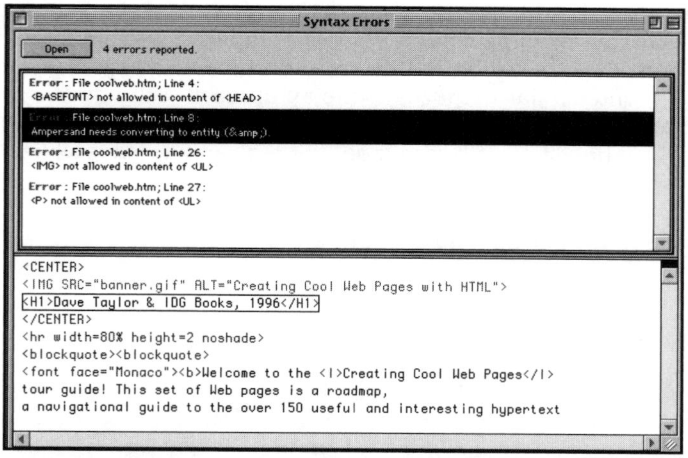

Figure 14-9: BBEdit reveals that my clean HTML still has a few stray problems.

You add anchors, lists, and other complex tags by either clicking on the appropriate entry in the floating palette or using the pull-down menus. Taking an e-mail address and making it a live link is a simple matter of selecting the address then clicking on anchor... and accepting the default action. The program is smart enough to add the mailto: preface within the HTML, and you can even specify whether you want your tags to be in upper or lower case. Another neat feature: BBEdit automatically gives you a quick index of your document by listing all headers in a pop-up menu. Choose a header off-screen and it's instantly displayed.

TIP

In the grand scheme, BBEdit offers a powerful and very capable environment for developing Web documents, but it's certainly not for the faint of heart. I use it and find it a valuable tool. On the other hand, you have lots of knowledge now that you've read this far in the book, so you should be comfortable opening up a new page and creating a Web masterpiece. Don't be fooled, however, BBEdit is popular, but it might well prove too bare-boned for people looking for a simple WYSIWYG drag-and-drop development environment. You can download a demo version of this excellent program at:

`http://www.barebones.com/bbedit.html`

A Cast of Thousands . . .

Between shareware writers and companies still working their way into the marketplace, there are a remarkable number of other programs and filters making their way onto the market at this point. Other programs are shipping today but I hope that the selection I've explored herein gives you a good idea of the kind of approach most companies — and individual programmers — are taking in this area. Either way, keep your eye on *Macworld* and similar magazines to stay abreast of the developments in this hot area. It's really a combination of the programs I'm still seeking; the WYSIWYG capabilities of HomePage, the text-editing capabilities of BBEdit, and the verification tools included with SiteMill.

Here are a few other packages worth a brief mention.

Hot Metal Pro

SoftQuad, the company that makes Hot Metal Pro, has an interesting perspective on HTML editing; it offers an HTML source editor, like BBEdit, but instead of showing you the actual tags, it replaces them with small graphical icons. You'll either love this or hate it. The program is quite popular and gets positive reviews both in the user community and from major publications. You can get a quick idea of its approach in Figure 14-10, which highlights the source edit view. The program also has a very capable WYSIWYG view like HomePage and PageMill.

Check it out at:
`http://www.softquad.com`

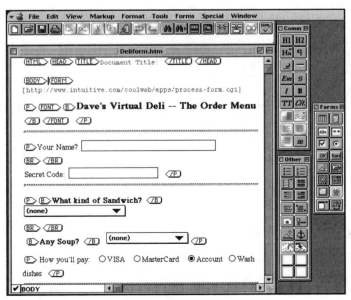

Figure 14-10: Hot Web page design with Hot Metal Pro.

Adobe Acrobat

One of the hottest battles in the computer industry in the past few years has been over portable document distribution formats. It seems like there are at least six different firms with powerful solutions for sending complex multifont documents to people across disparate hardware platforms. Sounds a lot like the problem that HTML solves too, doesn't it? The bright folk at Adobe certainly thought so, and they've negotiated with the Netscape team to have a version of Netscape Navigator that will include an inline Adobe Acrobat reader. This means that you'll be able to send out complex documents preformatted and saved in the Acrobat format, and users will still have live buttons, hot areas, and other hypertext characteristics, while locked into exactly the presentation form you desire.

Is this a good strategy, and will it help the world? I'm a bit skeptical, frankly. I think the real value of the Web is that there's an easy and powerful underlying language enabling everyone to easily create and publish information. Sending massive binaries that are versions of documents in Acrobat format defeats the entire purpose, and definitely will cut out all the people who don't enjoy a fast connection to the Internet, among others. Your conclusion might vary. Adobe has a nice Web site at: `http://www.adobe.com`

FrameMaker

FrameMaker is a powerful publishing tool for documents both large and small, with a tremendous number of layout options and powerful style sheets. Many of the most complex technical documents are now designed and developed within FrameMaker. Starting with the next version, Frame Technology will be adding an integrated HTML document conversion tool that enables you to define mappings from FrameMaker paragraph styles to HTML format tags. FrameMaker documents can already have hypertext links, so there'll also be a mechanism whereby those links can be translated into HTML-style links, both those within a document and those pointing to other documents or information on the Internet.

Online Utility Archives

There are a ton of specific applications, frankly, and the best way to learn about them is to check out the offerings at a few of the best archival sites on the Web. One of my favorites, both for its terrific graphical design and exhaustive indexing, is the Mac Internet SW Starting Point page at `http://www.comvista.com/net/Directory.html`

If that doesn't have what you seek, try clnet's excellent shareware.com, at:
http://www.shareware.com/
Neither of those doing the trick for you? Sheesh, you're a tough audience. How about one more possibility: Mac Helpers at:
http://www.tiac.net/users/mdw/imap/intro.html

Ultimately, whether one of these tools can help you produce more attractive Web documents faster is dependent on many factors, including your own working style and your knowledge of the HTML formatting tags. There will doubtless be beautiful Web documents produced by each of these tools and ugly, confusing ones too. It's up to you: cool Web pages are a function of your layout and design more than anything.

One thing is for sure: there's a lot happening in this market niche, so we can all expect better tools to evolve quickly.

Moving On

In this chapter, I gave you an overview of some of the most popular HTML editors, offering you a glimpse at the strengths and weaknesses of this type of application. Your experience may vary quite a bit, but the holy grail of a perfect WYSIWYG Web page and Web site development tool is still unattained. Chapter 15 explores some up-and-coming Web page technologies that can make your site even more exciting.

Where to Next?

The Next Big Thing: Style Sheets

Of all the changes that you can expect to see in the next generation of the hypertext markup language, none will be more pervasive and important than style sheets. It's a step away from the original paradigm of the Web, where you'd have 'suggestions' for formatting like <STRONG> and <H1> and the browser (as configured by the user) would decide exactly how it should appear on the screen. Instead, style sheets will let you define the exact size of the typeface to use, the color, the typeface itself, and lots more for any given HTML tag.

TIP As of this writing, only Microsoft Internet Explorer supports style sheets.

All of this magic is buried in HTML comments that are themselves buried in the `<STYLE>` tag. Why buried in comments? So browsers that don't understand styles won't get confused, like how JavaScript and VBScripts are included in Web documents.

For example, say you'd like to have all header level one tags 16-point, Arial bold, and green. Here's the style tag:

```
<STYLE>
<!-
    H1 { font: 16 pt "Arial" bold; color: green }
->
</STYLE>
```

There's a remarkable amount of different information that you can specify in a style definition. Here's another example:

```
H1 {font-size: 15pt;
      line-height: 17pt;
      font-weight: bold;
      font-family: "Arial"
      font-style: normal}
```

In this case we're defining the `H1` tag to be 15-point type in a 17-point high line space, bold, in Arial 'normal' (as compared to 'condensed' or 'expanded,' for example).

A *point* is a historical measure of type size, based on the distance between the very top of an ascender to the bottom of a descender. Okay, it's actually the size of the metal slug that held the letter, if you want to be completely accurate. Nonetheless, it's a very common gauge of type size, and there are 72 points in an inch.

There's even a shorthand way of specifying some of these style characteristics. If you want to specify a variety of font details, you can pour them all into one tag:

```
H1 {font: 15pt/17pt bold "Arial" normal}
```

You can also create your own types of HTML tags by using style sheets. Let's say that I'd like to have two paragraph styles, one that's code listings (just like this book!) and the other that's handy notes shown in red. I could do this with style sheets as:

```
<STYLE>
   P.code { font: 12pt/15pt "Courier" }
   P.notes { font: 14pt/16pt bold; margin-left: 0.5in;
color: red }
</STYLE>
```

Now you can use this within your own documents as:

```
<P>
Here's a regular paragraph of information.
<P CLASS=code>
This is some code to show, it should be in 'courier' and it
should have lots of space between the lines of text, more
than would normally be the case with a 12 point typeface.
<P CLASS=notes>
And don't forget this important - indented - note too!
```

You can see how this could enable you to have attractive and consistent Web sites across pages. Figure 15-1 shows how this formats in Internet Explorer.

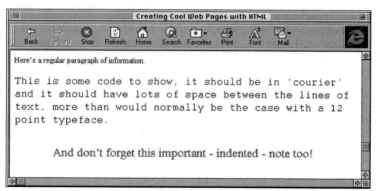

Figure 15-1: Style sheet demonstration.

 Figure 15-1 is an 'artists rendition' of what style sheets will look like on the Mac in the next version of Internet Explorer.

Ways to use style sheets

You can use style sheets in three ways, depending on your design needs:

→ By **linking** to a style sheet from your HTML file. This method enables you to change the appearance of *multiple Web pages* by modifying a single shared style file.

→ By **embedding** a style sheet in your HTML file. This method enables you to change the appearance of a *single Web page* by modifying a few lines at the top of the file. That's what I'm demonstrating in the previous example.

→ By adding **inline** styles to your HTML file. This gives you a quick way to change the appearance of a *single tag*, a *group of tags,* or a *block of information* on your page.

You can use any combination of these methods on your Web pages.

Linking to a style sheet

You can actually have a single style sheet for an entire site; you need to point to it at the top of each file that uses the style sheet, as demonstrated in the following example:

```
<HEAD>
<TITLE>Title of article</TITLE>
<LINK REL=STYLESHEET
HREF="http://www.intuitive.com/stylesheet.css"
     TYPE="text/css">
</HEAD>
```

Here the stylesheet is saved as the document:
http://www.intuitive.com/stylesheet.css

Embedded style information

You've already seen this above; it's a set of style specifications defined at the very top of a Web page, within the `<HEAD>` area, that defines the exact look of the tags on that page. Here's the style specification that appears on the very top of the Microsoft home page:

```
<HTML>
<HEAD>
<STYLE TYPE="text/css">
<!-
  BODY   {margin-left=0; font: 9pt Arial; color: #000000; }
```

```
   A:LINK {color: #000000; font-weight:bold }
   A:VISITED {font: 9pt Arial; color: #000000;
font-weight:bold}
   STRONG {font: 16pt Arial; color: #990000;
text-decoration:none}
  BIG {font: 10pt Arial; background: #CCCC66}
  H1 {font: 24pt Arial; color: #990000; margin-left=0}
  H1.RED {font: 15pt/17pt Arial Black; color: #FF3300; }
  H1.GREEN {font: 15pt/17pt Arial Black; color: #66CC33;
margin-left=20px;}
  P {margin-left=0; font: 9pt Arial; color: #000000}
  P.HEADLINE {margin-left=20px; text-indent: -20px; font:
9pt
    Arial,Helv,sans-serif;  color: #00000;}
  P.SMALL {line-height=5pt}
-->
</STYLE>
<TITLE>Microsoft</TITLE>
</HEAD>
```

There are only a few things here that you've not already been shown in this chapter: the A:LINK and A:VISITED attributes enable you to change a variety of attributes associated with hypertext reference links: in this case links are shown in black, emboldened (font-weight:bold), and when they're visited then they become 9-point Arial rather than the default face and size. The definition of the <BIG> tag is interesting, too, because it demonstrates that you can also specify a background color for a formatted region, which means that anything that's specified as <BIG> will automatically be in 10 point Arial, with a gold background (color CCCC66). On the CD-ROM you'll see an example of this used with paragraph formatting to great effect.

Also notice the different unit of measure specified for the left margin on H1.GREEN: 20px means that it's a 20 pixel margin or indent from the left edge of the page. P.HEADLINE, on the other hand, specifies an outdent, as it's called, where all lines are indented 20 pixels (margin-left=20px) but the very first line is back to the edge of the page (text-indent=-20px).

Inline style information

The third possibility with style sheets is to have the attributes tucked neatly into the specific tag that they should affect. A simple example:

```
<P STYLE="margin-left: 1.0in; margin-right: 1.0in">
This line will be indented one inch on both the left and
right.
</P>
```

Table 15-1 has the official set of attributes and possible values.

Table 15-1:   **Official Attributes and Possible Values**

Attribute	Description	Values	Example
font-size#fsize	Sets size of text	points (pt) inches (in) centimeters (cm) pixels (px)	{font-size:12pt}
font-family#ffamily	Sets typeface	typeface name font family name	{font-family: courier}
font-weight#fweight	Sets thickness of type	extra-light light demi-light medium demi-bold bold extra-bold	{font-weight: bold}
font-style#fstyle	Italicizes text	normal italic	{font-style: italic}
line-height#lheight	Sets the distance between baselines	points (pt) inches (in) centimeters (cm) pixels (px) percentage (%)	{line-height: 24pt}
color#color	Sets color of text	color-name RGB value (hex)	{color: blue}
text-decoration#tdec	Underlines or otherwise highlights text	none underline italic line-through	{text-decoration: underline}
margin-left#margin	Sets distance from left edge of page	points (pt) inches (in) centimeters (cm) pixels (px)	{margin-left: 1in}

Attribute	Description	Values	Example
`margin -right#margin`	Sets distance from right edge of page	points (pt) inches (in) centimeters (cm) pixels (px)	`{margin-right: 1in}`
`margin -top#margin`	Sets distance from top edge of page	points (pt) inches (in) centimeters (cm) pixels (px)	`{margin-top: -20px}`
`text -align#talign`	Sets justification	left center right	`{text-align: right}`
`text -indent#tindent`	Sets distance from left margin	points (pt) inches (in) centimeters (cm) pixels (px)	`{text-indent: 0.5 in}`
`background #backg`	Sets background images or colors	URL, color-name RGB value (hex)	`{background: white}`

 Read the official style sheets proposal to the HTML standards committee at: `http://www.w3.org/pub/WWW/TR/WD-css1.html`

OpenType

If we have these fancy style sheets, what else could we possibly want for Web page design in the future? Another area needing improvement is the management of typefaces. If you've tried to specify typefaces by name so that they'll work on both a Macintosh and PC, you know what I mean. On the Mac it's Times, but on Windows it's Times New Roman. On the Mac it's Courier, on the PC New Courier. The Mac has Palatino as a standard typeface, but Windows 95 includes Arial instead. And we haven't even started to consider the further complications of typefaces on a UNIX system!

As a result, Adobe and Microsoft announced a new extension to TrueType called TrueType Open version 2, or, succinctly, OpenType.

The design is pretty darn smart, I must admit. Because it's based on TrueType and Type 1 type, the two main type formats for the Mac, just about all existing fonts will work without any effort on the part of the user.

OpenType will make it possible for you to include high quality on-screen fonts as part of your pages. If the client doesn't have Arial, you'll be able to send it along with the document, compressed, and it will display the text in the appropriate typeface automatically.

Microsoft and Adobe have submitted a proposal to the World Wide Web Consortium, the group that now manages the growth of HTML for a standard way to embed OpenType fonts in Web pages. If you're very interested in using specific typefaces, stay tuned for developments in this area. There's an OpenType FAQ to read:
`http://www.microsoft.com/ truetype/faq/faq9.htm`

Content Ratings

In mid-1996 one of the most hotly argued topics was the quality and appropriateness of content on the Internet. Congress passed the Communications Decency Act of 1996, and Web developers added blue ribbon icons on their pages to protest the intrusion of government regulation onto the Net. One side chanted its mantra of 'free speech über Alles' while the other decried 'protect our children.' Both sides had valid and important issues and the debate was very interesting. The CDA was recently challenged in court and overturned, so as of right now, it's not the law, and publication of pornographic or offensive material on the Internet doesn't violate any specific electronic laws (though it might violate basic pornography and lewd conduct laws, but that's an entirely different debate).

What's my take on all this? I think there's a lot of appalling stuff online, things I don't want my daughter to see, things that are distressingly easy to encounter. Free speech is important, but not to the exclusion of common sense and community decency. I supported a modified version of the CDA when the debate raged, and refused to add a blue ribbon to my sites.

The best news from this entire debacle is that Paul Resnick from AT&T and James Miller of MIT's Computer Science Lab developed a content rating system and distributed sample programs demonstrating that voluntary ratings for Web sites can be coupled with screening software like Net Nanny and Surf Watch, or even built into Microsoft's Internet Explorer program, to allow free discussion online while also protecting children from stumbling into inappropriate material.

This system is called PICS, the Platform for Internet Content Selection, and it enables you, as a parent, teacher, or administrator, to block access to particular Internet resources without affecting what's distributed to other sites or otherwise on the Internet. It's based on two ideas: instantaneous publishing of information on the Web (in this case the ratings themselves) and access to Internet resources is mediated by computers that can manage far more than any human being.

As the two inventors of PICS state in their original paper:

Appropriateness, however, is neither an objective nor a universal measure. It depends on at least three factors.

➥ The supervisor: Parenting styles differ, as do management styles.

➥ The recipient: What's appropriate for one fifteen-year-old may not be for an eight-year-old, or even all fifteen-year-olds.

➥ The context: a game or chat room that is appropriate to access at home may be inappropriate at work or school.

PICS allows complex site content ratings, which is one of its strengths and weaknesses, simultaneously. If I wanted to create a movie stills archive, but wanted to limit access to the archive to match the original ratings of the films, I could use a rating system for sites based on the movie ratings from the Motion Picture Association of America (MPAA). Here's how it'd look:

```
((PICS-version 1.0)
 (rating-system
 "http://moviescale.org/Ratings/Description/")
 (rating-service "http://moviescale.org/v1.0")
 (icon "icons/moviescale.gif")
 (name "The Movies Rating Service")
 (description "A rating service based on the MPAA's movie
 rating scale")

 (category
  (transmit-as "r")
  (name "Rating")
  (label (name "G") (value 0) (icon "icons/G.gif"))
  (label (name "PG") (value 1) (icon "icons/PG.gif"))
  (label (name "PG-13") (value 2) (icon "icons/
PG-13.gif"))
  (label (name "R") (value 3) (icon "icons/R.gif"))
  (label (name "NC-17") (value 4) (icon "icons/
NC-17.gif"))))
```

Let's jump to a real example. Here's a <PICS> tag in use. This <META> tag PICS rating is from the CompuServe home page at:
http://www.compuserve.com

```
<META http-equiv="PICS-Label" content='(PICS-1.0
"http://www.rsac.org/ratingsv01.html" l gen true
 comment "RSACi North America Server" by
"72662.1715@compuserve.com" for
 "http://www.compuserve.com" on "1996.04.04T08:15-0500" exp
"1997.01.01T08:15-0500"  r (n 0 s 0 v 0 l 0))'>
```

Clearly, it's ugly and confusing. Is it going to change things? It seems unlikely in this first release. If the PICS system can become much easier to use and specify, there's a good chance people will start to voluntarily rate their Web sites. One way or the other, though, we're not going to be able to avoid wrestling with the problem of inappropriate and obscene content on the Internet.

There's lots of information, including the original PICS design documents, available at:
http://www.bilkent.edu.tr/pub/WWW/PICS/
There's a competing ratings system called VCR: the Voluntary Content Rating. Read about it at:
http://www.solidoak.com/vcr.htm

Spiffo Tricks and HTML Extensions

There are lots of tricks with HTML and specific browsers that I haven't talked about in this book, in the interest of having it be a few pages shorter than *Encyclopedia Britannica!* Nonetheless, there are some spiffo things you should know about.

Page counters

Counters are a popular addition to Web pages that can be applied in a variety of ways. Counters appear as either graphics or text; if you go to my home page, for example, you'll find that it's a text counter. Graphical counters are implemented by you using an <IMG SRC> tag to include a graphic that's actually a program that computes the counter value and then creates a graphic with the numbers in question.

To use a text counter, you'll need to talk with your system administrator about whether the server supports server-side includes and what kind of changes you'll need to make to your page to have it work. On my server, I simply rename the filename suffix "shtml" rather than "html," and it works like magic. You might also see a different use of .shtml on the Web. It also stands for "secure HTML document," often for Internet commerce purposes. The actual HTML tag I use on the page to count is:

```
<font size=4><B>Hey! You're the</B></font>
<font size=5><B><!-#counter file="mycounter" -></B></font>
<font size=4><B>visitor since 1 June '96</B></font>
```

If you want a graphic counter, you specify a regular image include that happens to point to the program in question:

```
<img src="apps/Counter.cgi">
```

There's a third option — you can have a third party site keep track of your hits and produce the counter graphic on-the-fly for you. There are a number of sites offering this service, some free, some for a nominal fee. My favorite is Web Counter, which you can visit at:
http://www.digits.com/

There are lots of fun counters and digit styles available, and it's neat to realize that people are actually visiting your pages and exploring your ideas and design. You can confirm this for me; visit my home page right now and increment my counter at:
http://www.intuitive.com/taylor

Looking for more information on page counters? Check out Digit Mania's delightful page at:
http://www.digitmania.holowww.com/

Special HREF targets

You know that you can 'aim' a hypertext reference at a specific frame with the TARGET attribute, but in fact there are some other possible values for this attribute, values that can be quite useful:

_blank	Load the link into a new blank window. This window is not named
_parent	Load the link into the immediate parent of the document the link is in
_self	Load the link into the same window the link was clicked in
_top	Load the link into the full body of the window

How can you use this? Perhaps you'd like to have a button within one of your frame pages that takes the user to a new area of your site, an area that has a different design and isn't intended to be within a single pane. That's accomplished with the following snippet:

```
<A HREF=newarea.html TARGET=_top>visit our kewl new
area!</a>.
```

A musical alternative: MIDI

If you're really plugged in to the music world you already know about the fabulous Musical Instrument Digital Interface (MIDI) and how it enables you to define a musical passage in terms of *triggers*, sequences of notes to play, in specific voices. It turns out that there are two very cool plug-ins that enable you to actually play MIDI files while within your Web browser: Yamaha's MIDplug and LiveUpdate's Crescendo. I use both on my site, they're both very cool — and free, too!

You can get the Yamaha MIDplug at:
`http://www.cyber-bp.or.jp/yamaha/index_e.html`
Crescendo is available at:
`http://www.liveupdate.com/get.html`

The biggest advantage of MIDI is that the files can be tiny, and can still offer 5–10 minutes, or more, of music. Check out the CD-ROM: I've included a couple for you to enjoy, and they'd work just as well as a `BGSOUND` or sound player control in Navigator as a standard WAV or AU sound file.

An amazing MIDI archive is MidiFarm. Visit them if you're even the tiniest bit interested in adding sound or music to your pages, at:
`http://www.midifarm.com/`

Force a mouse click in Navigator

Here's a situation you might occasionally encounter. You move to a new Web site, or rename your entire set of pages and want to put up a 'please visit our new Web site' message, but, rather than force users to click on a link to get there, you'd like to have the program magically and automatically jump to the new site after a specified amount of time.

In Netscape Navigator, that's done with the `HTTP-EQUIV` attribute to the `<META>` tag, as follows:

```
<META HTTP-EQUIV="Refresh" CONTENT="10;
URL=http://www.mynewsite.com/">.
```

This page will automatically change to mynewsite.com 10 seconds after being loaded.

Bullet lists with custom bullets

You're an expert at creating bullet lists by now, using the <UL> tag, right? But what if you want to fine-tune things a little bit and actually have a bullet list that uses a specific graphic image of your own? Here's the trick:

```
<UL>
<IMG SRC=bullet.gif ALIGN=center>My first important
point.<br>
<IMG SRC=bullet.gif ALIGN=center>My second, incredibly
vital point.<br>
<IMG SRC=bullet.gif ALIGN=center>The third, crucial
point.<br>
</UL>
```

You can see how this appears in Figure 15-2.

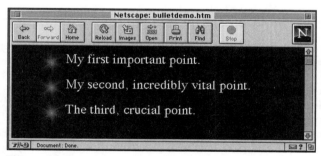

Figure 15-2: Any kind of bullet you'd like can be on your page.

Special characters to add to your page

HTML also includes support for many special characters, some of which are shown in Table 15-2.

 Find a list of special characters online too, at:
http://www.sandia.gov/sci_compute/symbols.html

Table 15-2:	Useful Table Extensions
Tag	**Common Meaning**
&cent;	Cent symbol
&copy;	Copyright symbol
&deg;	Degree sign
&iquest;	Inverted (Spanish) question mark
&laquo;	Left angled quotation mark
&micro;	Greek micro character
&middot;	Midline dot, a sort of floating period symbol
&not;	Negation sign
&para;	Paragraph symbol
&plusmn;	Plus or minus sign
&pound;	British pound symbol
&raquo;	Right angled quotation mark
&reg;	Registered-trademark symbol
&sect;	Section sign
&yen;	Yen symbol

The additional extensions and additions scheduled for the final version of HTML 3.2 are a little harder to identify, because the specification is still being finalized as this book is written. Many of the changes reflect continued refinements to the HTML+ specifications, including the <FIG> tag that's slated to replace the <IMG> tag, maybe. The complexity level of future Web pages will increase dramatically with style sheets and obscure multipart-header information like PICS ratings. Forms will be extended to include graphical editor panels (these are called "scribble-on image" in the specification) and file-uploading and audio-input capabilities. That's why it's wonderful news that the capabilities of Web page design editors are increasing at an amazing clip!

To check on the status of any HTML specifications, visit:
http://www.w3.org/hypertext/WWW

Happy HTML-ing

That's about it for this greatly revised edition of *Macworld Creating Cool HTML 3.2 Web Pages*. Having read this far, you are now an official expert on the HyperText Markup Language. Now all you have to do is go create the coolest new Web pages on the Net.

As you travel the Web and design your own pages, keep in touch! You can always reach me at the e-mail address taylor@intuitive.com and, of course, you can check out the *Macworld Creating Cool HTML 3.2Web Pages* spot on the Web any time you'd like (and increment my page counter!) at: http://www.intuitive.com/coolweb
Or, visit the official — and way cool — IDG Books Worldwide site at: http://www.idgbooks.com/

Finding a Home for Your Web Page

Appendix A

Now that you've built a cool Web page or two, the natural question is *Now what?* Where can you put it so that everyone else on the World Wide Web can find and enjoy it? That's an important question, but it's not as easy to answer as you might think. Why? Because there are seemingly millions of solutions, from sites that advertise their willingness to host your Web pages for free (if they're not too big), to sites that charge a very small amount annually, to those that offer very fast connectivity but bill you based on megabytes transferred (which means that you definitely don't want to have lots of huge graphics!), and finally, to sites that will host a reasonable set of Web pages for a small monthly fee.

If you're seeking a commercial presence, even more choices are available because now there are thousands of so-called *cybermalls* eager to offer disk space and access to their *commercial servers* in return for a monthly fee (which can be quite steep) or a percentage of your online sales. A commercial server is one that can process credit card transactions — securely — over the Internet.

Regardless of what you choose, the most important factor in my opinion is to be able to match your realistic expectations for your page with the capabilities of the *presence provider* (as they're called in the biz). For example, if you want to create a page that will be viewed by thousands each day because either you're going to include it in your print advertising or your mom can plug it on her nationally syndicated radio show, then you'll certainly need to put your page on a fast machine with a fast, reliable network connection. If you're just having fun and want your friends to visit, then a simpler setup with less capabilities at less cost should be just dandy.

Key Capabilities

The key capabilities to look for, regardless of your performance demands, are the following:

➡ **What speed is the connection between the system where your pages will reside and the Internet?**

➡ Good answers to this question are T1 and T3. Bad answers are ISDN or a fast dialup.

➡ **How many other pages are on that system?**

➡ The more Web pages on the system, the more likely you could be squeezed out in the crush of Web-related traffic.

➡ **What guarantee of up-time and availability is offered?**

➡ A great site that's off-line one day each week is worse than a slower system where they guarantee 99 percent uptime.

Because you've read this far and are now an expert at creating cool Web pages, you will also want some sort of access to your pages online, rather than mail in your changes and updates. If you have something new to add to your Web pages, you want to do it *now!* At least, most people do.

Here's a run-down of some of the possibilities for free, inexpensive, and commercial Web page hosting. Which you choose is up to you, of course, and I don't necessarily vouch for the quality of any of these sites. They're just fast and seem to feature well-designed and — yes — cool Web pages.

Free Sites

I'm sure there are more options than the few I list, but these should get you started. If you want to find more, there's a page on the Web that, although a bit out of date, does list a number of places that offer free or cheap Web page space. It's on Turnpike Metropolis at:
`http://members.tripod.com/~jpsp1/sites.html`

Beverly Hills Internet

The space isn't unlimited, and it's a bit tricky to get an account, but the BHI Homesteading concept is a brilliant one. It offers space for about 1,500 different home pages, divided into virtual cities. Pick, for example, Rodeo Drive, and if there's a street address between 1000 and 1299 available, you can have it for your home page. A very fun concept and some wild pages.

```
http://www.geocities.com/cgi-bin/main/homestead
```

Phrantics Public Housing Project

A cooperative venture of five or so different Web sites, each member of the Public Housing Project offers free Web space, with a few caveats. Your best bet is to pop straight over to the list of landlords, and read the details for yourself.

```
http://www.phrantic.com/phrantic
```

Home Pages for the Homeless

These folks offer free Web space — one page with small graphics — for noncommercial use and they're rather swamped with requests. Very worth visiting, one way or the other.

```
http://www.homeless.com/
```

Vive Web Creations

Vive Web Creations offers free Web space for schools, community centers, and nonprofit organizations, but its system seems to be quite slow, even during nonprime hours.

```
http://www.vive.com/connect/
```

Inexpensive Presence Providers

The prices can range all over the map, and it's astonishing how many firms now offer some sort of Web site service or other. The majority, though, are clearly geared to grab a slice of the business market as thousands of companies worldwide come onto the Internet. If you're looking for somewhere to keep your personal home page, you might want to carefully consider which of these spots has the *aura* you seek. They definitely differ quite a bit!

The following doesn't even scratch the surface. Hundreds, if not thousands, of firms offer relatively low-cost Web space. This is a sampling of variously sized firms so you can get an idea of what's available:

ADANAC

This Canadian firm offers very inexpensive space on its Web server — $12 a month — but charges you each time you want to modify your page. Want more than one page? You'll need to price it out with ADANAC.

```
http://www.magic.mb.ca/~rickm/adanac/index.html
```

Best Communications

Based in the Silicon Valley, Best offers a wide variety of Web hosting packages, including one that'd work just fine for your new pages. $30 a month gives you 25MB of disk space, although it does charge for excessive network traffic. The Web pages for my consulting firm, Intuitive Systems, are hosted on a Best system machine and I recommend the company to all my clients. Tell 'em I sent you!

```
http://www.best.com/
```

Di's Online Cafe

A nicely done site that offers you the chance to have your home page as part of the site, though it's not necessarily that easy to find. The company is based in Mobile, Alabama. Contact Di's Online Cafe for fee structure.

```
http://www.dibbs.net/
```

Digital Landlords

Only $28 month to host your home page (three-month minimum), although there's no indication of how much it may limit your disk space or bandwidth use. It hosts both personal and business information at this Atlanta-based Internet system.

```
http://clever.net/
```

Hurricane Electric

Hurricane Electric offers remarkably inexpensive space for your new pages, and on a snappy machine, too. Prices start at an amazing $1 a month for 10MB of storage space, but if your site is too popular, you'll have to pay a traffic tariff at the end of each month.

```
http://www.he.tdl.com/
```

Netcom Communications

It's one of the largest Internet-only companies and has a good track record of growing its business and offering national accessibility at low cost. If you sign up as a NetCruiser user, you'll also get a 1MB Web space for free!

```
Http://www.netcom.com/
```

Northcoast Internet

The group that runs this Northern California company is really cool and fun to work with. In fact, my Embot program lives on their system. Check out this site for its inexpensive Web hosting prices, too. Fees start at $25 a month.

```
http://www.northcoast.com/
```

The Well

If you're looking for a funky and fun online community with lots of writers, musicians, and even a few members of the Grateful Dead, then the Well, created by the Whole Earth Access team, is the spot for you. Web page hosting is inexpensive here, too, starting at $5 a month for each 2MB of

storage space if you already have an account on the Well, which starts at
$15 a month.

```
http://www.well.com/
```

Commercial Hosts / Cybermalls

If you think that a lot of new companies have popped up offering Web
space, you haven't seen the absolutely frantic explosion of commercial
hosts and so-called cybermalls! It's astounding. A year ago there were
perhaps a dozen, and now there are *thousands*, ranging from large,
complex, well-funded systems to a PC in the basement. If you're hoping to
gain a new income stream for your business from the online community,
you'll want to make doubly sure that the company you sign up with has the
speed and reliability that you want, and that the other shops in the mall are
acceptable to you and your customers.

Don't forget about security and the possibility of digital, online commerce,
with secure transactions that let you take credit card orders directly online.
For more information about these topics, I recommend you pick up a copy
of the book *The Internet Business Guide* by Rosalind Resnick and me.

Best Internet

It's the same firm I listed previously, but they have a complete commerce
package available and are hosting a large number of commercial sites
including the Oakland A's, the Internet Mall, and more!

```
http://www.best.com/corpbus.html
```

Branch Mall

One of the largest and most established of the electronic shopping malls is
Branch Mall, from Branch Internet Systems, with hundreds of stores. It
offers your customers access through not only the Web but Gopher and
e-mail too, all as part of the package.

```
http://www.branch.com/
```

Community Business On-line

This small but well-designed online shopping spot based in Virginia offers a range of different services, including home page hosting for smaller businesses.

```
http://www.cbo.com/contact.html
```

CyberHouse

The people at CyberHouse will build a Web presence for you, but they're also happy to work with you on installing custom lines, hosting your Web information on its server, and using the company's secure server for online transactions.

```
http://www.cyberhouse.com/
```

Downtown Anywhere

This is one of the few firms that has been around longer than a few months, and it's always had a terrific vision of how to help build a compelling site. Downtown Anywhere will also offer you space for whatever cool Web information you'd like to make available yourself.

```
http://www.awa.com/
```

iShops

An example of a different kind of Web site, one that lets you focus on the products you're selling and not worry so much about the Web page design (of course, you've just read this book and probably *want* to design your own pages, but a combination of professional pages for your products and online ordering and your own custom pages for other parts of your site might be helpful).

```
http://www.ishops.com/
```

The Virtual Village

The Virtual Village is based in Hawaii, offering a small town metaphor for its commercial space. It, too, has a variety of shops available and will rent you space for your commercial presence.

```
http://www.interpac.net/village/
```

Not Enough Choices?

You can also dig around in the ever-fun Yahoo! online directory to find a wide variety of Web presence providers. And remember that if the provider can't even publicize itself, it's not likely to help you publicize yourself, either. Pop over to `http://www.yahoo.com` and search for *Web presence* or perhaps *Web* and your city or state.

Nationally distributed Internet-related magazines can be a good place to find presence provider advertisements, too. A few come to mind: *Internet World*, *NetGuide*, *Internet Life*, and *Boardwatch*. Finally, don't forget to check with your local computer magazines or newspapers. Most of the major cities in the U.S. now have one or more computer-related publications, and the advertisements in these publications are a terrific place to learn about local Internet companies and their capabilities. If you have access, I'd particularly recommend *Computer Currents*, which is available in at least eight of the largest cities in the U.S.

Also remember that there's absolutely no reason that you *have* to work with a company in your own city. After you have some sort of access to the Internet (perhaps through school or work), you can easily work with a presence provider across the nation.

Best of luck to you, and do send me your URL once you're up and online!

Glossary

To achieve precision in communication, experts and amateurs alike speak in what sounds like a secret code. This glossary is a decoder ring of sorts that will help you understand the various mystery words surrounding HTML and the World Wide Web.

anchor

Either a spot in a document that actually links to another place in the document or to another document (a hypertext link), or the spot elsewhere in the document that can be quickly reached through a hypertext link.

animated GIF

A special kind of GIF — graphics interchange format — image for a Web page that is actually a sequence of pictures displayed in sequence, like a flip book.

anonymous FTP

A scheme by which users can retrieve files over the Internet without having an account on the remote system. Usually, the user logs in as *anonymous* and leaves his or her e-mail address as the password.

applet

A small application, usually written in Java, Java Script, or VB Script, that enables you to add additional functionality to your Web page.

ARPANET

The origin of the Internet, the ARPANet was funded by the U.S. Department of Defense Advanced Research Projects Agency.

attribute

An addition to an HTML tag that qualifies or extends the meaning of the tag. For example, `<body BGCOLOR=blue>`.

boldface

To set text off with a heavier font; **this text is boldface**.

bookmark

A Web URL that's automatically stored by the browser software for easy access later (see also *hotlist*).

borderless frame

A particular type of frame design that enables you to omit the small border lines between each pane of the layout.

browser

Software program such as Mosaic, Internet Explorer, or Netscape Navigator that can read and navigate HTML documents. Browsers are the client application that you run on your computer.

C

A powerful and sophisticated programming language that offers considerable power for CGI programmers, though it'll take you awhile to learn it.

CERN

The center for high energy particle physics in Switzerland. CERN is where the World Wide Web was invented.

CGI

Common Gateway Interface — the environment through which you can write programs that can deliver Web pages, search for material on the server, produce graphics on the fly, and more.

client

The formal name for the computer that's on your desk when you're surfing the Web or otherwise using the Net; it's the user side of the client/server model. Not to be confused with the John Grisham book of the same name (see also *server*).

client-side image map

An image map with a client-side component that enables users to choose new.

data

The never-ending stream of *stuff* that appears on the Internet, as differentiated from *information,* which is data that has some meaning or value to the user.

domain name

All the computers and servers plugged into the Net have their own unique names and each lives in its own unique namespace, or domain. Domain names are .com for commercial, .edu for educational sites, .gov for the U.S. Government, and so on.

e-mail

Electronic mail — a convenient way to send messages to other users or groups without the hassle of paper or postage stamps.

Ethernet

A low-level protocol for high-speed networks. The Internet runs on Ethernet connections. Ethernet was also invented a few decades ago by my friend Bob Metcalfe.

Explorer, Internet Explorer

A powerful and feature-laden Web browser available for free from Microsoft Corporation.

external link

A hypertext link that points to a resource not found on the current page (see also *internal link*).

floating frame

A feature unique to Internet Explorer; a floating frame is a window set within a larger Web page that has its own URL and contents.

font

A particular use of a typeface. Bodoni Poster is a typeface, but Bodoni Poster 12-point italic is a font.

form

An interactive Web page that seeks to collect information from users (the information is typically sent via CGI to the server).

frame

An advanced Web browser feature that enables you to have multiple individual pages displayed simultaneously, one in each *pane* of the viewer's screen.

freeware

Software available on the Net without any charge or license fee, just nice folk being generous with their time and efforts.

FTP (File Transfer Protocol)

The way files are sent and received over the Internet. Typically, a user needs an account on the remote system unless it allows anonymous FTP access (see also *anonymous FTP*).

gateway

A system that shuttles information from one network to another. Like a traffic cop, but in cyberspace.

GIF

The most common graphics format on the Web, the Graphics Interchange Format allows small files containing attractive graphics and pictures.

Gopher

A popular information-distribution service based on a hierarchical menu system; often overshadowed by the more sophisticated World Wide Web. The main Gopher site is at the University of Minnesota.

hexadecimal

Base-16 numbering scheme, where a digit can be 0,1,2,3,4,5,6,7,8,9,A,B,C,D,E,F, where F, for example, is 15 decimal. It's then simple math: 5C hex = 5*16 + 12 = 92 decimal.

home page

The central or initial document seen by visitors to your Web site. You can have many other Web pages connected to your home page.

hostname

The unique combination of computer and domain name that describes a particular computer on the Internet. For example, sage.cc.purdue.edu is a hostname in the Purdue University Computer Center domain. Alternatively, some people believe just the name of the computer itself is its hostname, with all additional information the domain name. That would mean that the same computer would have a hostname of sage and a domain name of cc.purdue.edu. There's no consensus.

hotlink

A hypertext reference link.

hotlist

A Web URL automatically stored by the browser software for easy access later; also known as a collection of *bookmarks*.

hot spot

An active region on an image map or client-side image map.

HTML (HyperText Markup Language)

The language that is used to define and describe the page layout of documents displayed in a World Wide Web browser. HTML is an application of SGML (Standardized General Markup Language).

HTML tag

A specific formatting instruction within an HTML document. Tags are usually contained within angle brackets, as in <HTML>.

HTTP (HyperText Transport Protocol)

The underlying system whereby Web documents are transferred over the Internet.

hyperlink

An active passage of text that, upon choosing, will take you to another spot in the document or another document on the Net.

hypermedia

Any combination of hypertext and graphics, video, audio, and other media. The World Wide Web is a hypermedia environment because it enables multiple types of media to be used simultaneously in a document.

hypertext

An interconnected collection of text information, wherein any given word or phrase may link to another point in the document or to another document.

image map

An image that appears on a Web page where regions of the image are defined as different hot spots, such that clicking on them will lead the user to different subsequent pages.

information

The small subset of data that is actually useful and meaningful to you at the current moment. Contrast with *data*.

inline graphics

Graphics that appear beside the text in a Web page when viewed via a browser (as opposed to graphics that require separate viewer programs).

internal link

A hypertext link that moves you to another spot in the same document. Most useful for tables of contents or quick shortcuts to jump back to the top of the current page.

the Internet

The global network of networks that enables some or all of the following: exchange of e-mail messages, files, Usenet newsgroups, and World Wide Web pages. Also known as the Net.

ISDN

Integrated Services Digital Network, a high-speed digital phone line that offers home and small office users a faster connection to the Net than a regular modem.

italic

A typographic convention typically used for emphasis or citations; *this text is italicized.*

Java

A popular new programming language designed for writing small applications that can enable your Web pages to do more interesting and complex tasks. Also a nice island in the South Pacific.

Java Script

A simple scripting language for Web pages designed by Netscape and now understood by both Navigator and Internet Explorer.

JPEG

A more sophisticated graphics format than GIF; JPEG, the product of the Joint Photographic Experts Group, enables millions of colors to be used in an image, but often produces larger file sizes as a result.

jump target

The point to which a user will be moved when they choose an internal link.

link

A word, picture, or other area of a Web page that users can click on to move to another spot in the document or to another document.

map file

The data file that defines the different active regions of an image map. Two main formats are possible: CERN and NCSA.

markup language

A special type of programming language that enables users to describe the desired appearance and structural features of a document.

marquee

A fun scrolling text region that can help add pizzazz to your site. Only understood by Internet Explorer.

MIDI

Musical Instrument Digital Interface. A digital format for specifying instruments and music.

Mosaic

The original World Wide Web browser program developed at the National Center for Supercomputing Applications at the University of Illinois. Its release in 1993 sparked the explosive growth of the Web and helped boost interest in the Internet. Many similar software programs to Mosaic — commercial, shareware, and freeware versions for almost any platform — have been developed since Mosaic's release.

MPEG

An advanced encoding system for movie files, created by the Motion Picture Experts Group.

multimedia

A combination of more than one medium; typically this refers to graphics plus text, but it can include audio, video, animation, and, someday, smell and touch.

Navigator

A World Wide Web browser developed by Netscape Communications, created by some of the original NCSA Mosaic programmers. Navigator is probably the most popular browser on the Net.

NCSA

The National Center for Supercomputer Applications, a group at the University of Illinois, Urbana-Champaign. It created the original Mosaic Web browser that started the whole explosion of the Web and the Internet.

the Net

Another term for the *Internet*, and an amusing movie with Sandra Bullock as a programmer who never leaves the house, eats pizza by ordering it online, yet looks great in a bikini.

ordered list
A list of items, often numbered, that describe steps in a process (Steps 1, 2, 3, and so on).

Perl
A powerful programming language for creating CGI scripts and other tasks. Perl is widely available on many different platforms.

pixel
A point or dot on the computer screen.

plug-in
A helper application that enables a browser to work with additional media types.

pointer
A word, picture, or other area that users can click to move to another spot in the document or to another document (see also *link*).

port
Frequency used to transfer a particular type of information between Internet computers; FTP uses a specific port, whereas HTTP uses another. Somewhat analogous to television channels.

RGB
The way in which your monitor builds colors: a combination of red, green, and blue.

server
The remote machine that a browser connects with to receive information.

SGML (Standardized General Markup Language)

The markup language that is the parent of HTML. SGML provides a means of defining markup for any number of document types (such as HTML). You don't mark up text in SGML — you mark up text using an application or instance of SGML. HTML is one of those applications.

shareware

A type of software that you can obtain for free from the Net and other sources, where the programmers hope you'll pay a small registration fee to help offset their time and efforts. It's a good system and a good idea, so if you can, please do register the shareware you use!

string

A sequence of characters, in programmer-speak.

T1 / T3

Very high-speed data lines for offices and other sites.

tag

A single element of HTML.

TCP/IP (Transfer Control Protocol/Internet Protocol)

A system networks use to communicate with each other over the Internet.

telnet

An Internet service that enables users to log on to a remote system and work on it as though they are directly connected to the system on site.

typeface

A particular design of a set of characters and symbols. Times and Courier are common typefaces. A specific size and style of a typeface — Courier 12-point, for example — is known as a *font*.

UNIX

A very powerful operating system that is the object of a lot of criticism and adoration. Probably the most common operating system on the Internet, UNIX has some Internet features built right into it.

unordered list

A list of items that have no implied order; commonly, a set of bulleted items.

URL (Uniform Resource Locator)

The standardized way in which any resource is identified within a Web document or to a Web browser. Most URLs consist of the service, host name, and directory path. An example of a URL:
`http://www.timeinc.com/time/daily/time/latest.html`

Usenet

The Internet's version of a distributed conferencing and discussion system. Most entertaining with over 15,000 different discussion topics.

VB Script

Visual Basic Script, an alternative to Java Script from Microsoft. Only understood within Internet Explorer as I write this, but Netscape Navigator will probably understand it by the time you read this definition.

Veronica

I kid you not: Very Easy Rodent-Oriented Netwise Index To Computerized Archives. Veronica is a search system for Gopher users.

VRML

Virtual Reality Modeling Language, a sophisticated markup language that enables users to define three-dimensional space that others can explore.

World Wide Web

A massive, distributed hypermedia environment that is part of the Internet. Consisting of millions of documents, thousands of sites, and dozens of indexes, the Web is a fluid and often surprising hive of information and activity.

WYSIWYG

"What you see is what you get," a type of interface in which you can edit a multimedia document while seeing a rough approximation of how the document (or Web page) will look when done. Very useful!

HTML Quick Reference

Appendix C

Once you've learned how to create documents in hypertext markup language, it's inevitable that you'll need to quickly double-check the form of a particular option, the spelling of a tag, or similar. That's why I include this helpful quick reference material.

What's a URL? (Chapter 2)

service   ://   hostname (:port)   /   directory (and filename)

Service can be:

`http`	Hypertext transfer protocol — Web pages
`gopher`	Gopher server
`mailto`	E-mail address
`telnet`	Telnet to a remote system
`ftp`	FTP file archive
`news`	Usenet news server

Basic HTML (Chapter 3 and Chapter 4)

`<HTML>`	Begins an HTML-formatted document

`<HEAD>`	Beginning of HTML header info (TITLE, and so on.)
`<TITLE>text</TITLE>`	Specify *text* as the title for this Web page
`</HEAD>`	End of HEAD section
`<BASEFONT SIZE=n>`	Define default text size for document (1–7, 7 being largest)
`<BODY`	Beginning of main HTML text and info
`BACKGROUND="url"`	Use specified GIF or JPEG as background graphic
`BGCOLOR=color`	Use specified color (RGB or by name) for background
`BACKGROUND="url"`	Use specified GIF or JPEG as background graphic
`</BODY>`	End of HTML body
`</HTML>`	Last line of an HTML document

Paragraph Formats (Chapter 3)

`<P>`	Paragraph break
`<BR`	Line break
`CLEAR=>`	`LEFT, RIGHT, ALL` break wrapped graphic space
`<HR`	Horizontal rule
`SIZE=`	Height of the horizontal line, in pixels
`WIDTH=`	Width of the line: pixels or percentage of screen width
`ALIGN=`	`LEFT, CENTER,` or `RIGHT`

NOSHADE	Solid rule line, no (default) shading
>	

Character Formatting (Chapter 4)

<B>text</B>	Present *text* in bold
<EM>text</EM>	Emphasize *text*, typically italics
<FONT	
FACE="*typeface*"	Present text in specified typeface
COLOR=*color*	Text in specified color (RGB or color by name)
SIZE=*size*	Text in specified size (1-7, or relative changes +/-*n*)
</FONT>	End <font> tag
<I>*text*</I>	Present *text* in italics
<STRIKE>*text*</STRIKE>	Show *text* with a line through it (crossed out)
<STRONG>*text*</STRONG>	Show *text* in a strong (typically bold) font
^{*text*}	Show *text* as a superscript
_{*text*}	Show *text* as a subscript
<TT>*text*</TT>	Show *text* in "typewriter" font
<U>*text*</U>	Present *text* underlined, if supported

Adding Images (Chapter 8)

<IMG	
SRC="*file or URL*"	Name or URL of the graphics file to include
ALIGN=*alignment*	Aligns subsequent text to TOP, MIDDLE, or BOTTOM of image, as specified, or LEFT and

	RIGHT align the image with word wrap.
ALT="*text*"	Show *text* instead of image for users who cannot display graphics on their screens
ISMAP	Mapped image with multiple click spots; must be supported by the server
HEIGHT=*n*	Height of the graphic space (may scale)
WIDTH=*n*	Width of the graphic space (may scale)
HSPACE=*n*	Vertical spacing around the graphic (pixels)
VSPACE=*n*	Horizontal spacing around the graphic (pixels)
BORDER=	Size of image border, in pixels, when activated
USEMAP="*#mapname*"	Client-side image map. Regions defined in <MAP>
>	
<BR CLEAR=*x*>	Break to (LEFT, RIGHT, ALL) open space in margin

Hypertext References (Chapter 6)

<A>	Anchor, inserts internal (same page) or external (different page or document) hypertext link
<A HREF="file or URL"	Hypertext reference
TARGET=*name*	Change should affect specified window in a frames layout.
<A NAME="text tag">	Anchor within document for jumping to that spot within the Web document
</A>	Close tag

Section Headings (Chapter 3)

`<H1>`*text*`</H1>`	Show *text* as a level-one section heading
`<H2>`*text*`</H2>`	Show *text* as a level-two header

HTML supports up to six levels of headings, but in practice anything less than a fourth level section heading is difficult to read.

Lists (Chapter 5)

`<OL`	Ordered list of items
`TYPE=`	A = uppercase alphabetic, a = lowercase alphabetic, I = uppercase Roman numerals, i = lowercase Roman numerals, and 1 = digits
`START=`	Initial value for the list
`>`	
`<UL`	Unordered list
`TYPE=`	Type of bullet/mark to use. Possibilities: `DISC`, `CIRCLE`, or `SQUARE`
`>`	
`<LI`	Individual List item
`TYPE=`	Bullet type (`UL`); `DISC`, `CIRCLE`, or `SQUARE`
`START=`	Starting value (`OL` only)
`>`	
`<DL>`	Definition or glossary list
`<DT>`	Definition term
`<DD>`	Definition description
`</DL>`	End of definition or glossary list

Other Cool HTML Tags

`<CENTER>`	Center a passage of text, graphics, or other material in the window
`</CENTER>`	End of CENTER list
`<BLOCKQUOTE>`	Block indented text passage
`</BLOCKQUOTE>`	End of BLOCKQUOTE passage
`<PRE>`	Preformatted text passage; not filled or altered
`<PRE WIDTH=x>`	Default line width of preformatted text where 'x' specifies the max number of characters to display on each line (ignored by most browsers)
`</PRE>`	End of preformatted text block
`<ADDRESS>`	Signature block at end of HTML page containing contact info for the person who created or maintains the page
`</ADDRESS>`	End of ADDRESS listing
`<DIR>`	Directory listing, a short form of a list (rarely supported)
`</DIR>`	End of DIR listing
`<MENU>`	A list of small items; may be formatted multicolumn by the browser software (rarely supported)
`</MENU>`	End of MENU listing
`<!-text ->`	*Text* is a comment; not displayed

Frames (Chapter 9)

`<FRAMESET`

`ROWS=`*`list`*	Width specifications of vertically split frames (pixels, percentage (add '%') or remaining space (use '*'))
`COLS=`*`list`*	Height specifications of horizontally split frames (pixels, Percentage (add '%') or remaining space (use '*'))
`FRAMEBORDER=`*`n`*	Size of border between individual frames (pixels)
`FRAMESPACING=`*`n`*	Spacing between frame content and border (pixels)

`>`

`</FRAMESET>`

`<NOFRAMES>`*`text`* `</NOFRAMES>`	HTML presented to people who can't see frames on screen

`<FRAME`

`SRC=`*`url`*	Information to display in specified frame
`NAME=`*`name`*	Name of specified frame, used with HREF TARGET=
`NORESIZE`	Freezes the specific frame so it won't resize as window changes
`MARGINHEIGHT=`*`x`*	Exact spacing above and below current pane (pixels)
`MARGINWIDTH=`*`x`*	Exact spacing to the left and right of the current pane (pixels)
`SCROLLING=`*`t`*	Allow scrolling, or add scroll bars as needed (`YES`, `NO`, `AUTO`)

`>`

Advanced Frame Formatting (Chapter 10)

<IFRAME	Embedded (floating) frame on page - **Internet Explorer Only**
NAME=*name*	Name of specified frame, used with HREF TARGET=
NORESIZE	Freezes the specific frame so it won't resize as window changes
MARGINHEIGHT=*x*	Exact spacing above and below current pane (pixels)
MARGINWIDTH=*x*	Exact spacing to the left and right of the current pane (pixels)
SCROLLING=*t*	Allow scrolling, or add scroll bars as needed (YES, NO, AUTO)
SRC=*url*	Information to display in specified frame
>	

Tables (Chapter 9, Chapter 10)

<TABLE	
BORDER=*n*	Size (in pixels) of rule lines in table
CELLSPACING=*n*	Space between cells of the table, in pixels
CELLPADDING=*n*	Space between cell contents and cell edge, in pixels
BACKGROUND=*url*	Background graphic to use for table
BGCOLOR=*color*	Background color (name or RGB) for table
BORDERCOLOR=*color*	Color (name or RGB) of the rule lines

BORDERCOLORLIGHT =color	Lighter color (name or RGB) for rule lines
BORDERCOLORDARK =color	Darker color (name or RGB) for rule lines
WIDTH=n	Width of table (pixels or percentage)

>

<TR

ALIGN=x	Align row of data LEFT, RIGHT, or CENTER
VALIGN=x	Vertically align row of data TOP, MIDDLE, BOTTOM
BGCOLOR=color	Background color (name or RGB) for table

>

<TD>   *Same attributes as <TR> tag*

Client-side Image Maps (Chapter 12)

<MAP NAME=n>	Defines map name (see IMG USEMAP=)
<AREA	The specific regions defined for each spot in an image map
SHAPE=shape	Shape of region (RECT, maybe others)
COORD=xy,xy	Specific x,y coordinates relative to shape
SRC=url	Destination URL for specified region

>

Building Forms (Chapter 12)

`<FORM>`	HTML form specification header
`<FORM ACTION="file or URL">`	What will process the results
`<FORM METHOD="method">`	How form info is sent - POST is as data, GET is attached to URL
`<INPUT TYPE=TEXT>`	Text input box
`<INPUT TYPE=RADIO>`	One of a group of on-off buttons
`<INPUT TYPE=SUBMIT>`	The actual 'submit form' button
`<INPUT TYPE=IMAGE>`	Just like SUBMIT, but with a graphic (specified with SRC=*url)*
`<INPUT TYPE=RESET>`	Another button for clearing all values entered
`<INPUT TYPE=PASSWORD>`	A text input box that doesn't echo what's typed
`<INPUT TYPE=CHECKBOX>`	An on-off option field

Within an INPUT specification, the following options have value, though not all options have meaning with all types of input field.

`NAME=`	Symbolic name of field value
`VALUE=`	Default value or content of field
`CHECKED`	Button/box checked by default?
`SIZE=`	Number of characters in text field
`MAXLENGTH=`	Max characters accepted (text)
`<SELECT`	User must choose between a list of select boxes

`NAME=`	Name of select boxes
`SIZE=`	How many items to display at once
`MULTIPLE=`	Okay to select more than one item
`>`	
`<OPTION`	An individual check box within `SELECT` list
`SELECTED`	Make this the default `SELECT` selection
`>` *text for selection option*	
`</SELECT>`	End of `SELECT` series
`<TEXTAREA`	Multiline text entry field
`NAME=`	Symbolic name of text area field
`ROWS=`	Number of lines in input space
`COLS=`	Width of input space
`WRAP`	Automatically wrap words entered
`>` *default text* `</TEXTAREA>`	
`</FORM>`	End of HTML form specification
`<ISINDEX>`	A searchable index - need CGI support on the server

Special Character Codes for HTML Documents (Chapter 5)

Character	`HTML Code`	*Common Meaning*
&	`&amp;`	ampersand
<	`&lt;`	less than

>	&gt;	greater than
©	&copy;	copyright symbol
®	&reg;	registered trademark symbol

See Chapters 5 and 15 for a more extensive list of special character codes within HTML.

Internet Explorer Only Tags (Chapter 10, Chapter 12)

`<BGSOUND`

`SRC=`*url*	Background sound to play upon loading page
`LOOP=`*n*	Number of times to loop (or `INFINITE`)

`>`

`<BODY BGPROPERTIES` `=fixed>`	Make background a 'watermark' (doesn't scroll with contents)
`<MARQUEE`	An animated text area of a document
`BEHAVIOR=`*x*	How the marquee should behave: `SCROLL`, `SLIDE`, `ALTERNATE`
`DIRECTION=`*x*	Where the message starts: `LEFT` or `RIGHT`
`WIDTH=`*n*	Width of the marquee box (pixels or percentage)
`HEIGHT=`*x*	Height of the marquee box (pixels or percentage)
`HSPACE=`*n*	Vertical spacing around the marquee (pixels)
`VSPACE=`*n*	Horizontal spacing around the marquee (pixels)
`BGCOLOR=`*color*	Color behind the scrolling text (RGB or name)

SCROLLAMOUNT=n	Number of pixels scrolled between redraws
SCROLLDELAY=n	Delay in marquee redraws (milliseconds)
>	

Navigator Only Tags (Chapter 10, Chapter 12)

<EMBED	Used to place sound files into Web pages
SRC=url	Background sound to play upon loading page
LOOP=n	Number of times to loop (or INFINITE)
CONTROLS=x	Type of control console: CONSOLE, SMALLCONSOLE
HEIGHT=n	Height of the control space
WIDTH=n	Width of the control space
VOLUME=n	Volume, 1-255, with 255 maximum volume
>	
<IMG LOWSRC=url	Quick loading, low res version of image to load first

JavaScript, Visual Basic Script

see Chapter 12 for details

Step-by-Step Web Site Planning Guide

When you design a simple one-page Web site for personal use, you can probably get away with letting the page evolve as you experiment. When you design a complex set of interconnecting Web documents or a commercial home page, you'll need to go about the process more systematically. Here's a guide to planning the process step by step.

Stage One: Conceptualization

A lot of your HTML choices and design decisions follow from overall decisions about the goal of the Web pages and the people you hope to reach. Thinking through these questions early in the process will save you a lot of time in the end if you're working on a complex venture.

Step 1: Establish the goal

As with any other project, you can expect the best results if you figure out up front exactly what you want the Web pages to do for you, your company, or your client. It's sometimes a challenge to clearly articulate the purpose, but it saves a lot of time you'd lose to unnecessary revisions if you make sure you know what you're doing and why before you plunge into the design.

Part of setting the goal of your Web pages is identifying as clearly as possible your intended audience. The tools for identifying who visits a Web page are limited, and so far there's no accepted standard for how to count the number of users to establish return on investment, or the number of people in the target audience who have received your message. If, during design, you spend some time thinking about what kind of people you want to reach, you can focus on including things that will bring those people, judge which external links to incorporate, and zero in on the sites you most want to point to your site. And you can do some contingency planning on what to do if your site is so intriguing that it's swamped by loads of browsers who aren't in the target audience.

Your target audience may play a big role in determining how you design your pages. For example, if you're preparing a site for Macintosh multimedia developers, you can assume that all targeted users will be able to play QuickTime movies, but that wouldn't be the case for a site directed toward a more general audience. Or, if you're creating a site directed toward Netscape users, you can go ahead and use the Netscape extensions to HTML, but you might want to stick to the standard HTML tags for a broader audience.

If you want a lot of repeat visitors, you need to plan to change elements of the page frequently to keep the site interesting to the real Web zealots. Some commericial sites are designed to change many times each day.

When considering audience, think about which browser software you plan to support (and therefore test with). A number of sites publish statistics about the types of browsers in use by visitors to certain sites. They might help you narrow down to the browser software you need to support for your site. One site that gathers stats from several sites is Valerie's page at: `http://www.rezn8.com/world3/meme1/browse2.html`.
And remember, if you want to reach everyone, you'll need to include text alternatives to graphics for Lynx users.

Another factor that may control your design, especially in a corporate setting, is who's going to maintain the site and how much time do they have to do it? Many companies find that managing and maintaining Web sites and responding to all the inquiries they generate takes more time and money than originally anticipated. If a company goes on the Web but can't keep up with the visitors' demands for information or follow-up, the company seems unresponsive, so make sure these issues are part of any discussion about a commercial Web site plan. (Interestingly enough, even if a commercial Web site doesn't include a company's Internet address, launching a Web site often leads to more e-mail from the outside world, sometimes radically more, which is something else to factor in.)

Remember that it's the World Wide Web. You'll have a global audience, so if your client, company, or content has international aspects, be sure to include that in the Web page plan. For example, if you are planning to publish product information for a company that distributes its products worldwide, make sure to include international sales office contact information as well as U.S. contact info. If you don't distribute worldwide, say so. Some Web home pages offer users a choice of languages: click your native language and link to a set of pages that you can read without translating.

Step 2: Outline the content

Once you have a goal in mind, it helps to outline what content you want to include in the Web page or set of pages. As you outline, keep track of what content you merely need to collect, what you need to create, and what you need to retool for the online medium. Remember that some of the content may be links to information that's not part of your site — include that in your outline, too. The outline serves as a starting point for mapping out how the parts will interact.

Which of the information is simply text? Which text should be scrollable? Which text should be in short chunks that fit easily within a window of the browser?

What kind of interactivity do you need to build in? Do you need to collect any information about the visitors to the page? Are you going to try to qualify visitors by having them register their address or other information in a form? (That creates two tiers of visitors: browsers and users, whom you can attempt to contact in the future through the URLs they leave for you.)

Will the Web site link to any other pages on the same Web server or to external Web documents? Will you make internal links relative (all files in the same subdirectory or folder on the server, so only the unique part of the path name appears in each link address) or absolute (with complete path and filename for each link)?

Step 3: Choose a structure for the Web page

Once you have the big picture of what the Web pages need to cover and what external links you want, you can settle on a basic organization of the pages. Do you want a linear structure so users switch from screen to screen like a slide show, using Next and Back navigation buttons? How about a branching structure, with a choice of major topics on the home page that link to content or a choice of subtopics? If a branching hierarchy would be too rigid, how about a more organic web structure with many links that interconnect the parts of the content? What about a hybrid structure that combines a formal hierarchy with some linear "slideshows" and a complex nexus as appropriate for the different parts of the site?

Whatever structure seems right for the purpose and content, if it's a complex site, it's a good idea to sketch out a map or storyboard for the pages, using lines to indicate links. You can make your map with pencil and paper, index cards and yarn on a bulletin board, a drawing program, or any other tool that works for you. (There's one program, NaviPress, that helps visualize the relationships in a set of Web pages; see Chapter 12 for details.) Make sure the home page reflects the organization you choose; that really helps to orient users.

Stage Two: Building Pages

Once you have a plan for the pages, you can roll up your sleeves and get your hands into HTML. You can start with the home page and move on to the other pages within a set, adjusting the home page design as necessary as you go along. You might feel more comfortable designing the linked pages first and finishing up with the home page; it doesn't really matter, so choose which approach fits your style and remember that it's a process.

Step 4: Code, preview, and revise

You'll find that you work in cycles: coding, placing graphics and links, and previewing what you've done, changing the code, and previewing again in the browser software (that is, unless you're working with one of the rare HTML editing tools described in Chapter 12 that offers WYSIWYG. As you become accustomed to the effect of the HTML formatting tags, you'll have fewer cycles of coding, previewing, and revising the code, but even experienced HTML tamers expect to go through many revisions.

Fortunately, finding mistakes in the code is relatively simple: usually the flaw in the page points you to the part of the HTML that's not quite right.

Remember to format your HTML so that it's easy to revise and debug, and include comments about the code if someone else might maintain the HTML files later.

Step 5: Add links internally and externally

Once you have the basic framework of your pages, you can add the relevant links and check whether they make sense. Obviously you'll need to check and recheck links as you develop the material that links back and forth internally.

If you've planned carefully you'll be able to add links to external pages as you go along. Or you can add them later. Some pages have sections set aside for a changing set of links to external pages, you can arrange to change the links every week or every day or several times a day, depending on your target audience and the purpose of the page.

Step 6: Optimize for the slowest of your target audience

Once the pages have all the elements in place, make sure they work for the slowest connections you expect your target audience to use. Remember that a lot of people who use online systems like CompuServe, America Online, and Prodigy still have 2400 BPS modems. If you want to reach the lowest common denominator, you'll need to test your pages at that speed over the online systems and make design changes or offer low-speed alternatives to accommodate the slowest connections you expect in your target audience.

Stage Three: Testing

Just in case you didn't get the message yet: For great Web pages, plan to test, test, and test your work.

Step 7: Test and revise yourself

Even when you think you've worked out all the kinks, it's not yet time to pat yourself on the back and celebrate. If you're serious about Web page design, you need to test the pages with all the browsers you intend to support, at the slowest speeds you expect in your target audience, and on different computer systems your target audience might have. For example, what happens to graphics when they're viewed on a monitor that shows fewer colors than yours?

Step 8: Have other testers check your work

You can only go so far in testing your own work. The same way you tend to overlook your own typos, someone else may readily find obvious flaws that you're blind to in your own Web pages. As much as is practical, have people in-house test your Web pages if you're creating a site at work or in an organization, or load it all on the Web server as a pilot project and ask a trusted few testers to use the pages and report back any problems or suggestions for improvement.

Stage Four: Load the Files on the Web

When you have finished testing the files locally, you're ready to put them up on the Web for live test driving. You may need to do some preparation if you're sending the files to someone else's Web server for publishing.

Step 9: Prepare files for the server

Make sure your files are ready to go on the server. Put all the files for your pages in one folder (or one directory) on the hard disk of the Web server for your own site. Within that folder (or directory) you can name the file you mean to be the home page index.html — that's the file that's loaded as the home page by default by most Web server software.

If you're using someone else's server, find out if there are any file naming conventions you need to follow. For example, you may need to limit filenames to eight characters plus a three character extension, such as webpp.htm, for DOS-based servers.

If you're using someone else's server, you'll probably send your Web page files there via ftp, Zmodem file transfer, or some other electronic file transfer. Be careful to save Mac files in binary format, not MacBinary format, if you're sending them to a site that's not running a Mac server. If you're moving referenced text files to a server that's not a Mac server, maybe you can save them in the right format for that platform; check the file format options in your text editor's Save As dialog box.

Step 10: Double-check your URL

If you're not sure of the URL for your pages, check with the administrator for the Web site. Try out the URL to make sure it's correct before passing it around to testers or printing it on business cards.

Step 11: Test drive some more

This is the true test of your Web pages. Can you find and use them? What about the other testers you've lined up? Test, revise, reload, and retest. It may take awhile to iron out the wrinkles in a complex set of pages, but hang in there.

If you've transferred your files to an alien system, you may see unexpected results, such as line breaks in your Web page text where you didn't intend them, particularly in text formatted with the <PRE> tag. You may have double-spaced text where you meant to show single-spaced text, for example. If you can't easily solve the problem, you may need to use a UNIX filter to fix line break problems. Consult the Web site administrator if you're stuck.

Step 12: Announce your Web page

Finally it's time to let the world know your Web page exists! Use the techniques in Chapters 10 and 11 to publicize your Web pages. And take a moment to celebrate your World Wide Web publishing debut.

About the CD-ROM

As part of Macworld Creating Cool HTML 3.2 Web Pages, I've rounded up a wide variety of fun and useful software for budding Web authors, and included every single example in the book, too. You can use Netscape Navigator (included) to explore all the code tricks and page layouts shown throughout the book, then use some of the shareware, freeware, and commercial demonstration software included to create your own site.

Book Examples

To get started with the book examples, go into the Book Examples folder and find the file coolweb.htm. Double-click on it — you should have it launch you straight into your favorite Web browser (or Navigator off the CD-ROM).

If that doesn't work, find Netscape Navigator on the CD-ROM, launch it by double-clicking, then from the File menu in Netscape choose Open File... and select the file coolweb.htm.

Included Software

There's also a wide variety of different software on the CD-ROM, including the following:

Anarchie

A very helpful FTP front-end, particularly useful if you have your Web pages stored on a remote server, because the File Transfer Protocol (FTP) is the standard way to upload graphics and pages themselves.

BBEdit Lite

Looking for a solid text-only editor within which you can do your HTML editing? BBEdit, from the aptly-named Bare Bones Software, is a fast and quite capable application. A big step up from TeachText.

DeBabelizer Lite

If there's one thing that's true about the Web and the Internet, it's that there are an amazing number of different graphics formats, from TIFF and BMP to GIF, JPEG, and much more. DeBabelizer Lite helps you get a handle on the different formats and can also automatically translate one form to another.

GraphicConverter

A very nice graphics program that has the capability to read and write a wide variety of different graphic formats, including GIF and JPEG. GraphicConverter also has some support for animated GIFs (though GIFBuilder is probably easier to use) and definitely enables you to pick a transparent color and tweak your images until you've achieved just what you want.

Nuntius

A Usenet news reader with a unique and rather funky interface. If you don't like the news reading layout within Navigator or Explorer, Nuntius offers you an alternative. Note that you'll need NNTP server access from your Internet access provider.

Tex-Edit

A very capable replacement for the SimpleText program, this simple program enables you to whip through HTML pages, albeit without much specific support for formatting tags or layout.

HTML Editor/PageSpinner

Two of the best shareware HTML editors available today for the Macintosh. They have slightly different spins on how to help you create Web pages, so try them both to see which you like best.

NetPresenz

This is a simple Web and FTP server for your Macintosh that will enable you to experiment with how your Mac can act as a server on a local network for Web-based information. I also find it particularly useful to have FTP-based access to my Mac when I'm at a remote site and need a file or two from my desktop machine.

StuffIt Expander

This vital little program lets you grab and automatically unpack a wide variety of different archive formats from network archives, and is automatically invoked by your Web browser or FTP program when it receives a BinHex (.hqx), MacBinary (.bin), or uuencoded (.uu) file.

WeatherTracker

Just for fun, this slick program uses your Net connection to keep you up-to-date with the latest weather in your area and around the world. Think of it as an interactive Weather Channel on your Mac!

GifScan

This useful utility enables you to quickly ascertain the exact size and depth of any GIF image. Particularly useful for HEIGHT/WIDTH specs in an IMG SRC tag.

There are two additional programs I'll recommend that you pop online and get a copy of — alas, I couldn't include them with the CD-ROM. The first is WebMap (http://www.city.net/cnx/software), which makes creating image maps super easy, and the second is GifBuilder, for creating animated GIF sequences, which you can find at http://www.shareware.com

Important Note: If you find yourself using some of these programs a lot, and they're shareware, do yourself and the entire Mac community a favor and register your applications with the author. It's inexpensive and ensures that this kind of quality software will continue to be available.

Cool Demo Software

I didn't just stop with fun shareware and freeware! I also arranged for demo and trial software from a variety of vendors, including the following:

Artbeats

Artbeats is best known for its terrific clip art collections, particularly its Web-related GIF image sets. A sample is included on the CD-ROM, which you're free to use, along with some other goodies from Artbeats.

BBEdit 4.0

If you're really someone who enjoys working with raw HTML but wants to have as much assistance as possible, BBEdit offers colored HTML source views, floating menus of HTML tags, and even a syntax checker and spell checker. It's a great program.

Adobe Acrobat Reader

While HTML gives you great capabilities for laying out text and graphics to achieve your desired end-result, there's no question that for really detailed work, it's not powerful enough. If you really need exact results, you'll want to explore the platform independent Acrobat format with its Acrobat Reader.

Adobe PageMill

A capable and very useful visual web page editor, PageMill can help you quickly prototype your Web pages and even develop your entire site.

Adobe Photoshop

Not for the faint of heart, Adobe Photoshop is my favorite program for creating any sort of Web graphics. It offers tremendous power and capabilities, but the interface will take a few months to really figure out and use to its fullest capabilities. Save some heartache; buy one of the many good books about Photoshop and learn how it works.

Netscape Navigator

The premier World Wide Web browser, Netscape Navigator is, in my opinion, the best choice for surfin' the Net (and working with your own Web pages) on the Macintosh platform. I'm delighted we can include a full version of this terrific program on this CD-ROM. You need to install the Earthlink software before Netscape can be installed.

IDG BOOKS WORLDWIDE, INC.
END-USER LICENSE AGREEMENT

Read This. You should carefully read these terms and conditions before opening the software packet(s) included with this book ("Book"). This is a license agreement ("Agreement") between you and IDG Books Worldwide, Inc. ("IDGB"). By opening the accompanying software packet(s), you acknowledge that you have read and accept the following terms and conditions. If you do not agree and do not want to be bound by such terms and conditions, promptly return the Book and the unopened software packet(s) to the place you obtained them for a full refund.

1.   **License Grant**. IDGB grants to you (either an individual or entity) a nonexclusive license to use one copy of the enclosed software program(s) (collectively, the "Software") solely for your own personal or business purposes on a single computer (whether a standard computer or a workstation component of a multiuser network). The Software is in use on a computer when it is loaded into temporary memory (i.e., RAM) or installed into permanent memory (e.g., hard disk, CD-ROM, or other storage device). IDGB reserves all rights not expressly granted herein.

2.   **Ownership**. IDGB is the owner of all right, title, and interest, including copyright, in and to the compilation of the Software recorded on the CD-ROM. Copyright to the individual programs on the CD-ROM is owned by the author or other authorized copyright owner of each program. Ownership of the Software and all proprietary rights relating thereto remain with IDGB and its licensors.

3.   **Restrictions on Use and Transfer**.
      (a) You may only (i) make one copy of the Software for backup or archival purposes, or (ii) transfer the Software to a single hard disk, provided that you keep the original for backup or archival purposes. You may not (i) rent or lease the Software, (ii) copy or reproduce the Software through a LAN or other network system or through any computer subscriber system or bulletin-board system, or (iii) modify, adapt, or create derivative works based on the Software.

(b) You may not reverse engineer, decompile, or disassemble the Software. You may transfer the Software and user documentation on a permanent basis, provided that the transferee agrees to accept the terms and conditions of this Agreement and you retain no copies. If the Software is an update or has been updated, any transfer must include the most recent update and all prior versions.

4. **Restrictions on Use of Individual Programs**. You must follow the individual requirements and restrictions detailed for each individual program in Appendix E: About the CD-ROM in this Book. These limitations are contained in the individual license agreements recorded on the CD-ROM. These restrictions may include a requirement that after using the program for the period of time specified in its text, the user must pay a registration fee or discontinue use. By opening the Software packet(s), you will be agreeing to abide by the licenses and restrictions for these individual programs. None of the material on this CD-ROM or listed in this Book may ever be distributed, in original or modified form, for commercial purposes.

5. **Limited Warranty**.
  (a) IDGB warrants that the Software and CD-ROM are free from defects in materials and workmanship under normal use for a period of sixty (60) days from the date of purchase of this Book. If IDGB receives notification within the warranty period of defects in materials or workmanship, IDGB will replace the defective CD-ROM.

  (b) **IDGB AND THE AUTHOR OF THE BOOK DISCLAIM ALL OTHER WARRANTIES, EXPRESS OR IMPLIED, INCLUDING WITHOUT LIMITATION IMPLIED WARRANTIES OF MERCHANTABILITY AND FITNESS FOR A PARTICULAR PURPOSE, WITH RESPECT TO THE SOFTWARE, THE PROGRAMS, THE SOURCE CODE CONTAINED THEREIN, AND/OR THE TECHNIQUES DESCRIBED IN THIS BOOK. IDGB DOES NOT WARRANT THAT THE FUNCTIONS CONTAINED IN THE SOFTWARE WILL MEET YOUR REQUIREMENTS OR THAT THE OPERATION OF THE SOFTWARE WILL BE ERROR FREE.**

  (c) This limited warranty gives you specific legal rights, and you may have other rights which vary from jurisdiction to jurisdiction.

6. **Remedies**.
   (a) IDGB's entire liability and your exclusive remedy for defects in materials and workmanship shall be limited to replacement of the Software, which may be returned to IDGB with a copy of your receipt at the following address: Disk Fulfillment Department, Attn: *Macworld Creating Cool HTML 3.2 Web Pages*, IDG Books Worldwide, Inc., 7260 Shadeland Station, Ste. 100, Indianapolis, IN 46256, or call 1-800-762-2974. Please allow 3-4 weeks for delivery. This Limited Warranty is void if failure of the Software has resulted from accident, abuse, or misapplication. Any replacement Software will be warranted for the remainder of the original warranty period or thirty (30) days, whichever is longer.

   (b) In no event shall IDGB or the author be liable for any damages whatsoever (including without limitation damages for loss of business profits, business interruption, loss of business information, or any other pecuniary loss) arising from the use of or inability to use the Book or the Software, even if IDGB has been advised of the possibility of such damages.

   (c) Because some jurisdictions do not allow the exclusion or limitation of liability for consequential or incidental damages, the above limitation or exclusion may not apply to you.

7. **U.S. Government Restricted Rights**. Use, duplication, or disclosure of the Software by the U.S. Government is subject to restrictions stated in paragraph (c) (1) (ii) of the Rights in Technical Data and Computer Software clause of DFARS 252.227-7013, and in subparagraphs (a) through (d) of the Commercial Computer—Restricted Rights clause at FAR 52.227-19, and in similar clauses in the NASA FAR supplement, when applicable.

8. **General**. This Agreement constitutes the entire understanding of the parties and revokes and supersedes all prior agreements, oral or written, between them and may not be modified or amended except in a writing signed by both parties hereto which specifically refers to this Agreement. This Agreement shall take precedence over any other documents that may be in conflict herewith. If any one or more provisions contained in this Agreement are held by any court or tribunal to be invalid, illegal, or otherwise unenforceable, each and every other provision shall remain in full force and effect.

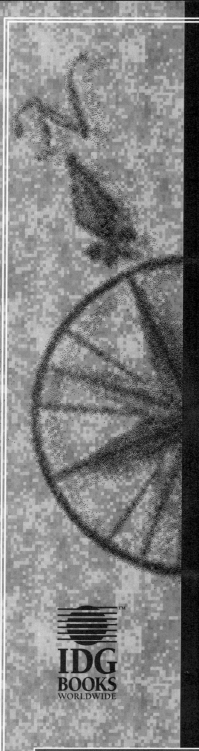

IDG BOOKS WORLDWIDE REGISTRATION CARD

RETURN THIS REGISTRATION CARD FOR FREE CATALOG

Title of this book: **Macworld® Creating Cool™ HTML 3.2 Web Pages**

My overall rating of this book: ☐ Very good [1] ☐ Good [2] ☐ Satisfactory [3] ☐ Fair [4] ☐ Poor [5]

How I first heard about this book:

☐ Found in bookstore; name: [6] ☐ Book review: [7]

☐ Advertisement: [8] ☐ Catalog: [9]

☐ Word of mouth; heard about book from friend, co-worker, etc.: [10] ☐ Other: [11]

What I liked most about this book:

What I would change, add, delete, etc., in future editions of this book:

Other comments:

Number of computer books I purchase in a year: ☐ 1 [12] ☐ 2-5 [13] ☐ 6-10 [14] ☐ More than 10 [15]

I would characterize my computer skills as: ☐ Beginner [16] ☐ Intermediate [17] ☐ Advanced [18] ☐ Professional [19]

I use ☐ DOS [20] ☐ Windows [21] ☐ OS/2 [22] ☐ Unix [23] ☐ Macintosh [24] ☐ Other: [25]_____
(please specify)

I would be interested in new books on the following subjects:
(please check all that apply, and use the spaces provided to identify specific software)

☐ Word processing: [26] ☐ Spreadsheets: [27]

☐ Data bases: [28] ☐ Desktop publishing: [29]

☐ File Utilities: [30] ☐ Money management: [31]

☐ Networking: [32] ☐ Programming languages: [33]

☐ Other: [34]

I use a PC at (please check all that apply): ☐ home [35] ☐ work [36] ☐ school [37] ☐ other: [38] _____

The disks I prefer to use are ☐ 5.25 [39] ☐ 3.5 [40] ☐ other: [41]_____

I have a CD ROM: ☐ yes [42] ☐ no [43]

I plan to buy or upgrade computer hardware this year: ☐ yes [44] ☐ no [45]

I plan to buy or upgrade computer software this year: ☐ yes [46] ☐ no [47]

Name: Business title: [48]   Type of Business: [49]

Address (☐ home [50] ☐ work [51] /Company name:)

Street/Suite#

City [52] /State [53] /Zipcode [54]:   Country [55]

☐ **I liked this book!** You may quote me by name in future
IDG Books Worldwide promotional materials.

My daytime phone number is _____

IDG BOOKS

THE WORLD OF
COMPUTER
KNOWLEDGE